Praise for They Called You Dambudzo

'A moving, powerful, intense evocation of an extraordinary time, and the intersection of extraordinary lives.'

China Miéville, writer, London

'They Called You Dambudzo *is literary scholar Flora Veit-Wild's deeply courageous and compelling memoir of one of Africa's greatest writers, the Zimbabwean modernist Dambudzo Marechera. Veit-Wild interlaces dialogue, poetry, anecdote and vivid portraiture to achieve something truly extraordinary. She not only gives the full story frame by frame of her fraught and passionate relationship with the writer, she also recalls us to the genius and prescience of his work, and of the loss to African literature that his early death represented.* They Called You Dambudzo *sheds new and renewing light on Marechera's remarkable talent and on the power of literary friendship. This book deserves its place among the classics of Zimbabwean literature.'*

Elleke Boehmer, Professor of World Literature in English, University of Oxford

'Here's the backstory to the Dambudzo and Flora affair that most followers of African literature have been waiting for. Lyrical, raw, honest, sympathetic. We follow Flora's journey from her childhood in post WW2 Germany, to

her meeting with Dambudzo in recently independent Zimbabwe, to their tumultuous love affair, to his death and to her growth as a scholar and curator of Marechera's life's work. A very important addition to African literature.'
Helon Habila, writer, Nigeria/USA

'Flora Veit-Wild's vivid memoir conjures Marechera back to life: manically creative, morbidly destructive, spontaneous, hounded, infuriating, erudite and agreeable, vulnerable yet proud. This is a portrait of a relationship, of an unforgettable person, and of a condition of the mind. It is a story of gain and of loss, of mutual trust and mistrust, of passion and its consequences, of commitment, risk and of choice. For all who would understand Dambudzo Marechera and his worlds, it will prove indispensable.'
Robert Fraser, Professor Emeritus Open University UK,
English and Creative Writing

'A transgressive, volatile love story. A memoir that subverts time and geography. Veit-Wild's account of her relationship with Dambudzo Marechera – the greatest African writer of his generation – is both a celebration and a lament. It is also a bittersweet portrait of the new Zimbabwe, with its fractured landscape of race, class and privilege. Veit-Wild does not flinch from exposing her own complicity when it comes to the dynamics of power, but neither does she excuse her lover. Their dance is beautiful and destructive. Ultimately, it is redemptive. Reader, prepare to be unsettled.'
Fiona Lloyd, Zimbabwean journalist and editor

'Flora's voice has integrity throughout. She does not shy away from the hard truths about herself. By confronting her uncomfortable truths she has gifted the reader with similar experiences, a shelter in which they can feel normal and accept themselves. However the greater gift she has given the world is Dambudzo the person and his writings.'
Chiedza Musengezi, writer and editor, Zimbabwe/Northern Ireland,
founder director of Zimbabwe Women Writers

'In Veit-Wild's relationship with Marechera the issues of privilege and colour are constantly apparent, exploited (at times ruthlessly by Dambudzo and with acknowledged guilt by Flora), and frequently weaponised. This imbalance in their relationship is examined with admirable candour. Its relevance continues to be interesting – particularly in the sense of the white patron/black artist *discussion. When this is compounded by an intimate, secret affair, outside the bounds of a seemingly conventional marriage, it takes on additional layers of intensity. These complexities are explored and interrogated throughout the narrative in an intense "raw nerve" way, making it at times uncomfortable but very powerful reading, and always with the author's style of steady, uncompromising self-examination. Veit-Wild acknowledges the complexities but defends her right to speak about them. And she does so unflinchingly. She does not shy away from confronting these issues but is equally steadfast in owning her version of her narrative.'*

Alison Lowry, writer and editor, Johannesburg

'*Ultimately,* They Called You Dambudzo *is, like all memoirs, its writer's story. In tracking "the two distant orbits" of Dambudzo and Flora as they come closer to each other until they meet, interact and subsequently part, the memoir vividly describes places and powerfully evokes times that Flora traverses as she grows from a sheltered materially comfortable childhood in Germany through a youth characterized by political idealism and an adulthood decisively shaped by an encounter with a remarkable man in Africa. Flora Veit-Wild's life story of political adventure, sexual experiment, survival over several major health scares, an unlikely ascension into a university professorship and a determined holding on to the joy of living is one of triumph squeezed out of nature, culture and history at considerable cost.*'

T. Michael Mboya, Moi University Kenya

They Called You Dambudzo

A Memoir

Flora Veit-Wild

First published in Southern Africa
by Jacana Media (Pty) Ltd in 2020
10 Orange Street, Sunnyside, Auckland Park 2092, South Africa
www.jacana.co.za

Published in hardback in World excluding Southern Africa
and as an ePDF worldwide in 2022
by James Currey
an imprint of Boydell & Brewer Ltd
PO Box 9, Woodbridge, Suffolk, IP12 3DF (GB)
and of Boydell & Brewer Inc.
668 Mt Hope Avenue, Rochester NY 14620-2731 (US)
www.boydellandbrewer.com
www.jamescurrey.com

© Flora Veit-Wild, 2020

James Currey paperback edition 2023

The right of Flora Veit-Wild to be identified as
the author of this work has been asserted in accordance with
sections 77 and 78 of the Copyright, Designs and Patents Act 1988

All rights reserved. Except as permitted under current legislation
no part of this work may be photocopied, stored in a retrieval system,
published, performed in public, adapted, broadcast,
transmitted, recorded or reproduced in any form or by any means,
without the prior permission of the copyright owner

This edition is published by arrangement with Jacana

ISBN 978-1-84701-329-3 (James Currey hardback)
ISBN 978-1-84701-334-7 (James Currey paperback)
ISBN 978-1-4314-3049-9 (Jacana paperback)

The publisher has no responsibility for the continued existence or accuracy
of URLs for external or third-party internet websites referred to in this book,
and does not guarantee that any content on such websites is, or will remain,
accurate or appropriate

A CIP catalogue record for this book is available from the British Library

Cover design by publicide
Front cover photograph courtesy of Tessa Colvin
Editing by Nkhensani Manabe
Proofreading by Megan Mance

Contents

PRELUDE 1

PART ONE: TRAJECTORIES
Escape from the House of Hunger 9
The Last Image of My Father. 18
Flower in the Snow 26
Defying the State 31
From Frau Mücke to Robert Mugabe. 36

PART TWO: HARARE IN HEAT
December 1982. 45
German Christmas in the Tropics 47
The Mozambican Bogey Man 50
The Oracle 55
Becoming Expatriates 58
Elective Affinities 61
Boscobel Drive 65
Guest of Honour. 69
Harare International Book Fair 1983 73

PART THREE: EAGLETS OF DESIRE

Getting Entangled 87
Nowhere to Go 97
Having a Home 104
Max and Dambudzo 108
Facing the Publishers 111
The Taxi Has to Be Paid 115
Vumba and the Grand Finale 126
Coda 1: The Accident 136
Coda 2: I Hate Death 138

PART FOUR: HEAVEN'S TERRIBLE ECSTACY

A Reading and a Murder Charge 143
They Are Boiling My Bones in the Kitchen 149
8 Sloane Court 152
The Ghost of Amelia 158
The Other Woman 164
Projects and Rejects 169
Patterns of Poetry 172
Angry Notes 178
Lake McIlwaine: The Entrapment 180
Coda 1: Seroconversion 190
Coda 2: Conception 192

PART FIVE: BASTARD DEATH

The Great Scare 195
The Hourglass 198
How to Live On 208
Shadows of Death 210
He Is Dead 215

PART SIX: ENTANGLED LEGACIES

The Execution. 223
The Tracking 234
The Moment of Terror. 256
Carnival and Cockroaches – The Appointment 258
The Lady in Black. 262
The Valley of Death or: Busting the Kraken 270
Out of the Closet. 275

Acknowledgements 278

Prelude

THE PREGNANCY LASTED ELEVEN months, your mother told me.

Yainetsa ichirwadza. It was so painful she thought it would never end.

She finally released you from her body on 4 June 1952. The pain stopped, and you were perfectly still.

They called you Dambudzo ('the one who brings trouble') because they were destitute.

Taishupika. We were suffering.

Inside the women's hut it was sombre, with just a few rays of sunlight filtering through the thatched roof. No men were allowed in there. Mai Marechera sat on the ground with some female relatives and their children. I was given a wooden stool.

Yes, she would talk to me, she said in Shona. Her voice was low and steady. Her niece would interpret.

It felt good to be huddled there with the women of your family. And yet the enormity of space that separated me from your mother made my blood feel leaden.

What did she think? Did she guess that you and I had shared a bed? It was winter, July 1990. Three years since you had left the world you so reluctantly entered.

I REMEMBER

I remember our first night. The raucous laughter in the hotel garden. The sneers, which you had to translate. 'Look at him and his white chick.'

I remember the silence of our room, stars spinning through the open roof.

I remember another night. Your cackling, brittle cough. A sign of what was looming in your body?

I remember how your mood lightened when you moved in with us. How you relished a proper bed, clean sheets, a shower. I remember you sitting in our garden, your myopic eyes close to the keys of your typewriter, two fingers jabbing down, as you pummelled the words out of your system.

I remember your wide face with the small scar on your forehead. Your full lips protruding into a pout or expanding into broad laughter. Or silent and so sensuous that I had to kiss them.

I remember the knock at our bedroom window at 2 a.m. one morning. Your drunken voice: 'Hey, it's me.' My husband and I sitting up, alarmed. 'What is it?' 'The taxi driver is waiting.' 'So?' 'He needs to be paid.'

I remember the puddle of blood gathering on the floor, as you stood there refusing to budge before the police arrived. You had smashed your face into the glass cabinet. You said my husband threatened you with a sword.

I remember waking up in a flood of warm liquid, soaking the bed where I was sleeping by your side.

I remember you munching handfuls of red chillies, and teasing my children: 'Hey, guys, you should try these!'

I remember the lake. Christmas beetles floundering to the ground. Your sullen silence.

I remember sniffing the thin film of sweat on your skin, when you let go of me. Digging my nose into your armpit, rubbing it against the minute curls of black hair.

I remember my shrieks, reverberating through the block of flats. 'How can you be so cruel?' Your eyes staring past me: 'Leave me alone. Go back home to your blond husband and children.'

I remember swearing to myself: 'Never again.'

I remember crawling back under your sheets, my mouth close to

Prelude

your ear, whispering: 'Forever.'

I remember the half-eaten pie on the table, the crumpled book on the floor. Your body a furnace. The doctor: 'Take him straight to hospital.'

I remember the oxygen mask over your mouth and nose: your ashen skin. Listening to your breath, rattling and gurgling from deep in your body. I remember waiting for the next gasp, each time thinking: Is this the last?

He was sitting upright in his hospital bed, smoking. His chest was wheezing.

'Bring me pen and paper,' he said. 'I want to write a will.'

'All right,' I said. 'When I come back tomorrow.'

Why did I not grab a scrap of paper at that moment and dig in my bag for a pen?

It was hard to find a nurse or doctor.

'One side of his lungs is gone, there's not much left of the other,' they eventually said.

'What does this mean? How long will it be …?'

Their answers were vague.

I had found him in his flat the day before. He was dehydrated, coughing badly, in pain. I rushed him to Parirenyatwa Hospital. Six months earlier they had treated him for pneumonia.

There was a long wait until he was admitted. We sat in the queue of patients on a wooden bench. His body, hot with fever, leaned against mine, his head to one side.

'Should I bring you anything else?' I said, awkwardly.

'No,' he said, now propped up on his pillows. 'I have cigarettes. And pain killers.'

His eyes, sunken back into his hollow face, hardly moved. His skin was a yellowish green. He looked so sad. But peaceful.

When I bent to embrace him, his thin arms clung to me.

'We won't leave you alone, we are all with you,' I murmured into his ear, my hand touching his burning cheeks.

I waved to him from the doorway.

Why did I not stay?

Next day I returned with pen and paper, and an invitation to a writers' conference in Germany. He had so much wanted to travel again.

But it was too late. He was unconscious, an oxygen mask on his face. His chest was heaving as he struggled to hold onto life.

I sat with him until late that night. Then, two hours after I got to bed, the telephone woke me.

I knew at once that he was gone.

When I kissed him for the last time his body was still warm. 'You will not be forgotten,' I whispered. 'I have loved you so much.'

You had not written a will but I had the key to your flat.

On the day you died I collected all your papers. Some were clipped together; others were still in their envelopes. There was a rejection letter, hastily read, thrown into the cupboard with piles of typed sheets, crumpled clothes, dirty underwear.

I rummaged through it all, sniffing your scent tinted by death.

I shoved everything chaotically into a suitcase: notebooks, letters, every bit of paper that bore traces of your writing or that of someone else. Photos of me and my children from your bookshelf. Postcards from abroad (from me, my husband, friends). Notes I had written while you were asleep, full of hurt and despair, love and longing. Letters from other women: those who came before me, those who came after.

I stroked the floral jacket you had filched from my wardrobe. But I could not linger. I felt numb. Under a spell.

I left most of your clothes, your books, your typewriter. I left the curtains I had sewn for you when the flat became yours after so many years of homelessness.

But I took two other things. The stone sculpture that Bernard Takawira gave you, from artist to artist. You had treasured it. And your waistcoat: a remnant of the three-piece suit you bought at Harrods in London from an advance on royalties, or maybe from your Guardian Fiction prize money. You wore it in the film documentary of your grand return from exile in 1982. You wore it one year later, when I first saw you at the Harare International Book Fair.

It seemed so innocent and child-like, in the absence of your angry voice shouting blasphemy at all and sundry.

It looked so tiny, as I held it on the day you died.

Prelude

Thirty years have passed.

Your waistcoat is now a cultural artefact here in Berlin at the Dambudzo Marechera Archive of Humboldt University. Marechera finally mummified, as someone joked.

How shall I tell our story?

I hear your voice ringing in mine. I struggle to disentangle a dense tapestry of memories.

One thread will be caught up in another. Early images will embrace later ones. My gaze will often be filtered through your eyes, your poems.

In the end I will not always be able to tell the original from the reflection. Just as you wrote,

Time's fingers on the piano
play emotion into motion
the dancers in the looking glass
never recognise us as their originals.

PART ONE

TRAJECTORIES

Escape from the House of Hunger

DAMBUDZO, CHILD OF SORROW, your mother was so proud of you.

At five and a half you were chased away from school because you were too little. But you went back. You always wanted books, she said. You always wanted to write. Panguva yega yega ainge achingonyora.

Your family lived in a two-roomed shack in Vengere near the town of Rusape, in what was still the colony of Southern Rhodesia. You had two elder brothers, and six more siblings were to follow.

You were baptised Charles William in an Anglican church. It was only when you became a published writer that you reclaimed your Shona name.

Your father was first a lorry driver, then a mortuary attendant. A violent man. He spent most of his meagre salary in the beer hall and often came home drunk, beating up anyone who got in his way.

Your mother crossed the railway line to the suburbs where the white people lived. She washed their dirty clothes and cared for their children. She did whatever she could so that you and your siblings could go to school, so that you had food to eat.

No wonder, many years later, you called your first book *The House of Hunger*.

'I got my things and left,' it famously begins. 'I couldn't have stayed on in that House of Hunger where every morsel of sanity was snatched from you the way some kinds of bird snatch food from the very mouths of babes.'

But even as a child you found a way to escape. 'I was mesmerised by books at a very early age,' you wrote in *Mindblast*.

> I found my first one – Arthur Mee's Children's Encyclopaedia – at the local rubbish dump where the garbage from the white side of town was dumped every day, except Sundays. You never knew what you'd find in that rubbish dump. Broken toys, half eaten sandwiches; comics, magazines, books. One brilliant morning I found what I thought was a rather large doll. But in touching it, I discovered it was a baby. Dead. Rotting. I fled as fast as I could to the safety and razor fights of the ghetto. I read that encyclopaedia from cover to cover. Wandering among the Ancient Egyptians, the Persians, the Hittites and the Gittites. Pouring over the voyages of discovery by the British, the Spanish, the Portuguese ... It was an early flowering of my imagination, all caused by a chance encounter with a Victorian imperialist on a rubbish dump in a small town in Zimbabwe. I was at the departure point for what by various quirks would turn out to be my writing career ... I had discovered that whatever the body may be, the mind is its own world.

You had eight years of primary school in Vengere – always top of the class. Then another six years of school at St Augustine's, situated high on a hill near the eastern town of Penhalonga. It was the country's first and most prestigious secondary school for Africans. Many future political and intellectual leaders went there.

At St Augustine's you delved deeper and deeper into the world of learning. You devoured every single volume of your teachers' personal libraries.

Boarding school was your haven. You preferred spending your holidays there rather than at home, but you couldn't escape for long.

1966: your first year at St Augustine's. The headmaster calls you out of class because your mother is on the phone. She says your father is dead. He was hit by a truck while he was walking home at night. Drunk? Probably.

Later, she forces you – still just a child – to follow her into the mortuary. You try to turn your head away but she grips you tightly, and makes you look at your father's mutilated corpse.

This trauma haunts you all your life. Nothing ever terrifies you more than the sight of your dead father, stretched out on the mortuary table. His severed limbs have been sewn back onto his body. He stares at you with a deathly grimace.

Scars, wounds, blood, amputation. Images of such will appear throughout your writing. But the manner of your father's death was not fixed in your memory. Was he hit by a car or shot by a Rhodesian policeman? It depended on who you were telling.

It was then that you started to stammer. Or that's what you said. Others remember you stammering when you were much younger.

'He spoke and thought faster than ordinary two-brained human beings like us,' said your friends Washington and Wattington, the identical twins.

They attributed your stammer to 'over intelligence'. They also lived in Vengere, and would go with you to the rubbish dump to scavenge books.

Do you know that I tracked them down, the twins?

They were working for an insurance company when I met them. Still identical, in matching blue suits. They told me how the three of you played 'office' in a little house made from cardboard boxes. You even had an old typewriter that you found at the dump, they said.

You always typed. You liked to see your words in print. I hardly ever saw any manuscript of yours that was handwritten.

Now a widow, your mother was forced to leave the modest council house of your childhood. She took you and your eight siblings – the youngest not yet two years old – to a slum on the outskirts of Vengere. This was the 'ghetto' you so often described in your writing.

Soon, your mother had no option but to sell her body to keep the family alive and pay the school fees for you and your brothers and sisters.

Your mother: a prostitute. You never forgave her. Your missionary education taught you that sex was filthy, a sin to be resisted. But when your brother gave you money to go to a township brothel you didn't refuse. You caught an STD from that first sexual encounter.

No wonder you became so ambivalent about women and their sexuality. No wonder you decided love was a fiction.

As your time at St Augustine's drew to a close, your complex mind revealed itself.

'Very brilliant, utterly individualistic, in many ways streaks ahead of everyone else in imaginative scope and major writing style – but maddeningly unpredictable and very much his own boss, however much he may conform outwardly,' wrote your English teacher and headmaster.

You were studying for A-levels when the paranoia started. Hallucinations. Voices. You imagined men following you, threatening you. Your headmaster took you to the psychiatric clinic in nearby Mutare, where they prescribed tranquillisers.

You almost refused to sit for the exams. When you did, you passed with the highest marks.

'I don't think anywhere could have given Charles the security that he needed – but all the same I think that possibly we gave him the nearest thing to stability,' your former history teacher told me many years later.

In 1972 you won a prestigious scholarship to the University of Rhodesia and enrolled for an English Honours degree. By then, the university, which had been seen as an experiment in multiracial learning, was deeply divided in its response to the racist government of Ian Smith.

You had become politically aware while you were still at school.

'I was extremely thirsty for self-knowledge and curiously enough believed I could find that in "political consciousness",' you wrote in *The House of Hunger*.

But, as ever, you remained an individualist. Your one-man demonstration is legendary. A placard in your hands, you walked the four miles from the university campus to the city centre all alone.

A year later, in July 1973, mass violence erupted on campus when black students protested against the segregated salaries of university lecturers. Ironically, you – the avowed individualist – were singled out as one of the 'ringleaders' and threatened with expulsion. Police came onto campus with fierce dogs. They rounded up 155 students, many of whom were imprisoned. Others joined the armed struggle or went into exile.

You went into hiding.

It was the birth of what you called 'the lost generation'. *The House of Hunger* became its mouthpiece.

In October 1974 you won a scholarship to New College, Oxford. What a seismic shift for a 22-year-old boy from Vengere. In the photo of the 50 first-year students, you are one of only two black faces. Almost invisible.

Several years later, you described how it felt:

'My main experience of Oxford University was loneliness and a certain questioning of why I found myself in a strange environment, whose traditions – well, frankly – I found disturbing. ... I discovered they were trying to make me into an intellectual Uncle Tom. I was being mentally raped.'

Of course you rebelled. In your own way. There was a series of drunken – often violent – episodes with College staff and fellow students. An attempt (mythical?) to set fire to the building. Warnings to refrain from further unruly behaviour. An offer of psychiatric counselling. Eventually, you were sent down.

Your version was different: 'I am not insane and you can therefore not expel me. I have already packed my things.'

It was March 1976. The end of your academic career; the beginning of your life as a penniless, homeless writer.

Fellow Zimbabwean Stanley Nyamfukudza gave you a bed. Like you, he had been expelled from the University of Rhodesia and he was a writer. He shared your despair about the predicament of your generation.

This was the genesis of *The House of Hunger*: a novella and eight short stories. You wrote it in a tent, camping by the River Isis. You wrote it at Stanley's kitchen table. You wrote it while staying with other friends. You finished it in February 1977, eleven months after your expulsion from Oxford. You submitted it to Heinemann. It was accepted enthusiastically.

James Currey, editor of the African Writers Series, lauded your 'searing talent', saying: 'This is some of the most powerful slum writing and reminiscences I have ever seen.'

The House of Hunger was published in December 1978. 'The book is an explosion,' wrote Doris Lessing. She continued:

> Writer and book are both of the nature of miracles. ... It is no good pretending this book is an easy or pleasant read. More like overhearing a scream. We can't use the word genius now, it is so debased. ... But Marechera has in him the stuff and substance that go to make a great writer.

You were compared to La Guma, Armah, Kafka and James Joyce.

Angela Carter commented: 'A terrible beauty is born out of the urgency of his vision.'

The culmination of your lightning success? The Guardian Fiction Prize for 1979, which you shared with Irish writer Neil Jordan.

At the award ceremony you appeared in a Mexican poncho and cowboy hat, a thick volume of Pound's *Cantos* under one arm. It was one of your famous masquerades: mocking those who expected to celebrate a 'real African'.

Instead of giving a humble acceptance speech, you hurled china and chairs at the chandeliers in London's Theatre Royal.

West Africa Magazine reported:

> CRASH…! There was the star of the show throwing expensive-looking plates at a wall … O Lord. What an embarrassment at an English literary luncheon.

You would not allow any white liberal art lover to feel comfortable patting the back of a black writer from the ghetto, however gifted he might be. You would always bite the hand that tried to feed you.

Your fame as the enfant terrible of African literature was assured. The next chapter in your life was predictably turbulent.

Oxford, then London. Stints in Wales, where you spent three months in prison for possessing cannabis. A post as writer-in-residence at Sheffield, where you were again expelled from a hostel and an irate citizen sold your typewriter as compensation for the books he had lent you. A trip to West Berlin, where you received a standing ovation at the Horizonte African Writers' Festival, after being detained by airport police for arriving without a passport.

Back in London, Currey urged you to write a 'proper novel' so as to sustain your literary fame. You submitted four manuscripts. Readers found them full of brilliance but too disjointed.

Currey finally published the last one: *Black Sunlight*.

You haunted his editorial offices, pestering him for advances, often appearing in disguise.

Many years later, Currey described your visitations to me:

> He used to appear at Bedford Square and the switchboard would ring me and say: 'Dambudzo is here!' And immediately I had to stop whatever I was doing and go through a sort of emergency routine. My concerns were least of all with his writing. They were mostly about protecting members of the staff – whom he actually never attacked directly, but I had heard stories of an architect who'd had a knife pulled on him.

Currey was your father figure. All complaints about your misconduct landed on his desk. Luckily for me, your biographer to be, they ended up in the DM Heinemann file where I would one day find them.

'Imagine being buried by Heinemann …' you quipped, with typical self-irony.

While writing *Black Sunlight*, you stayed in a squatter community at Tolmers Square. You were the only black person among 700 residents. It was a wild mix: unemployed people; lawyers and barristers working at the Inns of Court; doctors.

There were also 'a lot of Hari Krishna and Transcendental Meditation types. And witches who would come to meet on Walpurgis Nacht, All Souls Day. There was always dope. You could get anything you wanted in terms of drugs, but most of us tried to avoid the hard drugs like heroin,' you said.

You felt very much at home there.

> We all lived happily together. There was a slogan which I think is in *Black Sunlight*, it was scrawled on some of the walls: 'It is not what you want, but what you need.' I like that philosophy very much.

It was the 1970s. You were closely following political developments in Europe, especially the Baader Meinhof group. You read books on intellectual anarchism to reinforce your own 'sense of protest against everything'.

You also read about psychoanalysis, and the anti-psychiatry movement led by R D Laing. You identified with the sentiment: We are not the lunatics; it is society that's mad.

For the first time you became aware of the relationship between politics and sexuality. Most of the people of the hippie community at Tolmers Square 'rejected traditional sexual roles and accepted sexuality as a liberating force in itself,' you later recalled.

You found another kind of home at the Africa Centre near Covent Garden, a hub for London's large African exile community. You went there almost every day to meet people, to drink, talk, read and write. Lewis Nkosi, Ben Okri and Robert Fraser were among your regular drinking companions.

At the centre's literary events you would read from your work. Many people still remember your performance of 'Portrait of a Black Artist in London', a piece which exposed the acute racism of England under Thatcher, and the influence of the ultra rightwing National Front. It was a musical piece – you called it a choreodrama – and a saxophonist from the West Indies improvised while you read.

The staff at the centre were initially very supportive. Until you staged some of your more destructive 'performances'. After you smashed the front window with a brick, the director banned you from the premises.

Even though you were surrounded by exiles who felt as estranged as you did – 'like hippopotami that have been doped with injections of English culture', as you wrote in *The Black Insider* – you still refused to be seduced by nationalism. You saw yourself as 'the black heretic' – the title of another of your manuscripts.

When a ZANU delegation led by Robert Mugabe visited the Africa Centre, you sat in the back and heckled.

Then, on 18 April 1980, the day Zimbabwe celebrated its independence from white minority rule after seven years of bloody armed struggle, you joined the celebrations in characteristic style.

Exiled Zimbabwean film-maker Simon Bright tells the story:

> Marechera looked very smart. He was wearing a complete riding outfit with jodhpurs, black jacket, boots and a bowler hat. He stood out because everybody else was very patriotic-looking: a black Zimbabwean dressed like an English lord about to go on a fox-hunt, with pseudo upper-class English accent plus a slight stammer. While we white Zimbabweans tried to be very African and dressed in ethnic clothes, there was this black fellow making a mockery of English lords and Africans at the same time.

In February 1982 you returned to Zimbabwe. Your decision did not spring from post-independence euphoria. You were persuaded by an invitation from Chris Austin, a South African film director who wanted to document the story of a celebrated Zimbabwean author coming back to his home country.

They started filming you in London, showing you at the squat, then wandering through the grey streets. The forlorn, eccentric exile. Then the crew flew ahead to Harare and waited for you at the airport with some fellow writers.

It's all there in the raw footage.

You descend from the plane, wearing your three-piece pin-striped suit. You kneel to kiss the ground. You are greeted enthusiastically. You seem overjoyed.

Finally you are home.

But minutes later, in the car with Chris Austin and writer Wilson Katiyo, you stare out of the window, already alienated.

'I can't stay. I don't belong here anymore,' we hear you say. 'I am feeling like a bloody tourist.'

A couple of days later at the Park Lane Hotel, you break your deal with Austin. You are irritated because you have learned that *Black Sunlight* has been banned by the new Zimbabwean censorship board. You don't like the assistant cameraman because he is an ex-combatant. 'I am not used to being around people who have killed other people,' we hear you say.

Heated exchanges and mutual accusations follow. Eventually the film contract is terminated.

You are allowed to stay in the hotel for a week or two. Then it's life on the streets. You decide to go back to England, but you discover that it is impossible.

You do not possess any valid travel document.

You are trapped.

The Last Image of My Father

There was the story of a youth ... rebelling against the things of his father [who] had one morning fled from home and had travelled to the utmost of the earth. ... The years rolled by with delight until he tired of them and thought to return home and tell his father about them. But when he neared home his father, who was looking out for him, met him and said, 'All this time you thought you were actually away from me, you have been right here in my palm.'

Dambudzo Marechera: 'Protista: the Manfish'

FROZEN.

A still from a movie.

He stands in front of our house, his tall figure stooped. One arm holds the gate for support, the other gestures farewell.

He is thinking: I will never see my daughter again.

He did not. One year later, aged 85, he died of a heart attack.

We did not talk much in the days before my departure. He did not believe in our African venture, but he did not argue. He was resigned to staying behind. Yet still I felt he had some trust in me, his Engelskind.

The image never leaves me. I want to run back to him and tell him: 'I have not betrayed you. All my waywardness, which seemed to set us apart, only led me to the path you had carved out.'

'The Raspberry House' they called it, with a shake of their heads. Scarlet-red, square, flat-roofed, it was designed by my father and a post-Bauhaus architect. Its aesthetics radically different from the drabness of the era.

Inside, it was just as radical.

Upstairs was my father's realm. My father, the professor. Downstairs – with much smaller bedrooms and a tiny shared bathroom – resided my mother, my brother and me.

There was no living room, no cozy corner, no sofa or armchairs. The centre of family life was the dinner table, a massive Biedermeier piece of cherry wood. Above it, a lampshade inscribed with an aphorism by Goethe: 'Glückselig der dessen Welt innerhalb des Hauses ist' (Blissful those whose world is inside the house). My father, who knew Goethe inside out, chose the quote. My mother did the calligraphy.

Did he always want to keep me there?

My mother was the practical one. She made things happen. But she was also unruly and had her own life outside the house.

My father gave me a sense of direction; my mother instilled in me her energy – and a taste for adventure.

I took up piano, Girl Guides, horse riding. I was always top of the class.

Not so my brother. Two years younger and in my shadow, he resisted my father's expectations and dominance. He experimented with marijuana and LSD. At fifteen he joined Club Voltaire, a meeting place where intellectuals challenged the tenets of the post-war republic.

'Stefan goes to his Edelmarxisten,' my father would say, with a mixture of condescension and benevolence. 'He has such a kind heart.'

Meanwhile, I tried to shake off my 'good girl' image by wearing a black patent leather hat, varnishing my fingernails black, and applying a thick line of kohl around my eyes.

'You are not a vamp,' my father said, 'do wipe that off.'

Wesentlichkeit. Such a very German word. The core of his universe. The core of my upbringing.

'Children may only speak when they have something meaningful to say.'

This reverence for what matters. For depth.

Has it been my blessing or my curse? A bit of both?

Spring, 1966.

I am nineteen.

I have passed my Abitur, and I am to spend a couple of months in France. There, I will perfect my French and let the wind blow around my nose (as Thomas Mann would say).

It is exactly what the daughter of a good family should do at this stage in her life.

My father finds a French host family for me through the Rotarians. He has always despised such 'shallow ways' of socialising, and he only agrees to join Rotary after he is assured that he will be among serious-minded men with meaningful things to say.

My host family lives near Montpellier, so my parents decide to leave me there at the end of our Abiturreise – that typically German rite of transition. A time when parents introduce their children to the world, before setting them free.

But tensions rise between my father and me in those three weeks of travelling.

I long to be on my own.

Now.

The awe-inspiring architecture of La Chapelle de Ronchamp, the Roman amphitheatre in Arles, a Spanish corrida – I drink it all up. But my thoughts are not to be shared.

My father's frown hardens into a deep crevice above his thick-rimmed glasses. Lines of sorrow mark the handsome face that has charmed so many women. Grey-green eyes fix upon me like steel.

Imploring. Punishing. Willing me to open up.

'Why are you so withdrawn? It is so ungrateful of you.'

At last my parents deliver me to Montpellier. I will be there for five months.

Five months.

My inner self explodes like a bud exposed to sudden light.

The Bouffiers live in a mansion, which reminds me of a castle. Monsieur Bouffier is little and sturdy, his glistening dark hair tamed with brilliantine. When he speaks, his eyes probe the reactions of whoever he is addressing.

He belongs to the class of businessmen and landowners who, through their wealth and connections, have shaped public life and opinions in le Midi de la France. Catholic, authoritarian, patriarchal. Even his questions sound like statements. His wife, his mother and five daughters live in the mansion, under his command.

'You are different,' one of the daughters tells me. 'Tu es Allemande, you are used to more liberal ways.'

The family respect my liberty and give me a Vélosolex, so that I can go back and forth as I please. I attend classes at the Institut des Etrangers, stroll through the old city, go to parties, go on dates.

The French pronounce my name Florá, with the stress on the second syllable. It makes me feel like a different person.

Vibrant and beautiful.

Soon, my whole being is submerged in living à la Française. I cut my hair very short. I buy a bright yellow mini skirt, and a white-and-green-chequered blouse from Galéries Lafayette. I speak French. I read French. I write French. I think and dream and flirt in French.

I make love in French.

His name is Barnabas. He is from Ethiopia, tall and beautiful. With the haughtiness of youth, conscious that I am writing a script for my life, I decide to let him deflower me.

Here I am, red-skinned from a day at the beach, in a scarlet dress. We tiptoe up the dark stairway to his room. Le rouge et le noir, I think. Like the title of the Stendhal novel I have just read. This is exactly like a movie.

It is so hot and stuffy in his tiny room under the roof. We have raisins and sweet wine. Then I let it happen.

It is no longer like a movie.

Is this really meant to be a woman's life-transforming event? I ask myself.

And yet, when I am clattering home on my Vélosolex, the air grey with the first light, cypresses still shrouded in mist, pine cones bristling under my tyres, the morning breeze cooling my burning skin, I am filled with absolute power and freedom.

At the same time, throughout my five months in Southern France, I feel in complete unison with my parents. In my weekly letters – written in French, of course – I share the details of my life.

My joy and excitement. My gratitude.

Thanks to their trust, I feel self-reliant and resourceful.

My university courses are done, so I work as an au pair for a couple of months: first in a small village in the Cévennes, then in the countryside near Perpignan.

I savour the flair of late summer.

The macchia exuding heat blended with thyme and lavender.

Ripe grapes.

Lizards sunbathing on hot stones.

The air vibrating with the rasp of cicadas.

All this time I stay in touch with Carlo, the first person to rattle at the gate of my shielded existence.

Carlo. My boyfriend before I left home.

He wanders around in a parka and wild beard. Smoking Gauloises or rolling his own cigarettes. His appearance alone defies the propriety of the mid-1960s. His best friend's parents, a surgeon and his wife, ban him from their house.

My parents like him. He, too, comes from an unconventional home.

Carlo gave me Sartre and Camus to read, and *The Myth of Sisiphus* makes me question my world for the first time. Such biting irony in his eyes when he quizzes me about my 'good girl' status.

We have smooched and wriggled our bodies together on the wooden bench in his family's bohemian living room, but I refused to have sex with him. I wanted to wait, even though he tried to make me feel prudish and backward.

Now we decide that he will drive down to France in his Volkswagen Beetle and we will travel together along the Mediterranean coast before he takes me home. I tell my parents about the plan.

There is a furious exchange of letters.

My father: How dare you! Just presenting us with what you have decided. No, you are not going, you come straight home.

Me: You have brought me up to be who I am, to know what I am doing, to make my own decisions.

My father: No.

My mother: I understand you but please also try to understand your father.

Me: I do not understand. I will go. Like Antigone I will do what I think is right.

My brother: Hey, big sister, stop acting up. Antigone? You make me laugh!

But my decision does not waver for a single moment.

Just before Carlo arrives, yet another letter. This time it is from my mother. The package is thicker than usual. I shake it, and it rattles.

Contraceptive pills.

My mother!

It is 1966 and the pill is a novelty. Not easy to get. Not even accepted. But my mother has realised that her daughter is as stubborn as she had once been. So she turns practical and resourceful.

It is golden October. I have never travelled alone with a man before.

Our first night together, on a silvery beach. We huddle from the wind behind a canvas tarpaulin, sand grating in all crevices.

Carlo, who pretended to be so superior, is fumbling and clumsy. He finally admits that actually he has never done it before.

Villages glued to the hills, reflecting the setting sun.

A room in a country inn, with a double bed too short for my more than six-foot lover.

Our wet bodies drying on oven-hot rock.

Figs picked from the trees, velvet-skinned, moist and juicy inside.

Carlo's long body stretched out in a cave, his erect penis unsheltered.

Like an obelisk, I think.

Daunting.

Back home, my father's probing eyes find me: 'Why did you not confide in me?'

Was it jealousy? The jealousy of a father losing his daughter to another man?

Yet the real rift was still to come.

Two years have passed. It is 1968, and the world is on fire.

West Berlin is the heartland of the student movement. Last June, a policeman killed Benno Ohnesorg. In April, a radical right-winger shot Rudi Dutschke in the head.

Yet this is not the reason why I want to go there.

'It will be for one semester only,' I say. 'I want to know the city where you, my whole family, come from. Let me see it and then I'll return to Freiburg.'

'My child, you know nothing. You don't know what is going on in that city. You do not know what I have seen.'

The mass hysteria of the early 1930s. My father lost his job. So many family members fled into exile because of their Jewish roots.

Die Flucht vor der Freiheit. That is what my father called the book he wrote in Berlin during those years of persecution and war. Man is not ready for being a free individual. He will follow the masses into totalitarianism. This was his theory. He saw it beginning again in the 1960s.

In Frankfurt, where he was teaching. In Berlin, where I wanted to go.

His book was published in 1947, the same year I was born. He called me Engelskind, 'a gift from heaven'. I was the promise of a brighter future after twelve years of anguish, when he and his wife did not want to give life to a child.

He understood what would happen if I went to Berlin.

It could have been my father, the professor.

That is what I think today. I did not think so at the time.

Soon after I arrive in Berlin, I am drawn into the ranks of the Rote Zelle Germanistik, the most radical student group.

We have blown out a dozen eggs, filled them with red, blue and yellow paint, and sealed the holes with glue. With two eggs in our pockets, we mingle with a class of well-adjusted, conservative law students. They are about to listen to a lecture by a professor who is defying the teaching boycott, which was called after the expulsion of protest ringleaders.

Here comes the professor. A man in his forties, with suit and tie, a briefcase under his arm, looking respectably nondescript.

He polishes his spectacles, puts them back on his nose and, with determined authority, starts to address the class.

We let him speak for about ten minutes, the students around us tensely silent. Then one of us raises an arm. Other arms fly up. A loud chant of 'Ma – o – dze – dong!'

The last syllable propels ten eggs towards the professor. He tries to duck away. He turns stark white under the blue, red and yellow paint that is filling one eye, smearing his glasses, and sticking to his shirt, suit and lectern.

Many a time, when that last parting image of my father emerges in my mind, I want to run back to him in front of the Raspberry House, I want to fling my arms around his neck and tell him everything that has happened in my life since I set foot in Zimbabwe. While you deemed me far away, I want to say, I was actually right here in your palm.

He must have known that.

Flower in the Snow

AT THE BEGINNING WAS A FLOWER in the snow. Someone had drawn it on the bonnet of my VW Beetle. I had no clue who it was.

It must have been in January 1969. After a few days of heavy snowing, a bright January sun had transformed the city into a fairyland. The pavements were flanked by massive white-grey walls. I had come down from my cozy rooftop flat to unearth my car from under the snow, when I saw it, the flower, neatly carved into the glittering white crust.

Who could have drawn it? What did it mean? I had only come to West Berlin a couple of months before and did not have any close friends in the city yet.

When in October 1968 I arrived at the Free University, the Dahlem villa of the German department was under siege. The doors were barred with benches. Students, with sleeping bags and toothbrushes in their rucksacks, took turns spending the night in the building to make sure that nobody would take down the barricades.

The library, usually a place of hushed silence, seethed with activities and debates. While the goals of the strikes and next steps of action were discussed, flyers were written and placards painted. At other times or in other rooms, Marx and Engels were studied and young lecturers who sympathised with the students held seminars in which they turned the canon and the sacrosanct tenets of the discipline upside down. Schiller, Goethe, Lessing and Kleist were scrutinised through the lens of Historical Materialism.

In all of this I felt like the ignorant, innocent girl from the provinces – or from a far-away planet. I see myself sitting on one of the reading desks which had been pushed aside to make room for the centre of actions. Clutching my knees above yellow gumboots below a straight brown tweed skirt – I listened.

My eyes and ears – my mind – were opened wide.

Things made sense.

I had enjoyed Freiburg, where I had spent the three previous semesters focusing on Romance literature. I could identify with the melancholia of Verlaine or Baudelaire. I had liked the bohemian touch of the French literature students, the wine evenings in the nearby Kaiserstuhl or over the border in France; romantic parties in an old castle; playing charades at a young lecturer's house; listening to the chansons of Georges Brassens, Jacques Brel, Barbara or the old bard François Villon. It had been idyllic, playful, poetic. But something had been missing.

In Berlin the void was filled because the silence was broken, a silence I had not noticed before.

Schlagt die Germanistik tot – Färbt die blaue Blume rot! (Kill German philology, tint the blue flower red) had been one of the major slogans in the protest actions earlier that year. The blue flower was the symbol of German Romanticism, of Weltfremdheit, the aloofness of looking at literature and language far away from social realities. It was the way I had been taught to read literature, by my teachers, by my father. The students in Berlin were out for murder; they wanted to kill a discipline which they indicted for spreading a veil of silence over what had happened during the Nazi regime.

Our parents' generation described the genocide committed under Hitler and the phenomenon of the Nazi regime with words such as 'a monstrosity', 'aberration', 'totalitarianism' – words that did not explain any of the causes but just decried the unfathomable nature of what had happened, similar to a catastrophe of nature which left people incapacitated, unable to act against it, and thus also unable to prevent future events of a similar sort.

'Whoever does not want to speak about capitalism should be silent about fascism,' was one of the tenets of the Left of the time. 'Marxism is the only intellectual weapon against fascism. Ergo, we have to fight for the Revolution.'

From my bystander's position during that semester of strike, which upturned many tenets in my own mind, I had got chatting to a girl who mentioned she lived in a commune.

'A commune?' I had exclaimed, eyes wide open.

'Oh, well, come and see,' she had said. 'We just call it that. We share a flat.'

'Who do you share it with? Other students?'

'Yes, one of them is Victor, over there.'

'Oh really?'

I had seen Victor, he was all over the place, one of the key actionists of what was happening in the German villa. Lecturers dreaded him like a bogeyman.

'Herr Wiiiiiild,' I remember an elderly professor of medieval literature shrieking when she saw him entering her classroom. (She failed to have a heart attack.)

Actually, he did not look that wild. Of medium height, he walked around in a grey tweed coat, out of fashion, oversized grey trousers, and a black seaman's cap over his unruly blond hair. The cap and the heavy frames of his thick glasses gave his rather soft face the stern look of someone in command.

I met him in person when I followed the girl's invitation and went for a meal at their 'commune'.

It was indeed a far cry from the myth of orgies, drugs and free sex surrounding the famous Kommune I and II. The shared flat was sparsely furnished and the shared meal was basic. The sand in the salad was gritty between my teeth.

A week or so later, Victor came round to my flat to pick up a book he had lent me that evening. I think it was Friedrich Engels, that red leather-bound edition of *The Origin of the Family, Private Property and the State*. I must have asked some questions, to which he had suggested I read the book. To my great surprise, when he was about to leave and descend the stairs he turned round and placed a furtive kiss on my cheek.

What, I thought, you? The flower in the snow? I had not in the least expected it. He always looked so focused on serious business that I was utterly surprised by his sudden romantic advance.

Why was he attracted to me, I wondered. Was it because I seemed so innocent and artless?

When my new friend came again, the moon shone down on us through a skylight as he gently stroked my belly, all the while explaining to me how the students' movement had developed and why he himself had turned from a philologist keen on analysing Kafka or Musil into a revolutionary activist.

The Ad hoc Gruppe Germanistik, a group of up to 200 students, constituted the centre of action on the FU campus. They carried the protest to other departments – such as the paint-egg throwing at the professor of law – instigating their fellow students to make sure that no lectures were held anywhere, or else they interrupted lectures themselves.

I remember watching Victor and a few others ramming one of the long wooden benches from the corridors against the door to the office of the Romance Literature department, where two of the professors, who were known as unsympathetic to the demands of the students, had locked themselves in. With a 'whoom' the door was smashed in. Two senior members of staff were found hiding beneath a desk, shaking with fear.

Looking back, I have never seen Victor as self-confident and uninhibited as he was at that time. Not just in physical action. He was a brilliant speaker. I remember how impressed I was when a couple of months later a group of us drove to Göttingen where the students had asked for assistance from Berlin, and Victor, pushing the lecturer aside, went to the lectern and took over the microphone.

'Comrade Professor,' he started, cheered on by an audience of several hundred students, who broke into loud clapping, amid much hilarity. Using the informal 'du' instead of 'Sie' in addressing the bemused professor, Victor then launched into a long speech about the capitalist system and the need to liberate the universities from age-old traditions.

Unter den Talaren, der Muff von 1000 Jahre (Under the gowns the musty odour of a thousand years) was one of the slogans that had set off the students' movement in 1967 – the allusion being to Hitler's 'promise' that the Third Reich would last a thousand years.

During that first semester I not only imbibed new ideas and became part of the protest movement, but I entered into a romantic liaison with one of the ringleaders.

Sexual liberation was another key incentive for the rebellion, and Wilhelm Reich's *Mass Psychology of Fascism* of 1933 another 'bible'. Sexual repression serves social control, we read and believed; suppression of natural sexual instincts leads to sadism, the base of dictatorial regimes. Free sexuality without feelings of guilt; sexual self-determination constitutes the basis for freedom and a democratic society.

Unlike many of my fellow students, I did not feel sexually repressed. My parents, who had spent their youth in Berlin during the 'wild twenties', had always had other sexual partners and still maintained a stable marriage. An unrepressed, free sexuality, as preached and partially lived in the early students' movement, confirmed what I had felt in me already and would in the coming years of my adulthood see as the basis of a partnership.

Probably because I looked so decent and well bred, I was sent out, in the spring of 1969, as the front woman to find an apartment for a group of six Rotzeg students. (Rotzeg was short for Rote Zelle Germanistik which had been formed out of the Ad hoc Gruppe.)

Within no time I had signed the lease agreement for a beautiful apartment on the beletage of one of those nineteenth-century Gründerstil houses in Charlottenburg. Each bedroom had a pretty tiled stove, to be heated with coal, with a bench to sit on when it was cold. The landlady, one of the proverbial West Berlin widows, did not suspect at all that my sub-tenants would be a bunch of those wild FU students for whom most Berliners would not even open their doors. I did not look like them.

Ironically, however, the plan backfired – unknown to me then. As innocent as I might have looked, the flat came under observation all the same. When, five years later, I applied for admission into the civil service as a teacher, one of the issues raised against me was that I had rented a flat where Marxist study groups had gathered. The *Berliner Zimmer* with its large table had indeed not only been used as our dining room.

Defying the State

BY 1970, THE PHASE OF SPONTANEOUS action was giving way to more organised political formations, and the outlook was getting decidedly more 'red' – Marxist-Leninist. By then the flower in the snow had melted and Victor and I were a stable couple deciding together on where we might position ourselves politically.

When we joined one of these ML groups, our lives took on forms which, with the hindsight of today, appear utterly weird and quixotic. Our ML party did not send us into the schools as teachers but into the factories. Together with three others, Victor and I were sent from West Berlin to Ludwigshafen, to work in the huge chemical plant of BASF, which employed around 50 000 workers. In order to disguise our identities as students, we tweaked our CVs and made fake mistakes in the entrance tests. We all got jobs as unskilled labourers. I worked as a laboratory assistant, which I quite liked, while Victor had to handle heavy bags and heave them onto pallets day in and day out. While we were supposed to gain fellow workers for the revolution, we were also to join forces with the small group of old working-class communists based in Mannheim on the other side of Rhine. This was particularly ridiculous. If there was anything that I became ashamed of around my political involvement, it was this phase.

Nevertheless, I gained the confidence of the women I worked with, who, after some months, elected me as their shop steward (Vertrauensfrau), maybe also because I still looked so trustworthy. Following clandestine practices, and without revealing my partisanship for the Maoist Party, I had also been discussing general grievances with them. It did not take long, however, before I was removed from that position. Either the Verfassungsschutz (Secret Service) was starting to monitor the 'K-groups' or else it was the trade union that wanted to get rid of me (we accused all trade unionists of bamboozling the workers).

It is hard to imagine in retrospect our lives at that time. Our never-ending energies were spent on goals that seem so completely unrealistic and out of the world today. We were working eight hours a day in the factory, then hammering calls for action into stencils at night and distributing the pamphlets in the early mornings at the factory doors.

Our living conditions were equally ascetic. Victor and I rented a cheap flat and for warmth we had to put coals into an oven. Some crates (which served as bookshelves), a mattress on the floor, a large table and a few chairs for our group sessions was all we had for furniture – all of it came from garbage sales. A lasting memory of that time is a cloud of bedbugs descending on us and creeping out of the mattress in the night after we returned from a holiday. It was revolting.

Years passed. Victor and I separated for some time, but we kept communicating about the political agenda. We left the sectarian ML party, did our teacher training in cities in the Ruhr district of North Rhine Westphalia, and in 1974 decided to move in together again. This time we found a flat in Essen and we joined the Communist League of West Germany (Kommunistischer Bund Westdeutschland (KBW)). It was also Maoist, and also a cadre organisation, but with a sound basis in the existing movements of students (school and university), apprentices, teachers and trade unions. In the late 1970s it would become a strong supporter of the Zimbabwean freedom fighters. Independence for Zimbabwe was on the horizon but the struggle for liberation was still being intensely fought on the ground.

The KBW's overall agenda was defiance of the state, so after I had finished my teacher training in 1974 and was summoned to an Anhörung (a hearing) by the Ministry of Education, the party asked me to desist the summons. Based on three rather trivial observations of 'intelligence information' (the Marx study group in my flat five years before being one of them), the intention behind this summons was that the state wanted me to prove my loyalty to the constitution.

It was general routine at the time and it would have been easy to go and dispel the existing doubts by belittling the intelligence observations from my younger past as peanuts. But the KBW party directive was: The state has no right to decide who will be a teacher and who won't. I was not to go.

I had my doubts. I felt that the large group of people who supported me, who came to public protests against the threat of me not being admitted as a teacher, would not understand my defiance. They wanted me as a teacher who would fight for the right cause.

Nevertheless, I followed the party line. I think for me it meant: We are the ones with courage, we do not stoop, grovel and crouch.

As a result, I was rejected, barred from the civil service.

During our four years of intense political activism in Essen, in 1976 Victor and I got married. For us it was more of a formality to seal our perspective of staying together as two people who shared similar goals in life, and who wanted to rear a family and rely on each other in every way.

The wedding took place on a hot day in July. I wore a white linen lace dress my grandmother had worn in Bombay during her Indian exile. It felt cool and unblemished on my skin, the air fanning my body through the lace and letting my skin breathe. My grandmother had suffered greatly from the heat during the ten years she had spent in India with my grandfather. During the monsoon they would leave the city and spend a few months high up in the Kashmir mountains. The dress must have been passed on to me after she died, together with some other items. The large tablecloth, also in white lace, which I use on very special occasions, must also have been hers. I spotted it in a photograph of their dining room in their house in Pali Hill, a suburb of Bombay.

Two of my grandmother's sons – my 'Indian uncles' – had settled in India already several years before and they managed to facilitate their parents' immigration into the British colony. Their parents been chased from their home in Germany by the Nazis after the November pogroms of 1938. My grandmothers' parents had converted to Christianity in the 1870s when, under Bismarck, a large group of German Jews became 'emancipated', meaning they received full German citizenship and equal political rights. With many of them being factory owners or tradesmen they were now able to participate in the general economic growth. The Nazis reverted that status. For them only ethnicity mattered, not faith. Hence, in terms of the Nurnberg Race Laws, my grandmother was classified a full Jew, although she was baptised and was a strong Christian believer. Whoever could not prove that at least three of his or her grandparents were Christians was considered a Jew. This also applied to my grandfather's mother; he was classified as *Mischling* (mixed race) and in 1933 was dismissed from his position in the Prussian Home Office.

In 1948 my grandparents returned to Germany and my brother and I were able to spend many joyful childhood vacations with them in their home in the Bavarian Alps, which they had built after my grandfather's dismissal in Berlin. At that time, I knew very little of the trauma they must have gone through. Different from the experience of many other exiles, they had been lucky to have comfortable living conditions in Bombay, near two of their children, but they were separated from the other three, who had stayed in Europe. Those siblings were my mother and her two other brothers. The many details my grandmother recorded in her diary of the time reveal the constant fear and anxiety she had to battle with; during the war there was hardly any possibility of communicating with her children in Germany.

I suppose for her my wedding dress was just an ordinary garment to be worn during the extremely hot days during her forced exile in Bombay. For me, it was more of a frivolous, playful gesture to put that dress on for my wedding. I didn't put much emphasis on the ritual – it was white and it suited me – yet somehow I suppose it was also a subconscious reference to my family history, which I would only begin to explore properly many years later, when I was in my sixties.

Now, as I look through the letters, diaries, photographs, passports with a J and other such documents, reading words of despair, of hope, of farewells and new beginnings, I get a strong sensation of the family energy field into which I was born. I can feel the pain but also the force that lies behind me, especially in the female lineage.

The day of our wedding was not much different from our usual routine. In fact, I had a job interview that morning (to which I wore my wedding outfit) with Krupp, the large steel company. Before the interview with one of the directors was even finished, I had to apologise. I had another important appointment I needed to attend: the signing of my marriage documents at the Registrar's Office.

Two women comrades came along as witnesses and afterwards the four of us went for ice cream and coffee in an ice cream parlour.

I did not get the job.

At the weekend Victor and I went to my parents' house in Wiesbaden. With Victor's parents, our brothers and a few other close relatives we ritualised our union. Both our fathers made speeches.

A marriage of convenience?

Maybe.

Certainly, it was a marriage without romantic illusions, but one based on affection, trust and respect, and a love that was growing with the trials life had waiting for us.

From Frau Mücke to Robert Mugabe

'AH, YOU AGAIN, MR WILD,' THE lady with the funny name (Mücke means 'mosquito') would exclaim when Victor entered her office. 'What happened? Did you get sacked again?'

Frau Mücke was our link person at the job centre in Essen. She knew us by sight and soon by name, especially after we had got married.

Based on the 'Radicals Decree' of 1972, Victor had also been barred as a teacher at government schools. Hence we both tried out various jobs outside the civil service. At regular intervals one of us would appear in Frau Mücke's office to ask for a new job or for unemployment benefits.

My first job, as head of department in adult education, was terminated at the end of the six-month probation period – no reasons given. The next one – after a period of living on the unemployment subsidy – was as personal secretary to the technical director of a large IT company. I remember how I went shopping to find appropriate clothes – a tailored skirt and high-heeled shoes – and put on some make-up, and how my boss was very pleased to have such a cultivated, self-reliant assistant, fluent in both English and French. Yet even before the three months' probation was ended I was sacked, with immediate effect, and banned from the premises.

My boss was baffled. My organisation was triumphant. It was obvious that state intelligence had informed management. Two days later, I stood at the company gate, distributing pamphlets with political slogans. The party newspaper, *Kommunistische Volkszeitung*, published a full-page feature about my case, including photocopies of bills from one or two business dinners my boss had paid for and I had smuggled out. Quite ridiculous, thinking of it now – some 500 deutschmark for one evening, no night club, no major debauchery – but obviously we found such harmless demeanour worthwhile fodder for denouncing 'capitalism and its state lackeys'.

'Nach Entlassung Staat beschimpft' (Reviling the state after getting the sack) was the *Westdeutsche Allgemeine*'s headline above the report about the incident. I got a court order and was fined 300 mark.

A week after Victor and I got married, we came back to our flat after an early agitprop shift in front of a factory gate to find an undercover officer, whom we had often seen at our rallies, waiting for us, a search warrant in his hand.

'Good morning, Mrs Veit-Wild. Good morning, Mr Wild,' he greeted us.

Well, they work fast, I thought; he already knew my new hyphenated surname.

'I am afraid we have to look a bit more closely for things in your flat which might be of interest for us,' he said. As usual, he was smartly dressed, a slightly ironic smile on his handsome face. And indeed, the search was 'successful'; he found some 'compromising' photocopies I had taken from a temporary job I'd had. The temp work agency fired me.

It is strange to think of all of that now. What did it mean to me then? Maybe it was something like playing cops and robbers? I can't say I ever felt truly threatened. I was spending loads of high-quality energy on a cause that was doomed to fail, but we were young, we were trying out things. We wanted to change the world. Erroneously but bravely.

Most important, however, for our future life was the fact that kind Frau Mücke, who thought Victor deserved better than lifting crates onto a pallet transporter and driving them around in a factory, eventually managed to get him into a state-funded vocational training programme. For eighteen months the former high school teacher of German and religious instruction, known to state intelligence of North Rhine Westphalia as a leading communist cadre, was remodelled into a toolmaker, which in any factory workshop ranks highest in the hierarchy of metal journeymen. 'What I learned during those eighteen months was really nothing compared to the skills of a proper toolmaker,' Victor used to say. 'These old master workmen only sneer at me, bloody Bavarian top dogs.'

Disparaged by the illusionist politics of our partisanship and bored with the jobs I had been doing – the last one was as personal assistant in a small French company in Dusseldorf – I looked for a teaching job out of the range of the secret service of North Rhine Westphalia. I found one at a private college in Nurnberg, where we moved in 1978. Victor got work in a factory there that made miniature toy railways.

The four years we lived in Nurnberg were the least spectacular of my whole adult life. We lived in a residential area south of the city, small houses recently developed, quiet, orderly, the epitome of suburbia. The highlight of our rounds with little Max, who had been born in Essen the year before, was a chicken yard where he would throw breadcrumbs through the meshed wire and beam with delight as the hens started clucking hysterically and the roosters boxed each other out of the way.

The flat we rented was on the second floor of a two-storey house, the potbellied owner with wife and canary below, a crippled lady in the attic above. The flat was neat and bright, floor carpeted in light grey, a balcony looking onto a square lawn, several garages and a birch tree with a birdhouse. The flat had the typical division of a small family unit – it was the first and only time my love life was restricted to a 'parental bedroom'.

Nurnberg was a time of transition. After a decade of intense political activism during which our personal lives and careers had been of no import, Victor and I started to turn into ourselves again. And, despite its uneventfulness, it was a time where seeds were sown – not only in the parental bedroom, where our second son was conceived – but also for our future.

One of the new things I tried was a course in mime, which I attended during our time in Nurnberg. In Zimbabwe, a few years later, I would run miming workshops with children. I had always been attracted by the melancholy of the mime: the face starch-white, dark lines running up and down from each eye, without movement, without a blink; and then out of the loneliness of the mime's heart all of a sudden a butterfly appears in his cupped hands, palpating, pulsating, le papillon, throbbing gently, then wildly, you see it breaking free, it is beautiful, full of colours, up and down it swoops, and away – the sad eyes of the mime turn inwards again, his limbs slacken – it is gone.

Was there an early connection in this to my infatuation with Dambudzo?

I had always had a longing for the wondrous, the fantastic, the outlandish. Dambudzo appealed to the clownish, melancholic, poetic part of me, which was menacingly dark and colourfully bright at the same time. That was what I lived out in pantomime or in romance, though I had always been pragmatic enough to know that, for 'real life', I had to make rational choices. Dambudzo more than anyone I'd ever met embodied this 'other' side in me. He led me through many closed doors. He fostered my infatuation with the mad side of life, the 'Coin of Moonshine'.

Moon gleams, a bright distended coin above the dark decade
Casting beams of greed through my shantyhut door,

he ends the poem with that title.

Another important stage for me was that I started to look at what it meant to be a woman. I liked wearing dungarees, in gardener's green or in pink, and they would bulge only slowly and gradually in the summer of 1980 when my belly was growing with my second pregnancy. There was one pair I was especially fond of, which in fact I have kept up to today; it is of a flowing material, very dark blue, patterned with oval shapes in all colours. I am wearing it in the photos taken of me and Dambudzo in our garden in Harare. It is connected to my world of fantasy, the miming. In it I felt playful and light.

I also discovered the beauty of my womb from inside. In a workshop at the Frauenhaus in Nurnberg, a building in the old city which housed a wide range of women's groups and their activities, we were shown how to use a speculum on ourselves. A woman, legs widely sprawled, demonstrated how, using a speculum and a torch and a mirror, you can see your own cervix.

'You see the slime covering the cervix?' she said. 'If that slime is thick and cloudy and opaque, you do not need to worry about getting pregnant. Once you see it spinning threads, elastic and translucent, then you are within the three days before and during your ovulation or shortly after.

So if you want a child, go for it then. If you don't, use protection.'

After she closed her legs and put her knickers and purple pants back on, she showed us photos of the different stages of the slime. 'Go to your pharmacy and ask for a speculum. It is not expensive. And then try it out at home. You can do it with your partner or on your own. Just hold a mirror and a torch between your legs and you will be able to look into your own self.'

'My belly is mine!' The slogan of the movement for the right to abortion obtained a new meaning. Looking into your own femininity, seeing the channel the sperm would take, easing its way through that liquid glittering mucus, I felt elated, empowered, and overwhelmed by its beauty.

During several months Victor and I said to each other, joyfully, curiously and jokingly, 'Okay, shall we *speculate* again tonight?'

When one of the sperm had won the race through the shimmering gateway into my womb, Franz was conceived.

How could I have foreseen that 20 years on, I would undergo a similar introspection of my lower body but under very different gruesome auspices; and that Franz, then 21 years old, would console me.

'Mama,' he wrote when I was in hospital, fatally ill, in his tender loving irony, 'I suspect you are a secret member of the Kennedy clan: like them, you are bright, beautiful and always on top of things. But you are spared no tragedy.'

I started reading women writers. Like many other West German women of the time, we were attracted by writers from the other side of Germany: Christa Wolf, Maxie Wander, Irmtraud Morgner, Sarah Kirsch. While they were less radical in their renunciation of men than West German feminists, they projected new gender roles, fantasised about cross-gendering and created in their characters adventurous, self-reliant women, which immediately appealed to the image I had of myself as a woman.

We were also fascinated by the German Romantic poets around the Brentanos and Schlegels, who at the outset of the nineteenth century proposed new images of men and women, of love and of sensuality, the fluidity of affiliations, of gender – the androgynous, another image of the mime, of the artist, which also appealed to me – longing to be free beings who float in the pink space of desire, changing our personae, loving one in the summer and another in winter, and diving into the pool of shared sensations.

Something else I followed at the time were the Trümmerfrauen, those women who after World War II helped to reconstruct the cities out of rubble and ruins. After interviewing my mother, who survived the bombings in Berlin, I wrote a feature about that part of German history and submitted it to the *Nürnberger Nachrichten*. It got published, on a full page, in one of their weekend supplements. And so, another plant was seeded: perhaps I could not only teach but also write?

About six months before Victor and I left for Zimbabwe I enrolled for a correspondence course in journalistic writing. It would be my point of entry into the literary arena in my new home.

Despite the provinciality of our living conditions, Nurnberg had its enchanting sides. One of these was the old waterway not far from our flat, which would resurrect in Dambudzo's poetic sequence 'My Arms Vanished Mountains' a couple of years later, when he had found a picture book about the 'Alte Kanal' on our bookshelf. Romantic, picturesque, with narrow bridges over the wooden, moss-covered locks and quaint little lock-keepers' houses, the canal was beautiful in all seasons. We would often go there with the children on our bikes or with buggy and pram, and while they were feeding the ducks or watching mirror images of trees and clouds in the green water, Victor and I would sit on a bench and talk about what to do with our lives.

Victor attended the occasional lecture at the university, browsing subjects, mostly in the social sciences. He read expansively around questions that engaged him, particularly the effects of colonialism and imperialism in Africa, which topic we discussed and thought deeply about. How had Europe underdeveloped Africa? What is the outcome of the anti-imperialist movements? What new dependencies are developing in the former colonies? What can be done to undercut the dominance of the centre over the periphery and prevent the neo-colonialism that we saw emerging in the countries who had fought for their independence? Victor read books by Dieter Senghaas, Bassam Tibi and Walter Rodney. He was very interested in dependence theory. His aim was to re-enter the academic field, not to go back to Germanistik but this time to do development sociology.

After some deliberations we decided to go to Zimbabwe so that Victor could carry out his research there. Zimbabwe had won its independence in 1980 – for which we had campaigned strongly in the years before – and so for us it was the obvious choice.

In May 1982 we went on an exploratory visit, to find out about job possibilities. It did not take long before Victor was offered the position of technical instructor at the trainees' centre of a big company in Harare.

This was one of the major ironies of our story. Political persecution (not being allowed to work as a teacher at a government school) prompted the state to sponsor Victor's training as a toolmaker. And had it not been for the double qualification as a teacher and a craftsman he would not have been offered that job. We would not have been able to get residence in Zimbabwe. And the two distant orbits of me and Dambudzo Marechera would never have come close to each other.

When we arrived in Zimbabwe in 1982, Victor had a photograph in his pocket of himself on the same stage with Robert Mugabe. It had been taken at a ZANU rally in the city of Essen in 1976. A group of nine delegates of the Zimbabwe liberation party are standing around a lectern, from which hangs the banner 'Pamberi neChimurenga' (Forward with the liberation war). Right arms raised to clenched fists, their mouths open, they are singing a revolutionary song, the usual ritual at the close of such a rally. In the centre of the photograph stands Rex Chiwara, a student leader and head of ZANU delegations to Western Europe. Mugabe is standing on the right, looking tired and, without glasses, slightly myopic. My husband looks on from the left, hands on hips, shirtsleeves rolled up, his blond hair over his ears, his eyes behind thick-rimmed glasses cast downwards, lips parted into a respectful smile. As the chairman of the local branch of the KBW, a leading force in the solidarity movement for Zimbabwe's independence, he was the official host of the delegation.

The photo remained rather a joke than a joker and door opener for our life in Zimbabwe. Yet within my personal narrative it serves to illustrate an early connection with that country's trajectory towards independence. Victor's and my engagement in the KBW and alliance with the Zimbabwean cause was not the reason we decided to go there in 1982, two years after the country's independence, but it certainly formed the backdrop. We had for many years campaigned for the freedom fighters, had collected money to buy trucks, had helped print ZANU newsletters and had chanted revolutionary slogans alongside their delegates when they visited our country.

We came to Zimbabwe with the joy of a victory won, with the hope for a prospering nation but also with the vigilance grown out of our own faults and failures.

PART TWO

HARARE IN HEAT

December 1982

*Harare in heat. Whores in plenty. Sunlight harsh, stridently bright.
... The only sound of water in the City was the plungent Cecil Square
fountains, the flush of toilets, the horrible oogle of the sink ...*
Dambudzo Marechera ('Park Bench Diary' in *Mindblast*)

WE ARRIVED IN HARARE IN December 1982, a week before Christmas. It was terribly hot. After two seasons with abundant rains and bumper harvests, the summer months had been extremely dry and the country was facing its second year of drought. Every day clouds gathered, temperatures rose above 30 degrees, the air became oppressive – but then the clouds dissolved and not a drop of rain fell. On the farms the maize plants withered. In the villages rain-making ceremonies were held.

In my mind I see Dambudzo, sitting in Cecil Square, hammering away on his portable typewriter. At the time still bearing the name of the colonial conqueror, the square was a small quadrangle of a park in the centre of Harare, with low hedges laid out in a geometrical pattern, a fountain pouring water high into the air in its centre. Yet for Dambudzo the air is polluted by the stink of the public toilet hidden in one corner of the square, as the heat mingles with his pain and the hunger in his belly.

Of rain, not a smell, not a taste, not a touch. And the heat in my mind raged; a raw seething wound.

On one side of the square stood the old Meikles Hotel, whose wood-panelled interior exhumed the scent of the earliest days of colonial settlement; the other side was flanked by the modern commercial centre with a skyline of office towers, square façades of glass and stone, up to twenty floors. The centre of Harare was not at all as one might have imagined an African city. To the dismay of travellers looking for the exotic, it felt very European. There was no flurry and pell-mell of people, no carts or markets, no hubbub of voices, noises and smells. Everything was clean and orderly.

Yet it was Dambudzo's habitat. His typewriter and a plastic bag containing books and clothes – all the belongings he possessed – accompanied him. For lunch he would get a mug of sour milk from the Indian grocery. At sunset he would stroll off to the Ambassador Hotel, scrounging beer and cigarettes in the Long Bar, where he could be sure of finding journalists or government employees drinking their heads off. The Herald House was next door, and two huge newly erected ministry buildings, all ugly in grey cement, were not far away.

'Hey, Dambudzo, you are not looking good today.' Someone would always beckon him over. 'When will your new book be out?'

At night, when the bars were closing, he could be found sleeping in a doorway or in a park. Passers-by were familiar with the image of the down-and-out city poet. He was a legend.

Yet I had never heard of him, when I was entering his stratosphere, on that hot and dry end of the year 1982.

My first impressions of the city were of a different sort.

German Christmas in the Tropics

WE WERE INVITED TO A GERMAN Christmas party. Groups of people in summery clothes, wine glasses in hand, neatly dressed children, tables decorated with twigs of pine, homemade Lebkuchen arranged on small trays, their chocolate icing melting, a waft of roast coming from the kitchen. And in the middle of it all a Waldorf nativity play. German Christmas under the tropical sun. Such was our introduction into our new life in Harare.

Our host was a geologist from Germany who, with this wife and three children, was posted in Zimbabwe for three years. He was not the type we would have normally spent our time with in Germany. He seemed overly correct and formal and, whenever we met him, throughout the three years, he always addressed us with the formal 'Sie'. But he was outgoing and he radiated some of the excitement of a life out of the ordinary, which brought us all here together on that hot Christmas Day.

'My work is exciting. I have to travel a lot, looking at mines and the like – but, come, let me introduce you to the other guests.'

'Aha, so are you helping our old friend Mugabe with his land reform?' Victor said, when we were introduced to a guest who worked as an adviser to the Ministry of Agriculture.

'What do you mean, your old friend …?'

'This must be your wife,' I interrupted, not sure what the German agriculturalist would think of our close affiliation with Mugabe and his comrades during the liberation war.

His wife reminded me of my mother. Tall and slim like her husband, keeping herself upright, she radiated a sporty elegance. I imagined her wearing a tartan skirt in winter topped by a twinset with a pearl necklace. Their faces were tanned – probably from playing tennis or golf – but I also sensed in them a resolve to make the best of their stay, for themselves and their three girls.

'So what brought *you* here?' she asked. 'Who do you work for?'

'Well, actually' – I was trying to find a way of saying that we did not come with a contract, that we were just ourselves – 'my husband got a job as a technical instructor in a trainees' workshop –'

'Let me introduce you to our pastor,' our host interrupted.

'Ah, some more sheep for our Lutheran herd?' A tall man was busy getting to his feet, stretching his long arm out to greet us. He reminded me of a slightly bent tree. The German pastor's voice was full and warm and the impish smile above his long grey beard made me think that we did not have to feel embarrassed about not joining his herd.

Suddenly a loud blast on a trombone made me jerk and turn. The angels were greeting the wise men. Some were singing, other children played the flute, the violin, the cymbals.

'Do your boys play an instrument?' the pastor's wife whispered to me. She was a large lady, Jewish, American, a mother of five.

It hadn't taken me long to realise that all the mothers here seemed to spend their days chaperoning their children to and from school and to all sorts of extra classes: swimming, tennis, ballet, speech and drama, and music.

The pastor's wife was whispering again. 'You see that angel with the violin? She is my daughter … and the one on trombone is my son … and the tiny one with the triangle is our three-year-old.'

'I see …' I nodded, looking anxiously across to the pool where our children were splashing about. They were the only ones who had gone swimming instead of watching the nativity play.

Later that evening, when the children were asleep, Victor and I sat together at a wrought-iron table in the garden of the Oasis Hotel, where we were staying until we found a place to set up home. The garden was dark and quiet. Most people would be in their homes around the

Christmas tree. Only a few candles and the underwater lights of the pool gave a shimmering glow.

'It is difficult to explain to those people why we are here,' Victor said. 'We are so different from everyone else. They are all here with a contract, with a mission, with a clear definition –'

'Yes, and we, we are just us. Did someone ask you how you got the job in the training centre?'

'Yes. I said that I was a teacher and also had a qualification as a toolmaker.'

'Ja, isn't it funny? If it hadn't been for Frau Mücke, we would not be here.'

The Mozambican Bogeyman

DURING OUR FIRST WEEKS IN Harare Victor often hitchhiked to his workplace, which was on the other side of town. On top of the persisting drought, Zimbabwe was experiencing a severe shortage of petrol. Where to find fuel was the talk of the day. The newspapers were full of crisis news and images of endless lines of cars queuing at the petrol stations. Some days not a drop was available; on others the disbursement was rationed to ten or fifteen litres per car.

It was easy to hitch a lift in those days, in the general air of hope and of trust. It wasn't unusual to see big groups of people walking along the roads and, at the approach of a car, hundreds of thumbs stretching out. If it was a white man hitching, he did not even have to stretch out his thumb before a car stopped. The black ladies with heavy bags of flour on their heads and snotty-nosed babies on their backs might have to wait a while longer but they, too, would be sure to find a place on the back of a pick-up eventually.

After our first days in the Oasis Hotel, we moved to a house-sit at Danhiko School, a vocational training centre for disabled ex-combatants. It was one of the first-hour projects funded by a Norwegian aid organisation. The house, which belonged to the American director of the school, was messy and chaotic but it came with three major assets: a typewriter, a dog and a car. Our own typewriter was in the container with all our furniture which would arrive much later. And our car was in for repairs from the damage it had sustained on board the ocean liner from Bremen to Durban.

Our weekly letters to our parents, in which we reported all the details of our new life, could now be typed. Max, we told them, had recently declared that he liked blacks better than whites. He wanted to know all about their lives and why they were so much poorer than white people were. He observed how women carried heavy loads on their heads and wondered why we would often see them sitting at street corners, staring at us. His brother had different concerns: 'Franz's main addressee is Bingo, the German Shepherd,' we reported. '"Sit down! Out! Off! Eat!" are his first English words.'

The tank of the battered Renault 4 the landlady had left for our use – a make you would frequently see on Harare streets at the time – was already on reserve. Victor only just made it to the nearest petrol station, where he spent half the night in a queue. In the morning, just before it was his turn, the pumps stopped dispensing so he left the car where it was and hitchhiked to work. The following night he walked the seven kilometres from our house to the petrol station and eventually got his fifteen litres. Little as it was, it helped me run necessary errands. A bank account had to be opened, money transfer from Germany organised, immigration procedures finalised, mortgage options for buying a house explored, and, most importantly, Max to be enrolled in school.

So while Victor was at work, I crammed the children into the car, which was littered with books, papers, empty cigarette packets, plastic bottles, matches, lighters and cigarette stumps, pressed the windows down as much as they would budge to dispel the stench of smoke, and, bumping the peculiar R4 gears into place, drove off at fuel-saving speed.

We had taken the advice of other German parents to enrol Max at Lewisam School in Chisipite, one of the park-like suburbs forming the green belt around the northern part of the city. Low-density suburbs, they were now called, meaning formerly whites-only areas; prior to independence blacks had only been allowed to enter with special passes proving that they were housemaids or gardeners.

Low-density indeed, I thought, as we approached the school. The flat-roofed, bungalow-style buildings were situated within a vast area of uncultivated green land and surrounded by large sports fields.

'Look, Mummy – ponies!' Max said, pointing to what turned out to be a riding school right next door. 'May I start horse riding?'

'Warum nicht, mein Lieber, but wait, first you have to start school and once we know where we're going to be living, we'll see.'

'Good morning, dear,' the silver-haired lady at the school office crooned. 'Isn't it hot today? I bet you must be suffering terribly, knowing where you come from – this is just such a ghastly summer.' I had to smile at her mannerisms and the pressed vowels in her speech, so typical of white Rhodesians. 'I am so glad you have been able to come. How did you manage, with this awful shortage of petrol? Isn't it deplorable, now that the borders with Mozambique are finally open again, some wicked terrorists are planting bombs and blowing up oil tanks?'

'Well ...' I tried to work out how to avoid a certainly fruitless discussion about who was responsible for the fuel crisis. Beira, I knew, had always been an essential port for landlocked Rhodesia-Zimbabwe. From the eastern town of Mutare it was only a five-hour drive to the Mozambican coast. As long as the Portuguese ruled, the tropical beaches had been a favourite holiday destination for the Rhodesian settlers.

'Oh, it was paradise,' the secretary continued, not noticing my hesitation. 'Coconuts, bananas, pineapples, cottages under palm trees right on the beach. Our children *loved* it. And so affordable! But then, you know, this communist took over – what was his name again?'

'Samora Machel,' I said. 'And he was rather a socialist ...'

'Socialism, communism, isn't it all the same? Anyway, he closed the borders and come '76 we were stuck in our country.'

I did not say, 'But do you know *why* he closed the borders?' Did I even think about it? Did I remember how, ten years before, I had taught *Song of the Lusitanian Bogey* as my final exam project in teacher training? I had chosen the play by Peter Weiss to alert my high school students to the liberation movements in Angola, Mozambique and Guinea-Bissau and the near end of Portuguese colonialist rule. And indeed, only a year later, the Portuguese 'bogeyman' had been ousted and the colonies set free. Samora Machel had closed the borders because his neighbours, Rhodesia and South Africa, were trying to destabilise the newly independent country.

'Anyways, I am glad you have chosen our school, Mrs Wild,' the secretary concluded after I had filled in all the forms. Then, with something between a chuckle and a whisper, she added, 'And I can assure you, the majority of our pupils are still white. The teaching staff of course too. Let me get you all the information leaflets and the price list for the tuck-shop where you can buy the young man's school uniform.'

The young man in question, meanwhile, had been listening intently to the conversation.

'Mum, what did that lady say?' Max asked as we walked back to the car. 'Is someone throwing bombs?' His ear was getting used to the new language and he must have picked up the word 'bomb', which is close to the German *Bombe*. 'Is there going to be a war?'

War and bombs had become one of his major concerns after we had taken him to an anti-nuclear war demonstration in Nurnberg a few years before. From his carrier seat on Victor's back he had seen the huge crowd of protesters carrying placards and banners and heard them chanting slogans. With the inquisitiveness of a three-year-old, afterwards he had hammered us with questions. I recorded them in a notebook, which I later found.

'Are the other children in nursery school also going to demonstrations?'
'No.'
'But then a bomb will drop onto their house.'
'Well ...'
'There should be a good bomb which destroys the bad bombs.'

'Don't worry, Max,' I told him now, 'there is no war where we are. But in Mozambique lots of soldiers and rebels with guns are roaming the country. And the government of South Africa has sent men to Beira – that's the harbour, where the big oil tankers arrive. You remember, we saw some in Durban? And those South Africans blew up the oil tanks and the pipeline that brings petrol to Zimbabwe. That is why it is so difficult to get fuel for our car.'

At home Max made a drawing of a petrol station and sent it to my mother. From the day we landed on African ground, he put all his new impressions into drawing and painting.

'Please send me a Lego petrol station, exactly like this,' he wrote to his grandmother.

Of course, it was not easy to explain to a five-year-old the political mechanisms that had turned the neighbouring country into chaos. In Zimbabwe we were breathing the air of freedom, of a battle won, of hope in the future – but across the border, soon after the bogeyman had been dismissed into the archives of history, a civil war had begun to ravage the country and turn it literally into parched soil. Even for us, this looming shadow at the back of our new life, like writing on the wall, was hard to decipher at the time.

We had first-hand reports from Germans working for aid organisations, Welthungerhilfe or the Red Cross, about how convoys transporting food and medical supplies through the corridor from Mutare to Beira were ambushed and looted every so often by rebel groups. A close friend, who had his base in Harare, once saved his life by rolling out of his truck and hiding behind a bush until the shooting was over. Injured and with no water, he had to walk the fifteen kilometres back to the border camp. In later years we heard about the millions of refugees flocking across the border. We had German medical students stopping over at our house on their way to work in one of the huge refugee camps near Zimbabwe's eastern border.

Although there was not any detailed information yet about why the neighbouring state was rapidly dilapidating, the Mozambican situation might have added to the political disillusionment we had gone through even before we came to Zimbabwe. Which made us aware that in Zimbabwe all was not well.

It also made me ready to meet someone who would not join in the slogans, someone who instead would point his finger at those who were left out in the grand venture of building a new nation.

The Oracle

Oracle of the Povo

Her vision's scrubland
Of out-of-work heroes
Who yesterday a country won
And today poverty tasted

And some to the hills hurried their thirst
and others to arson and blasphemy
Waving down tourists and buses
Unleashing havoc no tongue can tell –
Her vision's Droughtstricken acres
Of lean harried squatters
And fat pompous overlords
Touching to torch the makeshift shelters
Heading to magistrate and village court
The most vulnerable and hungry of citizens –
Her vision's Drought Relief graintrucks
Vanished into thin air between departure point
And expectant destination –

In despair, she is found in beerhalls
And shebeens, by the roadside
And in brothels: selling the last
Bits and pieces of her soured vision.

I DON'T KNOW HOW MANY TIMES I have read this poem, but every time I do I am more touched by its beauty, amazed how in one long breath, in a rhythm carried forward by sounds exquisitely placed and paced, in images astounding and yet lucid, the poem encapsulates the malaise at the core of the newly independent country.

I cannot say much about the life Dambudzo was leading before I met him. I once heard that the 'German commune', young people sharing a house in Alexandra Park, had given him shelter but, as was usually the case, once he had emptied the fridge of all things to eat and drink without replacing them, had chucked him out. He then slept on their ping-pong table in the garden.

The park-bench diary is the best record of his life then, in his own words, in that typical mixture of deep insight, scorn and self-mockery.

> I had nowhere but the streets and skidrow in which to sleep – for all the days that would come, I had not rejected the notion of human brotherhood; I could not accommodate its materialist ends. Now and then I would meet someone who would give me a floor and I would sleep easy in a snug sleeping bag. Come morning, with her six o'clock alarm rasping my dream apart, I would find the hazards of the street terrifyingly waiting for me with open arms. But first: food. That must always come first. I trudged into a Greek-owned grocery story, bought myself a pack of sour milk and three buns and headed for Cecil Square to sit, eat and type this story.

'Oracle of the Povo' belongs to the bulk of poems Marechera wrote in the weeks after his return from England. More sharply than any political scientist could do, he surveys the state of affairs: the freedom fighters who are now unemployed; the violence taking place in Matabeleland; the ZANU-PF leaders who detoured food aid trucks.

'I am feeling like an eccentric growth on the skin of my country,' he once said shortly after his return from exile. His poems, prose pieces and plays of that period express the writer's profound sense of unease and estrangement from his home country. 'Why does every revolution result in the alienation of its artists?' is a question he explores in many facets.

This alienation made him, who would not be compromised by taking a job in government or at the university as many of his contemporaries did, become the homeless writer-tramp that he was when I met him. And yet, in that state of homelessness, he was the poetic conscience of the nation, the oracle whose voice would be bitterly missed once it was gone.

Becoming Expatriates

IN THE MONTHS WE'D SPENT preparing the ground for our stay in Harare, and also in the months following our arrival, Victor and I got acquainted with what it meant to live as a European expat in a country such as Zimbabwe. While we enjoyed the extraordinary privileges such a lifestyle offered, the unease of being a white person in a country that was mostly black and the social differences attached to this never left us.

After another house-sit, we spent two weeks in the Brontë Hotel situated in The Avenues, an area north of the commercial centre. This was where the early settlers had built their first living quarters and indeed the place was – and is up to this day – a charming if quaint reminder and remainder of early settler times. Time seemed to have stopped in the Brontë Hotel. You imagine Cecil Rhodes himself appearing any minute in the wood-panelled lobby; or the Brontë sisters, after whom the place was named, in bonnets, drinking tea from floral-patterned china in one of the lounges.

In this august and venerable setting, every morning, when Victor had already left for work and I was trying to hurry the boys on to get Max to school by eight, I went through an ordeal.

The boys and I would sit at our table in the dining room, with its dark wood panels on the walls and red carpet covering the floor, while at least ten waiters scurried constantly around, asking in monotonous tones if we wanted our eggs boiled, fried, scrambled or poached, and with bacon, tomatoes, mushrooms or sausage ... Franz, our two-year-old toddler, would be in his high-chair, refusing to be fed, refusing to be rushed, sputtering porridge all over the place. When I tried to pull him out of the chair he screamed at full volume. With bashful side glances to the few other guests and the waiters who, in white uniform and red fez, all looked like they came straight out of a colonial picture book, I would try to swipe with a napkin at the unsightly splashes on the table cloth and floor.

'Don't worry, madam,' one of the waiters would inevitably murmur, 'we'll take care of it.' From underneath his polite smile and his starched uniform I would catch a faint whiff of the paraffin fire on which he had cooked his own food, basic as it would have been, in the 'staff quarters', those bare rooms hidden away in the far rear of each colonial property.

So I was glad when I found us a provisional home, a pretty little house that we rented for six weeks. It was not far from Max's school; I could take him there by bicycle. The garden was comparatively small, but densely grown with broad-fingered tropical shrubs, banana, bamboo and palm trees, and a huge cactus in the middle of the lawn. Cream-coloured angel's trumpets bent lavishly into the grassy driveway, emitting their sensuous perfume once the sun had set, and a cascade of pink bougainvillea poured down near the house's entrance. In the mild end-of-summer light everything was dipped in pastel colours.

Max and Franz were fascinated by the flock of bantam chickens that roamed the lawn, fluttering and clucking excitedly when handfuls of grain were thrown out to them from the kitchen door. One day the boys found the huge skull of a buffalo hidden away in a dark corner of a garden shed. A photo in our family album shows Max holding the skull, his face smiling under the grey floppy hat of his school uniform, his hands clasped over the mighty horns.

For our children, this interim home marked the beginning of ten years spent outdoors, running barefoot across open spaces, climbing rocks and trees. They dug tunnels to hide treasures, slept in tree huts and, at one stage, kept house snakes in a terrarium, feeding them mice. For me, the new set-up meant the first step into the freedom I would enjoy throughout the years to come, in which Anna, the housemaid, played an important part. Anna 'came with the house', so to speak; the landlady had asked us to keep her on. To a large extent I owe it to her that in our ten years in Zimbabwe I could launch an academic career, something I had never envisioned. Yet she also became a silent witness to some of the turbulences my love life would bring about.

Servants. The big bone of contention among expatriates living in Africa. Many eyebrows were raised on this issue in the letters we received from our friends back home. Were we not continuing colonial ways? How could we, former communist activists, who had fought for the liberation of the black people in Zimbabwe, now follow in the footsteps of the former oppressors? As important as the question was, we did not have an easy answer.

One thing I can say is that once I was with Dambudzo, I tended to forget the imbalance between me as the 'white madam' and him coming from the 'ghetto'. The tension was invisible, or so it seemed to me, but it was there. And it could – and did – suddenly erupt and cause havoc in our relationship.

Elective Affinities

ONE DAY VICTOR CAME HOME from work in high spirits.

'Guess who gave me a lift just now?'

'Tell me.'

'A young white guy. A Zimbabwean. He was also driving one of those old battered R4s. We chatted all the way and got on really well. He wanted to know why we were here, where we came from, what we were doing – he was so open-minded.'

'Wow, that's amazing. So not all whites in this country are bloody racists?'

It was a revelation. We soon became friends with Nyle, Victor's hitchhiking acquaintance, and his girlfriend Marie-Lou and, through them, met more white Zimbabweans who were sympathetic with the black government. Most of them were from the creative sector: artists, gallerists, musicians, filmmakers, actors. Some of them had immigrated from South Africa, glad to get away from apartheid society, which was mindboggling and exasperating for any sensitive person. Others were native Zimbabweans, who had hibernated during the right-wing regime of Ian Smith or, after years abroad, were returning to their liberated home country. Relieved that their tribesman's dream of 'a thousand years of white rule' had not come true, they joined in the general euphoria of a new beginning. Getting to know such people heightened our own feeling of being in the right place at the right time. Vice versa, our new friends seemed inspired by our company, and perhaps the flair of worldliness we brought to the parochial Rhodesian atmosphere in which they had been enclosed.

'Look at this,' Marie-Lou said to a friend when she and Nyle were taking a tour of our house. By then our belongings from Germany had arrived and the house was fully furnished with our things. 'Look at the clear lines and the bright colours.' She was admiring the Marimekko curtains in the children's bedroom. 'It is so beautiful and so simple,' she said. 'These flowers, pure red and blue, on the white – and feel the cotton! You won't find anything like this here. Come and look at this, Nylie …' But Nyle was sitting in the playroom, immersed in building Lego landscapes with the boys and not all that interested in curtains.

My heart flew for Nyle. He was a charmer. With a teasing smile on his lips and a hint of melancholy in his dark eyes, he looked like a blend of James Dean and a young Bob Dylan. As it turned out, Victor, in turn, was quite drawn to Marie-Lou. The couple joined us on our first trip to Tengenenge, the magical artists' place where hundreds, if not thousands, of stone sculptures lurked in the high grass, their black polish glistening in the sun. Victor developed a strong liking for this art, so peculiar to Zimbabwe. I watched him wandering around the vlei with Marie-Lou as they discovered more and more sculptures behind rocks, on the trunks of trees or hidden behind bushes. It was fascinating how they blended the archaic with the modern.

Tengenenge, world famous for many years for its school of stone sculptors, was the creation of Tom Blomefield, one of the peculiar and unique personalities we would get to know in Zimbabwe. When his tobacco farm in the area of the Great Dyke in northern Zimbabwe began to suffer severely under the sanctions imposed on Rhodesia in the late 1960s, he started to excavate serpentine, which was found in that area and is a stone particularly apt for sculpting. While he sat down to follow his own artistic inclination, he also gave hammers and chisels to some of his farm workers and taught them to sculpt. Many of them became highly regarded – and priced – artists. In the evenings, sitting by the fire, telling stories of days gone by, Tom looked for all the world like a gnome from a fairy tale. He was a chunk of a man, with curly white hair and beard framing his round face and bulging red cheeks around his twinkling eyes.

He was earthen; he seemed part of the bush around him.

An outing to Tengenenge, where we would take many of our visitors over the years, meant driving for several hours, which included long stretches of dust road, but it filled our hearts with joy: the country, the people, the warmth, the stones – it was a magnificent universe. We would take baskets of food and drink and have lovely picnics in the grassland. The boys would be off hunting lizards and chameleons, keeping an eye out for snakes, or collecting pieces of 'nature'. When Max was a bit older, he spent a couple of days there, workshopping with the resident artists. He sculpted a beautiful fish out of a piece of black serpentine.

Victor and I talked about the butterflies we both had in our tummies over Marie-Lou and Nyle. Wouldn't it have been a perfect cross-couple fling, another enrichment to our lives in that light-heartedness of the time?

I described my feelings to Nyle. 'Elective affinities,' I said to him. 'What is wrong with that?' I even ordered an English translation for him of Goethe's romantic novel but by the time it arrived he had already withdrawn from intimacies with me.

'Well, you know,' he said, as I lay by his side (the one and only time), 'it has been easy for you to seduce me – beautiful as you are, and a married woman – that is a real compliment for a homeboy like myself. But I don't think it is the right time. You know that Marie-Lou and I are getting married soon. And I also had this short episode with her sister recently. We have to steady ourselves.'

Marie-Lou, so Victor told me, seemed even more anxious about her relationship with her husband-to-be and rightly so, as it turned out, because the bridegroom, charming as he was, did a duck ten days before the wedding. Marie-Lou had already shown me her dress – I think it was pure silk, white, with a faint shine of rose – and her parents, an old established Rhodesian family, had sent out 150 invitation cards. Nyle became persona non grata in their house. Not too long after that Marie-Lou married an inventive businessman from Britain; he was also named Nyle.

At the time I could not understand our friends' reluctance to take up our proposition. To me it seemed so natural and life-enhancing, meaning no harm to anyone. Was I naïve, or selfish, or just insensitive to their anxieties? In any event I underestimated the cultural differences that existed between our white liberal friends and us. They were more rooted in cultural conservatism than they appeared.

'You come from a different culture,' Nyle tried to explain, 'so you don't understand.'

In fact, it seemed like we came from a different planet.

While the 'elective affinities' did not, in the end, come to bloom as Victor and I had hoped they might, the emotional flurry, the excitement, the opening up to new friends and new possibilities seemed to burst open blockages in our own relationship. It all became part of the high spirits that our move to Zimbabwe had put into motion, not only in us as individuals, but also as a couple. It helped Victor and me explore the emotional deficits that existed in our marriage. We talked more and now and then we wrote letters to each other – Victor from his workplace, while the trainees were busy filing, I from my desk at home.

'I feel,' Victor wrote, 'that perhaps we are now hitting the mute spot in our relationship. And I am quite confident that we will make progress in our attempt to delve into it. I feel much better than in the past years, much more able to talk to you about us. The experiences with Marie-Lou and Nyle have sensitised me. I am not at pains anymore to talk about my feelings, something that used to be so hard for me, cost me so much effort, and eventually left me silent – stumm.

'I am in such good spirits since we have been here, our life is full of new experiences, just as what we wished for since long, we can see that things are moving. And it is such luck that all this has been brought about by both of us together, in every way.'

Did I jeopardise the strong emotional basis between us, I must ask myself now, when half a year later I got involved with Dambudzo? Did I over-stretch the openness of our partnership and the trust that existed between us?

Boscobel Drive

THE PROPERTY WE EVENTUALLY found and which became our home reached far beyond what we had expected or aimed for. Back home in Germany, it definitely nurtured the reputation we were acquiring among some of our friends that we were stepping right into the shoes of those we had formerly regarded as colonial exploiters and oppressors. But for me, finding this dream-like house became another of the junctions in my life that would transform it as if with a magic wand.

One morning, when Victor was at work and Max at school, I put Franz into his buggy and set off on foot to view a house that wasn't too far from the one we were renting. I remember the day so clearly. Sunlight filtered through the feathery branches arching over Boscobel Drive, my destination.

Houses in Highlands, as the suburb was called, were built in the colonial style of the 1930s and 1940s. Mostly the houses were rather small but set on a large plot of land surrounded by tall old trees and hedges, shielding them from the streets.

I walked along the pavement, pushing Franz carefully over the uneven parts. Streets in these residential areas did not generally have sidewalks and residents seldom walked – they drove everywhere. It was only their nannies, cooks and gardeners in overalls or maids' uniforms you would see walking anywhere, ambling along, chatting to each other, or gathering at street corners on their lunch breaks. If they saw a white woman walking past, they would turn their heads and stare. Who was she? Why was she not driving a car? And in my case this bright morning – where was she headed with the little blond boy in the pushchair?

Looking out for house No 8, I found myself walking along a hedge, which was very high and seemed to have no end. Where it was a little patchy, I could get a glimpse of the property behind it.

'Hey, Franziboy, this can't be it,' I muttered, more to myself than to my son who, dummy in mouth and cuddly cloth in hand, seemed dazed by the warmth and the freckly light.

In the glimpses I got I could make out a wide stretch of lawn, large trees and something sparkling blue. I was certain I had missed the house number or that it was still coming, because this property seemed out of the world, way beyond what we were aiming at and could afford. Should I even go in and look at it, I asked myself, when I eventually confirmed the number and found the entrance, which was in a close around the corner. Surely it would be a waste of time?

But I did go in and I did look at the place, and I was very glad I did.

The owner was a Methodist minister, an attractive man in his mid-forties, who was in the middle of a divorce. He was happy to sell this other-worldly property, which covered two acres, at a very reasonable price.

Compared to the living conditions Victor and I had been used to in our previous life together, this house and garden seemed out of all proportion. And yet, as our lives expanded, we grew into them quite naturally. They became home and base for numerous visitors, family, friends, or scholars, on shorter and longer stays; they were a meeting point for artists, cultural workers and academics from Zimbabwe and abroad.

And for Dambudzo Marechera, who delightedly swapped the park bench for a luxurious writer's residency when he moved in with us half a year later.

Our very first visitor from home was my mother. She had been full of support when we were preparing for our big move to Zimbabwe. It was she who persuaded my father to give me an advance on my inheritance, which allowed us to finance our move and buy the house. Now she was curious to see our new environment for herself. She was amazed. And she was happy and proud.

'I wish he had known what you have made of it,' she used to say in later years, after my father had died and she came on regular visits. 'I really had to talk him into giving you the money.'

Indeed, our property was 'paying itself out'. It was to be the setting for years of a multifaceted social life, of pool battles, of birthday parties with challenging treasure hunts, of intense work, of nights of passion, of hurt, of love and of intense trepidation. It allowed me, after a hazardous roundabout journey of more than twenty years of my adult life, to become a well-known scholar of African literature and a university professor – thus, ironically, following in the footsteps of my father.

Thinking back to the first months in our new home, I see myself as if through a prism, in a kaleidoscope of colours, overwhelmed by the intense beauty of my new life. Every morning I would sit at my desk in a daze. 'This is paradise,' I kept repeating to myself. Through the window in front of me I gazed into our park-like garden with its vast expanse of lawn; tall trees with feathery leaves; the pool, glittering blue; to my right, an avalanche of pink – a huge bougainvillea flowing over a tree down into the flowerbed. It seemed unreal. Like something from a *House Beautiful* magazine or a glossy real estate brochure. But it was neither of these. It was my new home.

I had the mornings to myself. Victor would be at work. Max at school. And Franz somewhere with Anna: walking to the corner shop to buy milk and bread or sitting with her in the staff quarters during her tea break, enjoying thick slices of white bread with margarine and jam.

The correspondence course in journalistic writing I had started in Germany kept me busy. The regional newspaper, *Nürnberger Nachrichten*, had published two long features of mine – my first two pieces ever that I saw in print – and I also had assignments to do. One of the published pieces was a report about my first impressions of Zimbabwe during the exploratory trip Victor and I had undertaken in June 1982. Seeing my work in print gave me the appetite to learn more about the craft.

In my new surroundings, my course assignments gave me the incentive to explore the literary scene in the newly independent Zimbabwe and I would soon begin to speak to writers, publishers and literary agents, and attend book events. They would eventually and inevitably cause me to cross paths with Dambudzo Marechera, the most controversial literary celebrity of the day. In fact, he was the subject of my final assignment, an essay, which I titled in German 'Schreiben gegen den Wahnsinn' (Write or go mad) and for which I got the highest credits. It was published in English translation in several regional magazines and as a result I would start to be viewed as a literary critic.

Through the window on my right I saw our gardener, Anna's brother, in blue overalls, black gumboots and a woollen cap, preparing our vegetable garden. His face was just as broad and pleasant to look at as Anna's, making you feel safe. Right after we had moved in, he'd helped build the timber fence around the pool. After he'd varnished it, it glowed the same reddish brown as the terracotta tiles around the pool – a welcome oven to warm up after a swim.

Should I have felt guilty for living such a different lifestyle from before, in a house on a huge property, with domestic workers who called me 'madam' and my husband 'baas', as a few snide remarks of friends back home insinuated?

I did not. I felt exuberant. I felt like the princess in the fairy tale showered with gifts of gold by her twelve fairy godmothers. All I had to do was follow the invisible strings that were pulling me forward and life would be plentiful and rich. The evil fairy, who would curse the princess into a hundred years of sleep, had not yet arrived. My thicket of thorns was still to arise.

It was May 1983. I was turning 36. It was the beginning of a new life and of a story that was larger than life.

Guest of Honour

My current assignment, to conduct an interview, had taken me to the Literature Bureau, an agency for writers writing in Shona and Ndebele. I had almost walked past their office on Samora Machel Avenue, the northern artery of the city centre, so inconspicuous was it opposite the Monomotapa Hotel which, with its 20 storeys and modern architecture, towered over and completely outshone the low buildings in the area.

Through the bleary shop window I could make out some faded posters on the walls – announcing writing workshops and competitions – and equally sun-bleached catalogues on a table which, on closer inspection, had information about novels and children's books in the local languages. Their covers showed images of women with babies on their backs, a village scene, or a warrior with a spear.

'The Bureau is of a colonial legacy,' my interviewee explained when he saw me looking at them.

David Hlazo, the current director of the Literature Bureau, who spoke seven languages, was originally from South Africa. He was around sixty years of age and had a very dark complexion. The fine lines around his smiling eyes and criss-crossing the skin of his face reminded me of a map stitched into parchment paper.

He soon brought me back to the present.

'The colonial government saw in the black men only idiots,' he said.

The Literature Bureau was founded in the early 1950s, as the government wanted to develop a local reading market. The Bureau was to stimulate writing in Shona and Ndebele but at the same time it was supposed to make sure that writers abstained from touching on political matters. Every manuscript was screened by the Bureau and then put into print by local publishing houses.

'Anybody who mentioned Mugabe's name in writing would be committing an offence, punishable by imprisonment,' Mr Hlazo told me.

'So there was strict censorship?' I asked, my pen poised above my notebook.

'No, there was no censorship,' he corrected me. 'The authors just had their taboos – not to publish anything on political or religious issues, or anything defamatory about anybody.'

'So a sort of indirect censorship?'

'Yes, that's right. And even today, I can't visualise anyone writing in the vernacular producing a political manuscript.'

I learned that books with any kind of anti-colonial message could only be written in English and, until recently, in the early '80s, could only be published outside the country. Those novels had little in common with the works published by the Literature Bureau, which had kept its tribal touch and, compared to the books in English, were printed on cheap paper.

Hlazo invited me to a Literature Bureau workshop that was due to take place a couple of weeks later. I accepted the invitation, without knowing what to expect.

Sixty teachers from all over the country attended the workshop, all eager to acquire writing skills and publish their own books. I was made to sit at the head of the table, next to Mr Hlazo, who chaired the proceedings. The venue was very plain, a bare room with wooden tables and chairs. I was surprised to see how formal everyone was, with 'Thank you, Mr Chairman' before and after and in between any intervention. Most of the men were in dark suit and tie, whereas I, not understanding the protocol, came along in a summery blouse and skirt and sandals.

'Ladies and gentlemen,' Hlazo said in his welcome address, 'let me present to you our guest of honour, Flora Wild, a writer from Germany.'

Oh dear, I thought, heat mounting into my cheeks. Me – guest of honour and writer? I felt like an impostor, but everyone was so friendly, so welcoming – more than I would ever have expected – and I began to relax and take in the proceedings.

One of the presenters was Charles Mungoshi. Adding to what I had learned in talking to Mr Hlazo, he spoke about the colonial legacies hampering the growth of fresh new writing. I knew that he was one of the most prominent literary voices of the country and so I was especially surprised by his modesty. He was soft-spoken, used simple words, appeared almost shy. What he said, however, confirmed what Hlazo had told me about the inhibitions of writing in Shona and Ndebele.

'Zimbabwean writing in our own African languages is still so poorly developed,' he said. 'It is still dealing with the old themes and plots from colonial times: love, crime, romance. The plots are predictable. The stories are very moralistic.'

Over lunch Mr Hlazo asked me whether I did not want to step in for one of the speakers, who was to speak about children's literature but had not turned up.

'Me?' I asked, unsure whether I should feel embarrassed or honoured. 'But what should I say? I am not prepared.' I was beginning to feel anxious. 'And I don't know much about children's literature,' I added.

'Don't worry, I am sure you can say something our teachers here will find interesting,' Mr Hlazo smiled. 'Anything will do.'

And so I did. I held my first literary talk, with 60 black faces turned to me, the literary greenhorn and only pale face in the room. I started with a few words about my background, my involvement in the solidarity movement for Zimbabwe's liberation war in the 1970s, which, I said, made me feel happy and privileged to be here now, in the independent state. This was of course much appreciated.

After that I improvised. I talked about *Grimms' Fairy Tales*.

'Some parents back home think the stories are much too cruel to be read to children, but no, children *need* them –' I was thinking of Bruno Bettelheim's book that Victor and I had just read '– they need them to overcome their own anxieties. When your son gets lost in the woods with Hänsel and Gretel and put into a cage by the ugly witch, he will live through his own fears of being abandoned; when your daughter encounters the wolf in grandmother's bed with Little Red Riding Hood, she has an image of the unknown shapes looming in the dark. And in the end the child protagonist will always vanquish all the evil monsters. Your child will feel relieved and reassured.'

'Oh yes, it is the same with our folk tales,' the teachers told me, 'they are full of evil creatures. And our children laugh their heads off when the monsters are killed in the end.'

Our copy of *Grimms Märchen* was in tatters because we had read the stories over and over again to our children, especially Max, who knew them by heart. Would I have guessed that only half a year later, my six-year-old would be sitting side by side with my writer friend making drawings to the children's stories Dambudzo was knocking into his typewriter?

'Thank you,' I finally said, after around 20 minutes, to the beaming faces in the audience, and with much relief sat down. Rivulets of sweat ran down my back but I felt grateful and proud at the applause I received.

My contact with the Literature Bureau, the interview with David Hlazo and the workshop gave me a first intimation of the intricacies of the so-called 'language question'. What a battle it was to free writing in African languages from their colonial confinement, from their 'missionary chickenshit', as Dambudzo had scorned in his legendary 'farewell lecture' a year before:

> In Zimbabwe we have these two great indigenous languages, ChiShona and Sindebele. Who wants us to keep writing these ShitShona and ShitNdebele languages, this missionary chickenshit? Who else but the imperialists?

I was not in Zimbabwe yet, the year when Dambudzo wanted to leave his country a couple of months after his return from exile because he felt unwelcome and alienated. I only heard and read about the lecture he gave at the University of Zimbabwe, his home ground. The students at least were his fans; they were inspired by his uncompromising stand against the authorities. Bidding farewell to them, he drove to the airport, so it was reported, but alas – in tune with the patterns of his life – he could not leave because he did not have a passport.

Harare International Book Fair

AUGUST 1983. THE FIRST HARARE International Book Fair opened its doors at the National Gallery. People flocked to the event. The large hall on the ground floor, where you would on other days find a few forlorn art lovers, was transformed into a multi-coloured maze of bookstalls, posters, cloths and banners. An excited buzz filled the flat-roofed building. Crowds pressed through the alleys between the stalls, admiring everything on display from the publishing houses, booksellers, literary agencies, NGOs, writers' associations, cultural foundations, literacy campaigns, schools and colleges. They leafed through books, grabbed up pamphlets and catalogues to read through later, asking questions, greeting friends. School classes were paraded through the exhibits, black faces against red or green or blue school blazers, some white faces here and there, black and white teachers urging them on, explaining, pointing to placards and posters.

I was thrilled. I wandered through the maze, drinking it all in. For me, the newcomer to Zimbabwe, it was a great opportunity to get a sense of the country's book world.

'Look at the posters,' I heard a teacher addressing his students at the stand of the recently founded Zimbabwe Publishing House (ZPH). 'These are our famous writers.' There was Charles Mungoshi, whom I had met at the Literature Bureau workshop, smiling under his chequered cap; next to him, Stanlake Samkange, novelist and historian, the first to promote the Zimbabwean cause internationally; then Stanley Nyamfukudza, Wilson Katiyo and Dambudzo Marechera, who in their works had brought the liberation war to international attention. Published outside the country, in the famous Heinemann African Writers series, they had put Zimbabwe on the literary map. Now that the war was won, local editions of their works were being produced. Their voices were to be heard, their books to be read at home, in a free state. The ZPH poster presented them for everyone to see, next to well-known writers from other African countries, each of them in a specific pose. The poster of Dambudzo – in a kaftan shirt, cigarette in hand, leaning against a pole at a bus stop – hangs in a frame on my office wall today, part of the Marechera memorabilia.

The book fair, the first of its kind, three years after Zimbabwe's independence, was a showcase to the world. After years of isolation under the racist settler regime, the country could boast a flourishing book industry, free education for all, and empowerment through knowledge.

At the ZPH stand I met the directors, Phyllis Johnson and David Martin, a Canadian and a British journalist, who during the war reported about the guerrilla fighters for the foreign press. Known as close allies of Robert Mugabe, they were presenting their new book, *The Struggle for Zimbabwe: The Chimurenga War*. With detailed insight into what was happening on the front line as well as behind the scenes, the book offered the first historical account of the liberation war from the side of the ruling party – a kind of court history, for which Mugabe himself wrote the foreword: 'In writing the history of our struggle, the authors are compelled by historical reality to trace the revolutionary process through ZANU's history.'

The fair was full of success stories. Nobody talked about the faction fighting during that war dividing Mugabe's ZANU and Joshua Nkomo's ZAPU and their guerrilla armies ZANLA and ZIPRA. ZAPU was gracefully acknowledged for its 'complementary role' in the freedom struggle. Nobody mentioned that Mugabe's Fifth Brigade, an army unit trained by North Koreans, was killing thousands of people, so-called dissidents suspected of hiding weapons and supporting ZAPU, in Matabeleland. Who knew, as the good-natured crowds strolled around the fair, that at that very moment villagers were being rounded up and subjected to mass beatings? Or marched at gunpoint to public places and executed, after being forced to dig their own graves? Who would have imagined that families were being burned alive in their huts?

Victory, I realised, is seductive. And it is deceptive.

'I am sorry, ma'am, are you registered?' A young lady at the entrance to the writers' workshop was holding me up.

'No, why? Isn't this free for all?' Coming from Germany, I would not have imagined that a literature conference could have such restrictions.

'I am sorry, no, only with prior registration.'

'But surely the writers should be happy to have a large audience.'

'There are enough invited guests, I am afraid, and media people. Do you have a press card?'

Trying to suppress my growing irritation, I conjured up all my powers of persuasion. I told the workshop assistant that I had only been in the country for a short while and I did not have a press card yet, but I was writing for a German newspaper. My compatriots would certainly be greatly interested to know how the literary scene in Zimbabwe was flourishing and what such prominent writers as were assembled here had to say.

'All right, ma'am,' she conceded finally, 'I think I can make an exception. Here is a badge. Please wear it when you are moving in and out of the meeting.'

It was a great moment for me. Years later, when I was teaching African literature at Humboldt University, the tableau of illustrious African writers would emerge from my memory, as I saw them lined up at the book fair at that inaugural conference in 1983. I had not yet read many of their works, but I had the great chance to see them live, face to face, and get to know their voices, listen to what they had to say.

The writers were seated at the front of the hall. In the centre I recognised Nadine Gordimer, grande dame and moral conscience of anti-apartheid literature. With her silvery hair and fine-lined white face, she stood out among all the black faces. I always thought there was something of nobility about her, in her demeanour and her way of speaking, soft-toned but distinct, with that typical accent of the white South African educated at English schools. Next to her was her compatriot, Dennis Brutus, the Cape Town poet whose prison poems had stirred the compassion of the world. I would meet this tireless human rights activist, his long grey hair tied into a ponytail, at conferences in later years. He would smile when he saw me and say, 'Yes, our Dambudzo, nobody like him …' Lewis Nkosi, another exiled South African, was also there. He was one of Dambudzo's close friends from London times. A charming womaniser, in time Nkosi would become my own literary mentor.

Ama Ata Aidoo, plump-cheeked, in bright West African attire, was there, having left Ghana and now seeking residence in Zimbabwe. I would get to know her sharp tongue two years later, when I helped organise a writers' conference on 'Women and Books' at the Zimbabwe Book Fair of 1985 and she asked for more money for her participation. 'How can you let a white woman handle our affairs?' she complained to the organisers.

Seated next to her was the white-haired Gabriel Okara from Nigeria, looking dignified and withdrawn. 'Listen to the rhythm of your inner voice,' was his advice to African writers, as I would learn much later and also teach my students.

Most clearly of all I recall Nuruddin Farah, with his twinkling eyes, the exiled anti-dictatorship author from Somalia, whom I would meet often in later years when I was in the position of hosting readings with him or moderating a discussion at a literature festival. Farah and fellow-writer Taban lo Liyong from Uganda, who was also present at that first book fair, both seemed to regard Dambudzo as their protégé, the angry young man whom they had all met at the famous Horizonte Festival for African Writers in West Berlin of 1979. On that occasion Dambudzo had stormed onto the stage, cursing the 'fascist' Germans who had not wanted to let him in.

What an illustrious congregation of African literary nobility it was. The event also included writers from francophone countries. Mongo Beti was there from Cameroun. Already in the 1950s he had been writing about the cruelty of the city and satirising colonial administrators and missionaries. Across language barriers – which did not happen again in later years at such occasions – novelists, poets and playwrights all coming together to celebrate the long-awaited emergence of Zimbabwe from almost a century of colonial and settler rule.

What a privilege, how exciting it was for me, the newcomer, to witness such an eminent moment in Zimbabwe's literary history. It was a moment of bloom, of a multitude of voices pressing forward, writers back from exile, or from the war, or from their solitary desks where they had been hiding and waiting. The winds of change, which had seen the end of colonial rule in most other African countries two decades before, had finally blown across the country, clearing the sky for the Zimbabwean flag to soar into the blue sky.

And yet, as I would find out in the months to come, when I started to talk to many of the writers and read their poems and stories, despite the general feeling of freedom, they were not all singing the same tune.

And Now the Poets Speak, the title of Musaemura Zimunya's anthology of 'poems inspired by the struggle', was a collection he had compiled and published right after the war. In his poems he eulogises the sanctity of the Zimbabwean past, its heritage, the 'Zimbabwe Ruins' as national monument. Thus starts his poem 'Zimbabwe (After the Ruins)':

I want to worship Stone
because it is Silence
I want to worship Rock
so, hallowed be its silence.

Chenjerai Hove, another notable poetic voice of those years, in his collection *Up in Arms* gave testimony to the blood that had been shed by fighters and innocent civilians in the war, the bodies that had been mutilated, the country devastated.

Streams bathe in blood,
mailing it east
where warriors gulp it
Down war-braved throats
and unbandaged wounds smile
in unburied corpses

The high and often celebratory tone of such poetry, in my eyes, seemed to clash with the sober, pessimistic, even cynical outlook expressed by those writers who had written novels during the last years of the war, published to much acclaim outside Zimbabwe. In Mungoshi's *Waiting for the Rain*, of 1975, the protagonist, Lucifer, is overcome by feelings of stagnation and stasis when he returns home to his village. While the Chimurenga is hardly mentioned, the only politically active character in the novel turns out to be a traitor.

Much more pronounced and explicit is the distrust in political heroes in Stanley Nyamfukudza's short novel *The Non-Believer's Journey*. Like Marechera's *House of Hunger*, it was written far away from their country at war, in English exile, 'where we felt like hippopotami that have been doped with injections of English culture', as Marechera put it in *The Black Insider*. Thus, Nyamfukudza's novel with its eponymic title ends on a sadly ironic note: the protagonist's violent and accidental death by the gun of a freedom fighter.

While I, on the background of my own political disillusionment, could empathise with such anti-heroes, Zimbabwean critics of the time were not amused. They did not want fatalistic figures such as these; they wanted a literature that uplifted the nation by praising those who had fought for its independence.

'Pleading for admission into the neurotic twentieth century is the worst way to go about revitalising a culture depleted the self-same,' Zimunya wrote.

'... on the eve of Independence Africa does not tolerate cynics like ... Nyamfukudza's Sam and "tourists" like Mungoshi's Lucifer,' another critic echoed. 'Zimbabwe needs a literature that reflects its people's heroic efforts to re-discover themselves, literature that is imbued with local colour and perspective. This is the sacred duty of Zimbabwe's writers.'

Such statements came up, in the year of the book fair, in an article in *Moto* magazine, where writers and critics debated the literary scene. Marechera, who was hailed by his contemporaries for having set Zimbabwe on the international literary map, would in the least be seen as fulfilling such 'sacred duty'. The sense of futility and nihilism, the gut-rot and stench that his *House of Hunger* metaphorically reeked of, made his an extreme counter-voice to the chorus of nationalist uplifting. '... to move from Nyamfukudza to Marechera is to move from cynicism to oblivion, from sickness to death,' the *Moto* article concluded.

About the famous Zimbabwe Ruins, which were saluted as a symbol of national pride by Zimunya and others, Marechera later had this to say:

> It is the ruin and not the original which moves men; our Zimbabwe Ruins must have looked really shit and hideous when they were brand-new. But now their ruin imposes itself upon the grand imagination of even thousands who have never actually seen them.

'Communication Through Literature' was the theme the organisers had chosen for the Harare convention, which to me seemed to preclude controversy from the outset. This was soon confirmed. A short man with a pompous air about him and serious-looking spectacles chaired the proceedings. He was addressed throughout as 'Mister Chair' and he made sure that the deliberations remained as general and non-controversial as the theme suggested. This was Emmanuel Ngara, as I was told, literature professor and current pro-vice-chancellor of the University of Zimbabwe. When I later read some of his essays, I was bored by their dogmatic ideological stance.

In a similar vein, in tune with the prevalent socialist rhetoric, most speakers and discussants stressed the importance of the African writer's political commitment. Art for art's sake, it seemed, must be rejected as bourgeois and Western. The writer should get out of the ivory tower and find his place close to the masses. Ngugi wa Thiong'o, who had not come to the fair, was quoted repeatedly. 'The African writers have to decolonise their minds, they have to write in their own language, not in the language of the former colonisers.'

Hearing such statements, I felt reminded of my own political past. Had I not preached a similar agenda in my thesis about proletarian literature in Germany when I graduated from university? But now that I had left that behind, I felt annoyed hearing it reiterated by the African writers and academics. It seemed so hollow and uninspiring.

On the platform Gordimer was trying to resolve a dilemma that had arisen in the discussion. 'Beauty in literature and commitment do not exclude one another,' she maintained. 'Political struggle also entails beauty. It is the writer's task to bring this beauty about.'

Much to my relief, I began to realise that I was not the only one in the hall who was getting annoyed at such non-committal, general statements. The bulk of Zimbabwean authors in attendance were seated behind the row of illustrious international writers. I do not recall what they contributed, if at all, but I think Musa Zimunya, the celebrated poet who, shortly afterwards, became the chairman of the Zimbabwe Writers Union (and would become my fiercest adversary) made a statement. He always did. Mungoshi and Nyamfukudza were also there. They did not make statements. They were men of few words.

But there was Dambudzo Marechera.

I saw him excitedly waving his arm from his seat in the back row. Heads turned and the audience shifted on their chairs.

'What about censorship?' Dambudzo asked. 'My novel was banned by the censorship board, just like in the days of Ian Smith! There is no freedom of speech! And what about unemployment? What about drought relief being only delivered into the government-friendly provinces, while the other parts are starving? And that so-called Fifth Brigade, who right now is killing our people in Matabeleland? What about that?'

I found myself smiling. Finally, someone had pointed the finger at the real burning issues. I do not remember whether anyone responded to Dambudzo's questions but I suspect most of the other writers preferred to keep their mouths shut. The francophone contingency, even if they understood what was going on, retained their stone-like expressions – they were always more formal than anyone else. The chairman, trying to hide his rising irritation but not succeeding, deliberately ignored the constantly raised arm in the back row.

Never easily contained, Dambudzo continued his challenging behaviour throughout the session, jumping up from his seat, heckling those who were speaking, demanding that politicians respond to his questions. He went especially wild when it came to Eddison Zvobgo, Minister of Justice and himself a poet, who was chairing an afternoon session. 'Hey, you, Zvobgo! Comrade Minister! What does your government do to help the ex-combatants?' he demanded. 'You are sitting up there in your offices, in your padded chairs and in your villas – look at the cripples lining our streets, out of work, no pay, what do you do to help them?'

As the commotion rose in volume and temperature, Nkosi and Farah walked over to Dambudzo, patting his shoulder, trying to calm him. True to his name, the 'troublemaker' was not to be quieted. Even his friends failed. In the end Zvobgo beckoned to his burly bodyguard, who without breaking a sweat manhandled the lightweight out of the room and drove him to a safe distance from the gathering.

Triumphantly Dambudzo later told the press: 'I have been abducted.'

It was gratifying to discover, some years later, when I was following the tracks of Dambudzo's life, that Nadine Gordimer's and Wally Serote's recollections of the conference were very close to mine.

'Marechera was seated beside me at the writers' workshop,' Gordimer remembered. 'Of course, he always made an entrance like an actress, very late, with that big red scarf flying. Then he sat there, very nervous and tense, and did not keep still for a minute. It was all right until there was a speech by one of the ministers. There was the usual kind of dead atmosphere when the minister speaks and the feeling that the man was talking bosh, clichés. But being guests in the country – perhaps it's cowardly – you just sit there and clap your hands together twice, politely, and that's all. Then Marechera got up, he couldn't get restrained, not even by Lewis Nkosi who was trying hard. And he lambasted the man.

'But what he said was really true. He was talking about all the returned soldiers who had indeed fought to establish Zimbabwe and now were wandering around unemployed in the streets. He had the courage to say this.'

In a similar vein, Serote remembered: 'The first time I met Dambudzo was in 1983 when I came to the International Book Fair. It was three years after Zimbabwe's independence. Those of us who are not Zimbabwean and had been following the struggle for freedom here, had got the impression that the majority of the Zimbabwean people had been catapulted into a position where they had taken power. So to meet a person who was extremely cynical about this, not only cynical but also actively trying to pinpoint the fact that he did not think that the independence was independence of the Zimbabwean people, was rather a shocking experience.'

A day or two later, I saw Marechera again. This was in First Street Mall, where lunchtime readings were held to take literature into the city. It was a part of town I liked: a pedestrian area, with benches to sit on, and strolling around the streets during the day I could get a slight feeling of urbanity. I went there often on my errands in the weeks after our arrival, getting the regulation black school shoes from Bata for Max, or stationery at Kingston's Book Store. You could get a Coke or an ice cream from QV Pharmacy at the crossing with Angwa Street and sit and watch human-sized chessmen being drawn across a giant chessboard on the pavement. The players might be an elderly hippie, with matted hair and beard under a cowboy hat, a bank clerk in suit and tie munching his lunch hour steak pie, or an old bloke from the township, crouched on a stick or leaning on a small boy for support. A constant presence was the blind street musician with dark glasses, singing Shona songs and strumming his guitar, and always at his side a drummer beating out a rhythm on his makeshift instruments.

On this day of the book fair I was drawn to a knot of people crowded around a pedestal. To get a better view of what was happening, I wriggled through the rows, my Olympus mirror reflex camera dangling from my neck. It was Charles Mungoshi who was reading and I took a photo while I listened. In the photo he is wearing an open-necked shirt and jacket and trousers, both of an indistinct beige colour. He is holding some sheets of paper in his hand but is looking upwards, his mouth half open, obviously reciting from memory, in a posture of calm intent. In my photo, funnily, he appears emblazoned with an aureole of spikes – the leaves of a palm tree behind him.

While Mungoshi was reading, I spotted Dambudzo in the crowd. I took my first photograph of him that day. It shows him in half profile, from the waist upwards, the bright red shawl Gordimer mentions over his right shoulder. Where did he pick it up? From one of his hosts who gave him temporary shelter? He is wearing it proudly, like a sash, but also mockingly, in ostensible contrast to the formal three-piece suit he had put on for the conference, and the tie with a curly pattern in cream and brown. A small cluster of dreadlocks dangles from the right corner of his head. His forehead, unusually large and vaulted, bulging above his face, reminds me of a schoolkid too bright for his age. While the heads of other listeners are turned upwards to the reader, Dambudzo's eyes seem unfocused, his face still. Is he listening, or nervous because he is the next one to read? Clutching an envelope crammed with papers – his manuscript? – under his left arm, his hands are fingering a cigarette out of a packet.

I do not remember exactly what he read, but it was probably from *Mindblast*, the book he had recently handed in to ZPH. Yet I do remember clearly that when he stepped back down into the crowd after he had finished reading, someone tapped him on the shoulder. As he turned round his face lit up. I instantly knew this was 'Olga', who turns up in his park-bench diary. She was a German teacher working in the rural areas, with whom the lonely poet had had a fiery love affair while her boyfriend was away. I must have seen her somewhere before because I recognised her straight away; I knew who she was and I also knew her real name. When I wandered up First Street to return to the book fair, I saw them sitting in a café, chatting, obviously happy about an unexpected reunion. I smiled to myself, feeling like a spy, an illicit secret observer. Was I envious, jealous? No, my time was yet to come. I was filled with the bliss of being there at that time, taking in all the new impressions, letting things unfold. How sadly ironic, if I flash forward in my narrative, thinking of my meeting with Olga thirty years later, two elderly women, mourning the man they had both once loved.

A feature I wrote about the book fair and the writers' conference was published, again in my 'home paper' *Nürnberger Nachrichten*. It was my first piece on literature in Zimbabwe. Rereading it now, more than 30 years later, I can see how my own political past moulded my take on what was happening in Zimbabwe. My view was different from other European literary critics I met during those first years; I was wary of extolling the nationalist agenda of the day.

'There is no automatic linkage between revolution and mental and cultural liberation,' I wrote in a longer version of that first text. 'The state of literature in Zimbabwe today is still extremely precarious and unsettled. Writers, many of whom have returned from years in exile, have not yet found their position in society.'

I spoke about what government officials were saying to cultural practitioners, how they were warning them to restrain from unwarranted criticism, and I mentioned the gagging order the minister of Home Affairs had issued – under the Emergency Law that was still in force – prohibiting journalists from reporting on what was happening in Matabeleland. By the time I wrote that assessment, in November 1983, I had conducted interviews with several writers.

And I had got involved with Dambudzo Marechera.

PART THREE

EAGLETS OF DESIRE

Getting Entangled

I MET DAMBUDZO FOR THE FIRST time on a hot October morning in Charles Mungoshi's office. They were drinking vodka. Mungoshi worked as an editor at Zimbabwe Publishing House at the time. I wanted to speak to him about the literary scene in Zimbabwe.

For a moment I felt blinded, stepping into the squat bungalow from the dazzling colours in the streets, the purple of the jacarandas lining the west-east and the bright red flamboyants on the north-south axis of the grid. Like many of the newly founded NGOs, aid organisations, news agencies and the like, ZPH had opened their offices in one of the town houses in The Avenues, hastily deserted by their white owners when Mugabe came to power.

'Hi there. Is it you, our German book lover?'

The cheerful greeting came from Phyllis Johnson, whom I could barely make out in the dimly lit reception area, but recognising her clenched-teeth North American accent.

'It is so bright outside,' I told her. 'I am overwhelmed by the light and those colours – but it is also really hot.'

Phyllis grimaced. 'Yes, that's our Zimbabwean spring,' she said. 'The land is dry, even drier this year with that *odious* drought, but bang – out of nothing these trees explode into orgies of colour. What brings you here?'

I explained my mission and the interview I was hoping to have with Charles Mungoshi.

'Charles? Yes, of course – his office is down there. I am sure he'll be happy to speak to you.'

My knocking sounded hollow on the thin plywood door.

'Come in,' someone called, rather flatly.

Would I be regarded as an intruder, I suddenly wondered. What right did I have to come here and ask an eminent writer questions about literature in his country? I had no credentials.

Yet once inside the room I felt at ease. Mungoshi was sitting behind his desk, a pile of folders and papers in front of him. When I introduced myself and explained my endeavour, it was he who seemed rather timid. But he did not have to worry.

'What a gorgeous visitor you have, Charles,' I heard a booming voice behind my back. 'Please, young lady, do sit down.'

It was Dambudzo. Wearing jeans and a light blue faded T-shirt, he seemed very different from his rather fierce appearance at the book fair. He looked fresh, innocent, like a young boy who has just washed. His face, with its broad cheekbones and full lips, glistened. He used the ZPH offices, he told me later, to get warm after a night in the street and to freshen up in their bathroom, which still had a tub and all the installations from its former use as a family home.

'What can we do for you?' he said, as he grabbed a chair and pulled it close to Mungoshi's desk. 'Would you like some vodka? We are just moisturising our throats to get ready for the day.'

Looking around the room, which did not contain much more than a few chairs, two tables, and some shelves, I saw a bottle on the bare wooden floor.

Dambudzo saw me looking. 'Please forgive us, these publishers here are not really up to standard,' he said. 'They should provide their writers with appropriate glassware to receive our guests. So for the moment we can only offer you a cup – '

'A cup ... that's fine with me,' I said, laughing, amused by his laborious attempts to impress – or maybe mock – me. 'A cup. But with tea, please, not vodka.'

'Tea? Not my first choice. But so be it,' he said, and while Charles was getting another cup, and indeed a teapot, down from a shelf, Dambudzo, unabashed, looked me up and down appraisingly. 'My gawd,' he continued in the exaggerated Oxford accent he always adopted when he wanted to sound professional, 'look at these garments! Charles, would you ever see such simple elegance in prissy old Salisbury?'

I looked down at my feet, my brown leather sandals, the dark red polish on my toenails, trying to divert his gaze from my blushing face. I was wearing one of my loosely cut trousers with a bright floral pattern and a silky top. It was true. What I had seen here in Barbour's, the major department store, and in the few other clothes shops I'd wandered into, was more like what you might wear to a ladies' tea party in a provincial British town in the 1950s.

When I started asking the typical journalist's questions about the social relevance of Zimbabwean literature, I was quickly admonished.

'Zimbabwean literature? Zimbabwean culture?' Dambudzo scoffed. 'There is nothing like that. It is just some crap this government is trying to sell to you, coming from abroad, wanting to see our *proud liberated country*. It makes me laugh.' Glancing at Charles, who was busy pouring me tea, he said: 'Ask Charles. We feel like strangers in this country. We do not belong to that kind of *sacred heritage* everyone is talking about. Am I right, Charles?'

Mungoshi nodded, leaving the talking to his effusive friend.

'But hey, why don't we meet somewhere else, and talk?' Dambudzo's voice was toning down, becoming softer and less contrived. I started to like him. 'What about eight o'clock tonight at the Oasis Hotel?'

'Yes,' I said. 'I know the Oasis. I will be there.'

When I arrived at the hotel that evening, Dambudzo was already there. I saw his hunched figure, clutching some books under one arm, talking to a group of men and women sitting around a table, drinking. There was laughter. Voices saying something in Shona. Light-hearted jeering.

'What was that about?' I asked when we had settled at one of the wobbly tables at a distance from the group.

'The usual stuff. "Are you writing another novel? When will you write about me?" They know me. They know I am a writer. But you see here, copies of *The House of Hunger*. I got them from ZPH. These stingy people, David and Phyllis, they don't want to give me another advance, just some books instead. So I am trying to sell them. But most of those guys would rather buy me another beer than my book. Who cares about literature? They know I am a weirdo and that I write a lot about sex.'

'We talked a lot, or rather, he talked a lot,' I described this first evening in a letter to friend. 'He is quite egocentric but also endearing – he told me how in England he and other students had fought battles against the police; how three times he had resolved to take his life, but then, standing by the Thames and seeing the dirty water, had thought, "What? Should I lose my life in this stinking sewage?" and had started to laugh out loud and strolled off.'

From the Oasis we went to another pub, the Elizabeth Hotel, or rather a dance hall. There were only black people. 'They are all from ZANLA,' Dambudzo whispered knowingly into my ear. We got in there and danced. We just danced and danced. I had not danced like that for a long time, so carefree and light-hearted. I felt good with him, though not infatuated; his appearance was just too weird. At times, he reminded me of a lurking animal. He often talked about my eyes. He had forgotten my name, so he called me Stephanie.

Afterwards we sat in the car for a long time. He did not want to let me drive off, wanted me to stay with him. I enjoyed being close to him, but I wanted to leave it at this kind of heightened feeling and suspense. My restraint frustrated him but he was still quite sweet, and so lonely, so utterly lonely. He did not know where he was going to spend the night. I was not sure whether I should see him again, but we made a date for the following Sunday, three days later.

I waited for Dambudzo in the garden of the Park Lane Hotel. He did not show up.

Two days later I was visiting the ZPH offices and he was there again. He showed me his poem 'In the Gallery'.

We had misunderstood each other. He had waited for me at the Oasis and when I did not come he had wandered off into the city. There he'd gone into an art gallery, where he bracketed his disappointment among 'brooding mental landscapes' and 'luminous winter icescapes'.

How strange to re-read this first poem of our relationship – the conditional, in the negative – wasn't this what our love was all about? The longing, the wanting, the yearning, a permanent strain, the fulfilment of our love endlessly deferred by misunderstanding, by the inability of him and of myself to give each other what we were yearning for? Every

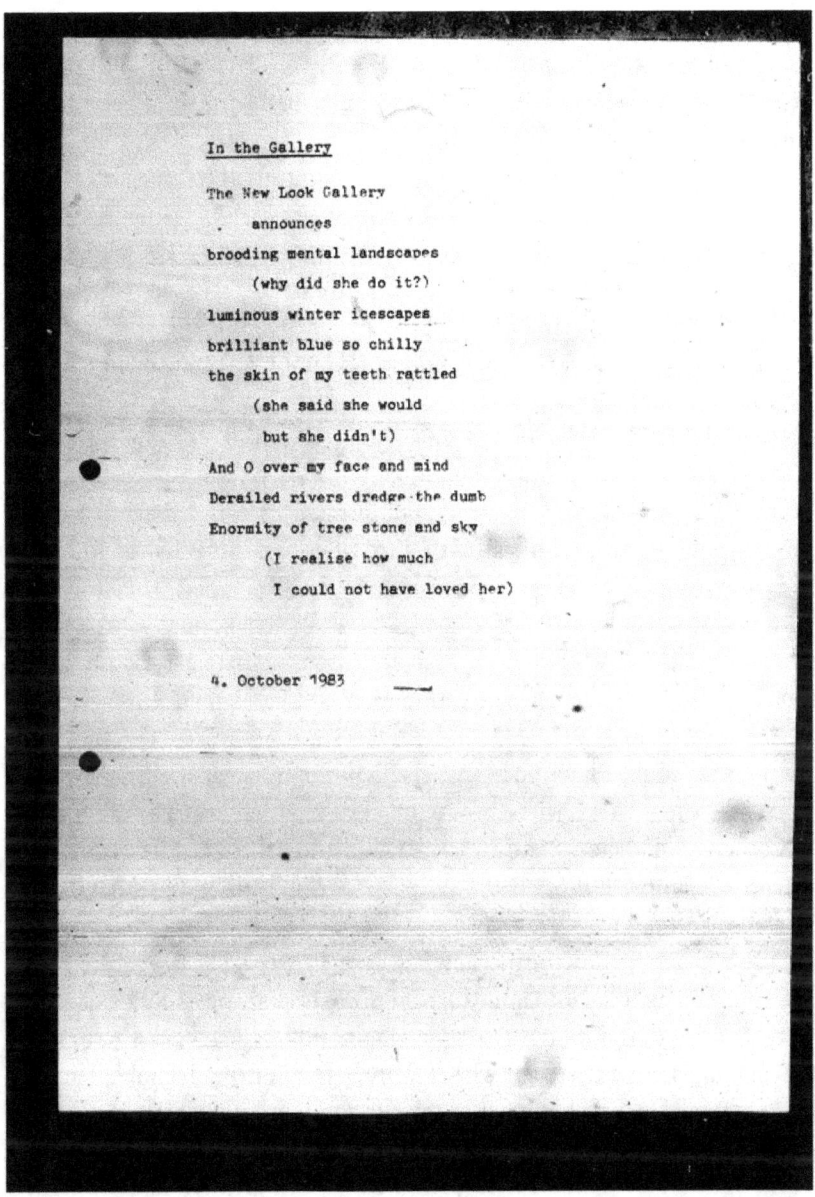

so often, when my frustration, my hurt about his destructive behaviour reached a new climax, I could have said to myself: 'I realise how much I could not have loved you.'

Our next meeting was two days later, again at the Oasis. When I arrived, I found him sitting at one of the notorious tables, dimly lit by a candle, with Albert Chimedza. Tall, lean, dreadlocked and intellectual, Albert was another 'been-to'. He had recently returned from film studies in the United States. He was married to a German – in fact, I had met the couple at a German cultural event.

'Hi there,' Dambudzo said without looking up. 'Have a seat. We are just talking.'

His eyes were clouded, his brows knitted tightly. He clutched a notepad in his hands, which was filled with his handwriting. I picked up a tense atmosphere between the two men.

'Ah, ya, by the way, this is Albert,' Dambudzo mumbled, 'Albert Chimedza. He is a poet.'

'Hi, Albert,' I greeted him with a smile. 'I didn't know you were –'

'You know each other?' Dambudzo chipped in, with a fierce glance in my direction. 'So you befriend a lot of men.' Before Albert or I could say anything, he turned his attention to Albert again. 'Why do you want to read it again? This is my work, I am a journalist, I made this interview with you –'

'I just want to see what you have written,' Albert interrupted. His mood was just as aggressive as Dambudzo's. 'That is my right.'

'Your right, blah blah … If you don't respect my work, then fuck you. By the way, could I have another beer? My throat is getting dry.'

While the two of them went on arguing, the one as stubborn as the other, their voices getting louder and the ashtray overflowing with cigarette stumps, I slipped the notepad out of Dambudzo's hands and started reading.

'So will you give it to me now?' Albert insisted. 'I'll go and sit over there and bring it back to you. I just want to make sure –'

'Okay, I see. You do not trust me,' Dambudzo said. 'I am a writer and it is nobody's business to see what I write before it is published. That's it.'

Grabbing the notebook out of my hands, he unhitched the pages from the spiralled pad and folded them, but before he could slide them into his pocket, Albert got hold of them, and with an evil grin on his long-boned face, held them to the candle flame. Nobody said a word. We watched the silvery black flakes dance above the ashtray and settle into a small heap. Then Albert stood up and walked away.

'Why did you not give it to him?' I said after some minutes of silence. I was perplexed and angry at what to me seemed completely irrational behaviour on Dambudzo's part. 'It was such a good interview. The questions you asked, they were so unusual, and what I read of your notes, so insightful. I had not known that he was also a poet.'

'Yes, his poems are good. You'll read them soon. They'll be published together with Hopewell Seyaseya's, another poet. He had shown some of them to me and then I proposed the interview. But that fucking idiot –'

'But now your work is destroyed. It is such a shame. Such a waste.'

'Look, you do not understand. Back in London I worked as a journalist, *West Africa Magazine*, they valued my work, but here – oh, let's forget about it. Come, let's go and dance.'

I got up and followed him, hesitantly. Not knowing what to do, what to think, what to feel. We went to the Playboy night club. It was fairly small, a longish room, and a live band in the alcove at the back was playing jazzy tunes, a glittering disco ball strewing freckles of light onto the dark walls and the faces of the drinkers and dancers.

'This is where I usually end up when the pubs close,' Dambudzo told me. 'They stay open 'til late, sometimes up to two in the morning. The people here know me. I just dance and dance … Now and then someone buys me a beer, and when they close, I walk around the block and sleep in a doorway or sneak into the park.'

The dancing felt good. We were smiling at each other, as our bodies moved close to and away from each other; I twirled into his arm and rolled out again. I still see his gawky figure, his arm stretching out, leading me around, pulling me in, to the rhythm of the music. In between, when we were close, he would suddenly snatch a kiss, as he had done during our first evening at the Oasis. His protruding lips would move forward quickly, like the beak of a bird, and for a fraction of a second clasp my lips. It felt natural, almost familiar, as if this was something he had always done.

From the club we walked to the nearby Harare Gardens. The gate was still open but when we were snuggled up on a bench in a dark corner and started embracing, a watchman came and chased us away. 'Well,' I said, 'I think I should go home now. Where will you sleep?'

'Could you drive me to the university campus?' Dambudzo asked. 'Some students usually let me sleep on the floor in their dorm.'

He directed me to Mount Pleasant, a suburb a couple of miles north of the centre, then through one of the gates of the university campus. It was familiar territory to him. Not much had changed in the ten years since he had been a student there, when it was still called the University of Rhodesia.

'When I came back from exile,' he told me when we were trying to find a secluded space, 'I gave lectures here. The students organised them. And readings. They were my friends. And later, when I did not have anywhere to stay, they let me sneak into their dormitories.'

I parked the car. He took my hand and led me to the university swimming pool. We lay down on the lawn, looking up into the starlit sky, talking softly. When he started kissing me, his lips now soft on mine, I felt like letting go. But then I stopped, pulled back abruptly, and jumped to my feet.

'No, let me go home now.' I started walking to the car.

'What? You mean –?'

'Yes … please,' I said, 'I need more time. Where can I drop you?'

'Drive up there, to Manfred Hodson Hall. I'll find a floor to sleep on.'

Yet once there, he did not want to get out of the car.

'Hey, you cannot do this to me,' he pleaded. 'Don't you see that I need you? Look what you have done to me!' He grabbed my right hand and pulled it to his groin so that I could feel his erection. (Our car was a left-hand drive.)

'That's not the way to convince me,' I replied. 'Please get out of the car now.'

'Where should I go? It is late. All the students are asleep.'

'Well, it was you who asked me to take you here.'

'So you really want to expel me? Another night over there near the stinking toilets?'

This was his way of making me feel bad – at that moment and many more moments to come.

'Here, take this,' I said, handing him the picnic blanket we kept in the car. 'Then at least you can cover yourself.' The blanket had belonged to my father. It was made of thin but strong material, a chequered brown in colour. Somehow, I thought I would get it back. One of the illusions of being with Dambudzo, as I would learn in the weeks to come.

Finally, he opened the door. With head lowered between hunched shoulders, the blanket under his arm, I watched him make his way towards the ablutions building, which with its red bricks did not look as bad and stinking as he wanted me to believe. Just before he entered, while I was reversing, I saw him suddenly turn round and, blinded by my headlights, start walking towards my side of the car. I rolled the window down and he put his head inside and kissed me again, very gently.

Driving home, I felt torn, full of doubts. I felt a strong pull, I felt like wanting to love this man and letting him love me. And yet, his love seemed threatening, full of hidden traps, of unknown abysses.

That same night Dambudzo appeared in my dream. His face popped up, like a flashlight, he snatched a kiss from me – the next moment I was wide awake.

In my confusion, I tried to get advice from Susanne, one of my closest friends. She had been the first German teacher hired by the embassy to start evening classes. As there was high demand, I had been asked to join her and had also taken over some classes. We quickly bonded. I liked her slightly frivolous manner, the way she joked about people, including herself; her humour, tinted with her Swabian accent, always made me smile. Her British husband had a three-year contract as a lecturer at UZ. We had soon gathered other expat women around us, most of them 'accompanying spouses' according to immigration laws. Whenever we got together, walking around in our silky pants with eccentric patterns, our loose-fitting linen jackets in bright pink or turquoise, blue mascara shimmering in our eyes, the mood was electric, fun.

We met once a week for an hour of gym at Gabi's house, my other best friend, who had a large basement. Afterwards we'd sit in her lush garden, drinking tea, chatting.

There was a lot to chat about. Our lives were opening up, in one way or other. Our gym leader, a physiotherapist, had travelled from Germany all through Africa in a truck, together with her partner of eleven years. He worked as a technical trainer in the same company as Victor; she found a placement at an institution for disabled people, many of whom were ex-combatants. Not long after they had settled, her partner left her for a black woman; they got married and soon started to have children. Our friend was bitter and shared her angry feelings with us. Was this what some of 'our' German men dreamed of, we wondered. Was an African woman easier to handle, more pliable in their hands?

Gabi, who was married to a rather boring engineer with a contract in technical co-operation, fell for a bearded journalist. He was reporting about the new Zimbabwe for a West German radio station. Like most of us in that close group, he was one of a wide range of people from the solidarity movement for Zimbabwe and, at regular intervals, returned to visit the country over years to come.

The day after that night with Dambudzo, I confided in Susanne. I told her about my fascination as well as my doubts.

'If I follow my impulse to be with him,' I said, 'I know it will be so complicated.'

'But that is what you like,' she pointed out matter of factly. 'You like it complicated.'

My friend's casual remark, who in her own private life hedged many 'what ifs' and 'buts', broke the dam of my own ambivalence and indecision. It gave me licence to follow the lure, to look behind the 'dark door of a dream', one of Dambudzo's images that I love so much. Did he inhabit the boundless space, the other side of myself, which was stirring below the surface of rationality and sense?

I knew how risky my decision was but it felt in tune with me and my life at that time and at that place. That the hazards I was facing would be life threatening I could not have known. Nor would I have ever imagined how immensely gratifying my love for the 'trouble-maker' would eventually be – a love lasting a lifetime.

Nowhere to Go

I DID NOT WANT OUR FIRST NIGHT to be rough and it was Dambudzo who suggested the Seven Miles Hotel. We set off in the late afternoon, driving south out of Harare.

My husband knew that I would be back before the children woke up; he would need the car to drive to work.

'Good afternoon, Mr Marechera,' the manager said, with a slight bow. 'How can I help you?'

So even here he was known.

'Well ...' my companion mumbled, not looking at the man with the beaming face who seemed unsure about the writer's escort. 'Um ... um ... could we go through to your garden and have a drink?'

'Yes, certainly. I'll show you the way.'

After the first two bottles of Castle Lager, Dambudzo began to relax. His face became more open and his limbs unclenched as he inhaled cigarette smoke deep into his lungs. Yet he remained rather subdued and made no move to leave the garden area.

When he ordered his third beer I got a little impatient. 'Should we not ask for a room?' I said.

By now the sun had set and the air had become clammy. The birds were silent. Not a single leaf stirred. Around me, under thatched umbrellas, groups of black men and women sat talking and laughing, their voices and the noise level rising with every fresh round they ordered.

'What is this hilarity all about?' I asked Dambudzo. 'What did that bloke say – they seem really demented, that group over there.'

'Well, the usual stuff,' Dambudzo shrugged. 'Making jokes about me, with my dreadlocks, and my white chick. I suppose they are just jealous.'

When we finally made our way back to the reception, the manager came darting around a corner. 'I hope you have enjoyed our garden,' he said, his smile now acknowledging me too. 'It is so pleasant out there at this time of year.'

'Yes, sure,' we muttered.

'Is there anything else I can do for you?'

'Um ... um, yes, could we ... could we get a room?'

'Of course, Mr Marechera, a room in one of our rondavels, they are quiet and airy. Should it be for half or the whole night?'

Dambudzo stared fixedly at the ground.

'For the whole night,' I said quickly, trying to hide my embarrassment about the unexpected option.

'All right then. That will be forty dollars. Here is your key.'

As my companion was not showing any reaction to this news, I got my wallet out and paid.

The manager waved us in the direction of our 'bridal chamber'. 'It is number eight, the last room on the far side.'

'I thought it would be good for you to have a whole night's rest,' I said, as we walked towards our room. 'I did not even know that you could book just for half of the night.'

'What do you think they are doing here, all these men?' Dambudzo said, grinning. 'Most of them are civil servants who come here after work or on a weekend to spend a few hours with their girlfriends before they drive home to their wives and kids.'

Inside the chalet, it was sombre and very still. When I opened the small window, the two-tone rasping of the crickets set in with a blast and from the distance, far away, came a faint murmur from the beer garden. The last grey shine of the darkening sky tinged the room.

Dambudzo's face, hardly visible, in my hands. His lips on my neck, our bodies slowly curling into each other on the bed. Above me the steep tunnel of the thatched roof, dark and musty. Shadows of bats, fluttering, vanishing through the opening into the night sky. When I closed my eyes, the roof was spinning in my head.

His embraces were gentle, testing, trying. Astounding then, the sudden leap, as I felt him inside me, making me shudder, then gasp with wonder.

A couple of hours later, as I was trying to disentangle myself from his arms, the spell was broken.

Dambudzo sat up abruptly. He stared into the milky white of the room. 'What's going on? Where am I?' His voice sounded harsh.

'We are here, in the hotel,' I said. 'I did not want to wake you up. It is still early morning. Lie down and sleep some more.'

'What are you doing? Why are you getting up?'

'I told you. I have to drive home. My kids …'

'What? You want to leave me here stranded? Surrounded by dissidents! Is this a trap? With whom are you plotting?'

I was perplexed, bewildered.

'What are you talking about? It was your idea to come here. You know the hotel. It is right by the Masvingo road. You will easily catch a lift into town.'

'Oh, come on,' he said. 'Don't play the innocent.' Then his eyes narrowed and he spat his next words into my face like poison arrows. 'You are all alike. Luring me into a trap –'

I was shocked. 'Dambudzo, we have had such a lovely night,' I said. 'I don't understand. How can you do this to me? Please stop it!'

I started pulling my clothes on, feeling a strange discomfort and urgency, steeling myself against a paranoia I had never encountered before. I tried to hug him before I left but with his knees drawn up to his chest and his head between his arms, he warded me off.

'Go away,' he said. 'Go and tell your colleagues from the CIO where they can find me.'

The pattern was set.

First came the see-saw of longing, then the swooning in passion, at first high up in the sky and then crashing down with a hard bump. The insults, the hurt, the anger.

Where could we be together?

I asked Susanne if we could spend a night at their house on campus. 'It was you who pushed me into this,' I said, lamely trying to turn the request into a joke.

Susanne agreed. She cooked spätzle and goulasch and she and her husband liked my guest. Dambudzo was amiable, made good conversation, but how must he have felt, being hosted by my friends so that after dinner we could make love in their spare room? It felt awkward for both of us. Dambudzo soon fell asleep while I, moulding my body to his back on the narrow bed, was kept awake until morning by his coughing, a dry, irksome cackle at regular intervals. Years later, when I knew he was sick, that night sprang up in my memory. Was he infected before we met? Was that why he was coughing?

We spent another night together at a sordid city hotel he had suggested because it was cheap. When I had to go to the bathroom, a row of black women, prostitutes, I suppose, were standing in the open hallway, staring at me, with unashamed hostile eyes.

'Not very romantic,' I said the next morning, pushing the smelly sheets away from our bodies. The room was depressing: bare walls, the plaster peeling off, a sagging mattress on a metal frame, unwashed blankets. I looked at our exposed bodies in the morning light. 'Le blanc et le noir,' I commented. 'How terribly pale and cheesy I look next to you.'

That time it was a weekend, so I did not have to rush home early.

'Don't threaten me with Voltaire,' Dambudzo chuckled, his hand gliding over my breast to my belly.

'At least we can see each other's bodies for once in bright daylight. Would you like to –' I started to spread my knees at an angle. 'I mean, I can show you what I look like down there, where I like to be touched – '

'My gawd, no!' Dambudzo's head jerked up. 'I do not want to *see* anything!'

Pricking my lips with his teeth, digging his tongue deep into my mouth, he rolled his body on top of mine. My legs high up on his back, I let him dive into my 'daunting femaleness'. 'Okay, okay,' I murmured, 'how could I resist your magic wand.' Afterwards, when we were getting dressed, I could not help teasing him. 'Well, well, you can't deny your missionary upbringing.'

Someone had smashed one of the small triangular windows of my car, which was parked outside the hotel. 'They sure did not like me here,' I concluded. 'Let's go.'

In the afternoon I picked him up in town. I had brought the boys and we drove out to Cleveland Dam, a couple of miles east of the city.

Dambudzo loved the calm beauty of the place, and he loved my children too. He had been afraid of them because they seemed such an important part of my life. But now he was easy around them, especially with Max. He talked comfortably to him, asking him about school, his friends, his recent birthday party.

'We played lots of games,' Max said. 'Egg race, and What's the Time, Mister Wolf, and Topfschlagen –'

'What?'

'It is a German game,' Max explained. 'Hit-the-pot. When it's your turn, you get blindfolded and someone gives you a cooking spoon, and then on all fours you have to grope your way, banging the spoon all around you, until you hit the pot. Then the blindfold is taken off, you lift the pot and there is a present under it.'

'Okay, I see. But what if you don't find the pot?'

'No, you always do,' Max told him confidently. 'Though sometimes the others tease and mislead the one with the blindfold.'

My heart warmed to Dambudzo, as I saw his pout give way to a tender smile. The gloom seemed to lift from him, his mind to distend into the serenity of the afternoon.

I had spread a blanket on the grass and Dambudzo and I sat close together, leaning against each other. A few families were scattered here and there, and a large Indian group with table and chairs was having a braai at the cooking area. Max and Franz ran up a slope and soon disappeared behind one of the huge granite boulders that rose up amidst the dry grass and indigenous trees. I loved those trees, with their firm shiny leaves, twisting stems and parasitic loops dangling down in the darkness of their foliage. They were so much less conspicuous than the foreign ones in town, with their crying colours.

'Hey, this is really beautiful,' Dambudzo said, putting his arm around my shoulder, 'and your boys, I like them, they are beautiful too.'

I saw Max waving at us from the top of one of the mighty rocks. His bare feet had an easy grip on the porous surface of the stone. I went looking for Franz and found him standing at the foot of the rock, frustrated that he could not get up himself.

'Come, let's go to the swings,' I said.

Dambudzo strolled across and joined us at the small playground. Franz, already on a swing, turned his head. 'You push me, Mummy,' he said. But when after a while Dambudzo took over, he let it happen. Max had scrambled down off his rock and was flying high on the other swing. I went back to our blanket and sat watching them. I remember the image: Dambudzo's angular figure, cigarette in one hand, the other pushing the swing, two blond heads whooshing up and down in front of him.

Some time later, when I took him to Cleveland Dam again without the children, it all went wrong. Hoping for some peaceful hours together, away from our house, I spread the blanket among the rocks, hidden from view, and unpacked a bottle of wine. The afternoon sun, filtered through the copper-coloured leaves above us, was warm on our skin. It could have been heaven but it turned out to be hell. As had become the pattern, Dambudzo sensed my expectations, my willing him to be pleasant and compliant – and he resisted.

Shortly after the outing to the dam with the children, Dambudzo phoned me from the Oasis. He said he needed to talk to me, right then. His voice sounded urgent.

I went.

In a roundabout way – 'How can I put it to you?' was one of his favourite phrases, supposedly showing that he had thought about it deeply – he steered to what turned out to be a solemn declaration, or rather, a proposal. He said he needed me for himself alone. I should divorce my husband. He wanted to marry me, together with my children.

I had never seriously considered that option. Of course, the fantasy of 'what would it be like if ...' had crossed my mind but only to be obliterated just as quickly. So my answer was a clear 'No'. I do not know whether he had expected anything else. The question was never raised again.

We continued as before.

I was the one who allotted the time we could spend together. Dambudzo went along with it, but the grudge that I was the one in charge rankled. It gave rise and reason to the never-ending series of tantrums that sabotaged my dream of our amour fou.

In October that year Dambudzo moved in with us. It was not a premeditated move. It happened out of the desperation of the moment.

We had driven out to the UZ campus again, to a spot somewhere around the vlei. Nobody would notice us there, Dambudzo had said. We made love in the boot of the station wagon. With the seats laid flat, we had space to stretch out. Huddling under a blanket, we fell asleep. Suddenly

– it must have been around 2 am – there was a bump against the car. I sat up, squinting into the harsh light of the campus watchman's torch that was being shone directly onto my face. Dambudzo angrily shooed the man away.

I realised I could not go on like this.

I could not continue to decamp with my lover in the middle of the night and then drive back to my cozy home.

So I took Dambudzo home with me. It seemed he had almost expected it. He had a way of taking for granted whatever was done for him.

At home, I opened the door to the cottage, which was right next to the carport. It served as Victor's study and extra guest room and it had a bed, a large desk in front of a window that looked out onto the garden, some bookshelves and a sideboard with drawers. After I had settled Dambudzo there, I sneaked into the main house, slipped into bed beside Victor, cuddled against his back, and whispered: 'I have brought Dambudzo. He is sleeping in the cottage.'

'It's okay,' Victor murmured.

Having a Home

DAMBUDZO THRIVED IN THE RESPITE of his new surroundings. He revelled in being off the streets, having a proper bed, clean sheets, clean clothes, a shower, regular meals and space to write. He also loved being part of our family.

Victor was very welcoming. He could relate to our guest's mindset. Dambudzo was one of the few Zimbabwean writers who appealed to his own literary sensitivity and he also liked him as a person. He found conversations with him stimulating. Likewise, Dambudzo liked and respected his host, his generosity, and his worldliness, something that was rare among colonials.

The first few days stimulated Dambudzo's creativity. He would sit at his desk in the cottage or at a table in the garden, typing away.

One of the first texts he wrote was a play about 'couple watching'. Two watchmen, who turn out to be ghosts and who are in love with each other, have to watch couples at a cemetery.

'I am sick of couples,' says one of them, 'I am sick of watching people living out the illusion that their feelings and emotions are permanent.'

'Look at those two,' the watchman continues, 'dying of love – grieving for each other. [Puzzled] It's their little boy who has died isn't it?'

'Such an idiotic churl of a child. [Thoughtfully] I never did like children. I consider them the inescapable permanent nightmare, a secret steel trap awaiting all who believe in the illusion of love.'

Was it an allusion to my own marriage? The husband in the play is called 'Man'; the wife has the German name Helga.

I liked the play. I was touched by the tender, slightly surrealist meditation about love and about dying. That love and dying was also a theme binding me to Dambudzo I did not yet know; nor that it would fall to me to publish the play after its author had become a kind of 'watchful ghost' himself.

My children, Max especially, to whom Dambudzo related so easily and fondly, seemed to revert the 'inescapable permanent nightmare', making our home even more, for Dambudzo, the unattainable ideal of a beautiful life. Photos taken during those first days at our house show him and the two boys sitting together at the workbench in the playroom, painting. Max, very attentive and engaged, with the older friend, Franz, dreamily trying out red paint. The plywood playhouse that Victor had built for them, decorated with green trees and a red elephant, is visible in the background.

Not captured by a photo but tender to my heart is the image I have of them sitting next to each other at the large desk in the cottage. I saw them sideways through the open door, from the kitchen porch. Dambudzo's dark head over the typewriter, Max's blond head over his pad and pens. Dambudzo, with his short-sighted eyes close to the keys, two fingers darting down like birds diving at frogs in a pond. He was typing the story 'The Magic Cat'. Now and then he turned his head to Max, getting his consent for what he was writing and looking at the drawings Max was doing. They looked relaxed with each other, familiar, focused on drawing up the story together. Dambudzo looked like the elder brother who enjoys working with the much smaller, younger one. Tenderness, companionship, care for each other – they could have been brooding over a trick they wanted to play on someone. Dambudzo typing simple yet poetic lines, as they were coming out of his head, inspired by the presence of the child; Max animating them with drawings in black ink, just as simple and poetic.

For the second story they wrote together, 'Baboons of the Rainbow', Max did his drawings in colour and the two artistic collaborators drew on the terrible drought in Zimbabwe at that time for their more elaborate plot. It starts fairytale-like but ends with Black Baboon and White Baboon eating Green Baboon.

*Once upon a time,
in a town at the end of the rainbow,
there lived a black baboon
and a white baboon
and a green baboon.
It was very hot.
The sun was bloodshot.
There was not a drop of rain.
'Drought!' shouted the Daily Baboon newspaper.
Black Baboon was hungry. Very hungry.
White Baboon was very, very hungry.
Green Baboon was also hungry.
'There is nothing but hunger at the end
of the rainbow,' said the Daily Baboon newspaper.*

The story ends with Green Baboon being eaten by White Baboon and Black Baboon, 'in a civilised way'.

Dambudzo and Max

WHEN DAMBUDZO GAVE THESE and a few more children's stories to publishers, he was told that they were not suitable for children.

Could the six-year-old illustrator relate to them? Did he understand the stories which 'contain themes that deal with adult cynicism but in a playful child's narrative voice', the adult Max Wild was asked years later. He was a well-known jazz musician by then and performing on his saxophone with Zimbabwean musicians.

> If I remember, 'The Magic Cat' was less cynical, and I definitely related to it in a very childlike way. 'Baboons of the Rainbow' got a lot darker, especially as the story went on. I didn't think twice about the violence, and thought it was very entertaining, as you can see from my drawings. I remember not understanding some of the adult stuff towards the end, like the drinking, cigar smoking, and listening/playing music. For me it didn't really make sense or go with the story at the time and seemed a little irrelevant. In fact, Dambudzo and I stayed up pretty late that night, finishing the illustrations, and I remember getting tired and him helping me with the drawings. The last couple of drawings he did himself, when I had gone to bed. You should be

able to notice the subtle differences.

Well, naturally, I now understand them better, and see the different layers. Although they went over my head at the time, I suspected that Dambudzo was up to something, hinting at something beyond the actual script. Reading them now, I recognise the pain and violence in them, but I remember that this was never an issue for me back then as a child, because Dambudzo made it sound so natural and almost comical. It seems to me that's how he might have viewed his own life.

He was very intense and, at the time, I thought he could act a bit crazy.

I think the key is that his mood could change very quickly. But when he was in form and focusing, he was very much in the moment, very funny, and definitely very nice to us kids. I think he liked me, and children in general. He could relate to our lack of inhibitions and the way life was so uncomplicated and easy to us. He was always very kind and caring towards me. As far as his 'unpredictability' went, I could tell when he was in a weird mood and might act 'unpredictable' and would leave him alone.

Sometime much later, we organised a series of creative writing workshops for children at our house. It was one of the attempts Victor and I undertook to make good use of Dambudzo's talents and give him the feeling that he was doing something useful – not to mention earning a little money. It worked for the two first sessions, but then drink and unease set in again, upsetting the young writers and isolating their teacher.

The workshops had a lasting effect on Max, however.

'Always remember the imagination, Dambudzo told us,' Max says in a radio feature after the writer's death in August 1987.

His notebook with Dambudzo's comments in red pencil still exists.

Of course, Max, the child, did not realise the special constellation in which his parents had given a home to his writer-friend. Yet, as I am listening to 'The End of Green Baboon', a song Max composed in later years, the images of the blond and the black head, engrossed in their work, emerge in my mind.

As much as at the time he might have been seen as an intruder, I feel that the impact Dambudzo had on my son at that age, and the inspiration that lasted until he himself became an artist, is also part of my story, widening and enriching it and filling me with joy.

In the liner notes to his first CD, *Zambezi Sunset*, Max thanks Dambudzo Marechera 'for teaching me to use my imagination and to be an individual'.

Facing the Publishers

IT DIDN'T TAKE LONG, AFTER he had moved in with us, for Dambudzo to put a whole manuscript together, consisting of prose and poetry and a number of plays. He gave the compilation the title *Killwatch or Tony Fights Tonight*.

But who would publish it? His homecoming from London the year before, when the papers had been full of the 'prodigal son', the Guardian Fiction laureate who had put Zimbabwean literature into the international limelight, had been a sensational event. The subsequent falling out with Chris Austin, which sabotaged the projected film about his return, had caused a stir, as had the famous 'farewell lecture' he'd staged – one of the punch lines in the narrative of his life – before leaving the country again (which hadn't happened because he did not have a passport). But since then it had become quiet around Dambudzo. Nobody seemed to care about him.

Nevertheless, he was feeling good and he was optimistic about his new manuscript. He suggested we talk to Marilyn Poole, a friend from England, who was the representative in Harare of Longman Publishers. Distinguished and beautiful, and graceful at six feet tall, Marilyn stood out at every social gathering she attended. In her slightly old-fashioned elegance it was no surprise that she was cast as the British ambassador's wife when a new version of *King Solomon's Mines* was filmed in Zimbabwe – Rider Haggard set in post-colonial Zimbabwe, another irony of the time.

We had Marilyn over for dinner. She seemed really fond of Dambudzo and in the months to come she would become, together with Victor and I, a strong supporter of his; she contributed to maintaining his daily upkeep before and during his illness. She took the manuscript and said she would try to place it with Longmans. However, it did not work out. Essentially, Longmans were school textbook publishers and, with its mixture of different genres, Dambudzo's new book did not fit into any of their categories.

This was a blow. Many more were to come.

It was at that point that Victor and I were thinking of organising a public reading for Dambudzo in the hope it would make him more visible again and also do something to lift his spirits.

'This country is not ripe for writers like myself,' Dambudzo moaned. 'Look at my last manuscript. *Mindblast*. I gave it to ZPH more than a year ago. They sat on it for months, and then – rejected it.'

We were sitting at his favourite writing place, the round garden table below the Lady Chancellor tree, a folder with the new manuscript in front of him. The air was sticky, there was no sun and no breeze. I could feel sweat running down my armpits. Everyone was hoping that it would finally start raining. From a distance, high-pitched children's voices wafted across the lawn. The boys had friends over to play.

'I don't understand,' I said. 'Charles is an editor at ZPH. Did he not want to publish your manuscript?'

'Ag, Charles, yes, he is my friend, he lets me use his office when I am out in the streets, we drink together, but he would never stick his head out.'

'But why? Did they give you any reasons?'

'I don't know. Too obscene. Or too critical about the big bums who are going around fucking the ministers' wives. Blah, blah, blah.'

When ZPH turned the manuscript down, Dambudzo had submitted the manuscript to College Press, where Stanley Nyamfukudza, another friend and fellow writer, worked as an editor.

'We were at university together here in Rhodesia, and again in Oxford,' he told me. 'I actually wrote parts of *House of Hunger* at his kitchen table when I had been expelled from college in Oxford.'

'So what did Stanley say? Will he get it published?'

'We will look into it, blah blah .... This is again more than half a year ago. And you know what –?' anger swelled up in his eyes '– Stanley wants to get his own new book out first, so mine has to wait. They all have their jobs, you know, all my contemporaries from university, they are civil servants or university lecturers or editors – they are selling their souls, all of them. And using their advantages to their own design – not mine.'

'Well, I am not sure ...' I said. 'Publishers might have their constraints. They cannot bring out a manuscript overnight just because the one and only Dambudzo Marechera has given it to them.'

'So you are defending them, those bastards?' His tone was becoming aggressive, his voice rising.

'Okay, okay,' I said quickly. 'What shall we do? Why don't you talk to Stanley and ask him?'

Hearing Dambudzo shouting at me, Max came running over, wanting to know what was going on.

'Ah, Max, you are my friend,' Dambudzo said to him. 'You are an artist like me. Please run to the kitchen and look for a bottle of wine.'

'Okay,' Max grinned. 'You mean one of the bottles with the red top and the picture of that ugly castle?'

'That's the one. Chateau Burgundy, it is called. *Chateau* meaning castle in French.'

I had to suppress a giggle at Dambudzo's stuck-up way of pronouncing the word, his accent so English, but his voice was raw with anger and thirst.

A week later we were sitting in Stanley Nyamfukudza's College Press office. Like Dambudzo's first book, Stanley's novel had been written during his Oxford exile. The bare prose of *The Non-Believer's Journey* and the author's cynical stance towards the liberation war had not been to the liking of the praise-singers of national culture at that time. I myself sympathised with it, my own 'revolutionary' past making me wary of the eulogies of the 'heroic struggle'. When in the years to come I would write my PhD thesis, I borrowed Nyamfukudza's term, calling it 'Teachers, Preachers, Non-Believers'.

Now we were facing the 'Non-Believer' himself. I had seen Stanley at the book fair conference, where he'd sat in one of the back rows, withdrawn, mute. He looked even more withdrawn now. His eyes, half shut, did not look at anyone in particular, and when he spoke his lips hardly moved and his voice was flat. He seemed extremely embarrassed by the situation.

I was embarrassed too. I felt like a dummy, a white woman placed there on the chair next to the black writer who wanted to challenge his editor about delaying the publication of his manuscript. I had nothing to say. Dambudzo had insisted that I come, but not only because I would drive him to the publishing house, which was in the industrial area south of the city, where he couldn't easily get to on his own. My presence seemed to augment his own importance. He had introduced me as a friend; maybe he had also said 'a literary critic'. In later years, when I was working on my doctoral study, he sometimes introduced me as 'Dr Wild, a German scholar'.

Stanley mumbled something or other about why the book was not out yet, why he could not give an exact date, but said that they intended to publish it. Dambudzo nodded. He also did not seem sure of himself and the words, when they came, were faltering. 'Okay, so I will hear from you,' he said, or words to that effect.

That was all that came out of that meeting, as far as I remember.

What I do remember is the awkwardness of the situation.

The Taxi Has to be Paid

After the peaceful first days at Boscobel Drive, our guest started growing restless. When I did not want to go with him, he hitched lifts into town and came home drunk.

One night, at 2 am, there was a knock on our bedroom window, then Dambudzo's voice, barking: 'Hey! It's me!'

Startled, I sat up in bed.

'What is it?' I hissed. 'Go to bed. Let us sleep.'

Victor stirred, then turned over, pulling the blanket over his head.

'The taxi.'

'What about it?'

'The taxi is waiting. It has to be paid.'

I could hear the faint growling of an engine running in the close on the other side of the house. What should I do? Hoping to salvage a few hours of sleep, I got up, grumbling, put my robe on, and, wallet in hand, walked to the gate, Dambudzo following me at a distance. When the taxi driver saw me, he got out of his R4.

'How much is it?'

'Four eighty, madam.'

I handed the money over through the gate and shuffled back to bed.

At the time that I met Marechera I was a novice in the field of African literature. I had done undergraduate studies in French and German, but apart from a few student essays I had never written with any authority about literature. The political movement had taken over the focus of my attention and had also shaped my perspective on the arts in a one-sided and often superficial way. In Zimbabwe, propelled by the impetus of assignments for my journalism course and also by my own growing interest, I had begun groping my way towards understanding and writing about the literature of the country.

Now here was Dambudzo, our house guest, my lover. I could talk to him, listen to him, hear him argue with others, interview him.

Dambudzo was an excellent interviewee. The many interviews journalists and critics conducted with him over the years, some published here and there, many transcribed by me after his death, were so lucid and full of surprising statements and insights that they have become canonical reading material for the large corpus of Marechera research.

I did my own first interview with him that November 1983, not long after he had moved in with us. I was particularly interested in the much cited 'language question', about which I had also asked other writers, and I was keen to explore the topic further. I did have a tape recorder but, unsure of my role as a literary critic, I was kind of shy to use it. With Dambudzo, however, this was not a problem. An interview with him was a professional procedure and the roles were clear – he the writer, who had significant things to say; me the apprentice, the 'emerging' literary critic, who could learn from him and write about it.

So I put the recorder on the table, switched the microphone on and held it towards him, a little anxious that my questions might sound stupid and uninformed.

'Dambudzo, what relation do you have towards your mother tongue – Shona?'

His first reply unhinged my question.

'What do you mean, "Shona"? There is no Shona as such. The Shona they speak here in the townships, the urban Shona, is a mixture of Shona, Ndebele, English and Afrikaans. It is a language full of violence.'

What he said was so simple and yet always full of startling insight. *Shona is a language full of violence.* I would pluck his words, these and others, at the many occasions in later years when German students or readers of African literature would, without fail, reproachfully ask

African writers who came for a reading, 'But why do you not write in your mother tongue?'

'But that does not mean,' Dambudzo continued, 'that you just take the colonial language as it is. You have to turn it upside down, until it screams your screams. For instance, you use poisonous language to describe beauty. Language is only the medium through which images of violence are thrown onto the reader – like in *Black Sunlight*. We are listening to how words emerge from our minds.'

I used this poetic phrase for the title of my essay about the language question, my first publication in an academic journal: 'Ich höre zu, wie Wörter meinem Bewußtsein entspringen'.

Without me being aware of it at the time, Dambudzo was helping me, a newcomer to Africa, a white woman from Europe, to find firm ground on the minefield of how I was to approach Africa, Africans, African literature.

One Sunday in November we took a family trip to Raffingora, about a hundred kilometres north of Harare, where friends of ours ran a pottery shop and did painting and cloth-printing. Dambudzo came with us.

I loved the drive across the Great Dyke. After our diesel engine had been slowed down by the steady uphill climb, on the crest of a hill a stunning view of the plain below opened up before us. It seemed like the entrance into another world. A bit further on, when entering the grassland, we had to drive on gravel roads, through clouds of red dust when another vehicle was passing, or abruptly blocked by a herd of cattle, goats or sheep in the road.

Our friends lived in an old farmhouse, thickly thatched, with low walls and small windows, overlooking a few acres of farmland, where they grew maize and vegetables and kept chickens. Their farm formed a sort of bohemian enclave within the community of white farmers who owned expansive fields of cotton, tobacco, maize, wheat and cattle.

For me, visits to the Ballymakosa Farm, as it was called, belong to the most treasured memories of what life could be like in Zimbabwe around that time. In my flat where I live today, I have small tiles and mosaic stones fitted in my kitchen and bathroom, in shiny blue, red and green, which I collected on our last visit there. They evoke memories of strolling through the pottery, among debris of walls, grass sprouting among stones and splinters of tiles, in that somewhat wild, romantic, creative space. I remember the meals with fresh vegetables, bananas, papayas, granadilla, mango, avocado, all homegrown. I remember sitting together at dusk. How eerie it felt when darkness came down, settling within minutes, and you would hear the ghastly shrieks of the hadeda birds and see their shadows flitting from one tree to the next. At dawn, you would be woken by the peacocks, their crowing shrill as screaming babies, carrying from the neighbouring farm far away. For our children, farm life with sheep, cattle, chickens and dogs, and the roaming around in the wilderness, was always a special holiday treat.

What was it like for Dambudzo, I wonder, who had often mentioned his 'Fear and Loathing out of Harare', for whom bushland meant tales of witches and rural areas were equated with Blair toilets – the brick pit latrines built by development agencies – where the writer had no contribution to make?

Yet he seemed to relish our excursion. A photo shows him in conversation with our hosts at a round table outside, having lunch, sipping tequila, sucking lemons, smoking and – Dambudzo – munching handfuls of red chilli pods. Victor and the children were chilling from the extreme heat in the only possible place, an old cattle trough filled with cold water.

I remember how our hosts enjoyed listening to stories from Dambudzo's life, his views on art and on politics. He visibly savoured the ethereal setting of the place and the tranquil and yet inspired atmosphere. And yet, the setting, the food and drink, the company remained unreal for him, unattainable. Beneath the surface of calm and serenity, the dread of the past was lurking.

Sunday it's Raffingora

Thoughts like cattle scattered
On barren parched fields
Spinning backwards my vehicle feelings speeding
Forwards to Raffingora –

Clear sunlit conceptions leap
Out of deft brushstroke:
Landscapes within.

On film, on canvas, on drawing board
Trees grass flowers boulder on boulder
In the shadows of Flamboyant elegance –

The past in meagre battlement of mud and thatch
Deserted bombed-out farmhouses,
The vision around sharp bend of the Age
Tottering manfully
On rattling ninety year old bike –

(Hours later) return exhausted not by space and time
Not by the paintings and the pottery and the garden
But by haunting vision of 'Out of Hunger a Terrible Art'
Faster driving faster into Harare's split-atom bursts of streets.

It was a pattern of Dambudzo's life. He befriended people, often Europeans, who were delighted to know him. They felt it was an uplifting experience. Yet soon they would realise – or at least, believe – that he needed help. They did not want to see such talent go to waste through his self-destructive behaviour.

And so it was with Victor and me. We wanted to get our friend off drink, off the streets, on his own feet. We suggested that he see our neighbour, a doctor, in the hope that she could convince him to accept help, see a counsellor, do psychotherapy.

'I do not want to be reformed,' he said, when he came back. 'It would kill my creativity. I am like I am. An artist, a writer. Oxford already threatened me with psychiatric "help". No, thank you. Leave me alone.'

Yet at the same time he depended on others to sustain him. He seemed to think that he was entitled to be cared for by others. I am a writer. The world owes me a living, was his tacit credo.

His nightly trips to town for booze and forgetting continued.

One morning, Max, who always got up first, found him sleeping in the garden in the hammock between the trees. On another we found him near the pool, one hand bleeding – he had slipped on the terracotta tiles and cut it. More than once he phoned me from town and asked to be picked up. When I got to whichever pub he was in, he would urge me to stay with him because he wanted to continue drinking. When I got impatient, he became hot-headed and started to insult me:

'Yeah, you go home and sleep with your husband, you bitch. Stop fooling me. You are just exploiting me; you only want to get hold of my writings.'

When he came home with me, he'd demand that I sleep with him in the cottage. When I refused because he was so drunk that it would only have left me frustrated, he would make a scene. If I agreed, it also ended in disaster.

One night, after we had made love and he seemed to be asleep, I wanted to sneak out of the cottage and get into my own bed. As I was putting on my pants and T-shirt, holding my flip-flops in my hand, he sat up, alarmed.

'Where are you going?' he said, hovering above me, lighting a cigarette.

'I am going to the house. I'll see you in the morning.'

'I don't want you to go. Stay! You always desert me, whenever you feel like it.'

'Dambudzo, you know I have to get up early, to get the kids ready for school. We can see each other during the day. You have a good rest.'

'Stop mothering me. All you want is my black dick and then you run back to your people. You bloody German fascists. People like you, they killed millions in the gas chambers. Just like here, those fascists of Ian Smith, they killed my people in that bloody war …'

'Stop it!' I yelled, as his voice grew more caustic. 'How can you? You know very well that my own family was persecuted by the Nazis because we had Jewish roots. My parents, my grandparents, all of them – You are crazy. Stupid. Cruel. Stop your insane insults. Anyway, I am going – you are driving me away. That's what you seem to want anyway. And afterwards you want to be pitied, you poor creature, always deserted …'

With his free hand he tried to hold me back but I pulled myself loose and ran away, closing the cottage door behind me, up the three steps into the kitchen and into my bed, where my husband was asleep.

It was a never-ending circle of love and passion, alcohol, jealousy, possessiveness, paranoia and loneliness. When Dambudzo was drunk, he lost control, and took revenge for all the injuries he felt the world inflicted on him.

At other times, when he was reasonably sober, he could be quite self-conscious.

I remember one night when he was looking down on my body sprawled out in front of him, saying something like: when he was making love to me, a white woman, he could not help feeling very violent. It was as if he was avenging all the brutality from his childhood in the township, or even against the whole white race.

I do not know how I managed to go on. Every so often, already in those early days, I told myself that I had to put an end to our affair. But then, after a most abominable argument or incident the night before, I would see him coming out of the cottage in the morning, squinting into the sunlight, rubbing his eyes with the back of his hands. And in the most affable and innocent way, he would smile and plead guilty.

'What did I do last night? Oh yeah. That was really shit. But you know me. I did not mean it.'

And then I could not help but love him again.

Sometimes, when I had fallen asleep in his arms, I would wake up in the middle of the night, enclosed by a sudden heat. What is this? I would think, befuddled, only to realise I was lying in a puddle, a hot pool of what could only be urine. His body had released the many litres he had been drinking. I never mentioned it to him. I just moved to the edge of the bed, and after a while I would get up, leave the cottage quietly and go over to my own quarters.

The next day everyone around the house would see a mattress drying in the sun. Anna, who also cleaned Dambudzo's room, had taken the wet sheets off the bed and put the mattress outside. Sometimes I left one of my nightgowns in my lover's bed; I would find it later, nicely folded, on my own bed. What did Anna think about this? I do not know. It must have been obvious to her that the 'madam' of the house was sleeping with the lodger, who was her compatriot and had the same black skin, and who now and then awkwardly exchanged greetings with her and the gardener in Shona. It was as if she was invisible, just like the many black servants in colonial novels – silent witnesses of most intimate goings-on in their masters' houses, their mistresses' bedrooms; shadowy beings in whose company the natural rules of shame were discarded.

All of us tried to ignore the mattress drying in the sun. Victor, of course, realised what had happened and he just smiled, but with each such incident Dambudzo's unease was swelling up inside him. His own shame about being hosted by his mistress's husband in their house and, on top of it, being waited upon by their black servants, was too much to bear. It was like a seething chasm. It was kept under control for a while, but the longer it lasted the more often it cracked open, unleashing his anger and his revulsion for his undignified situation.

So the drinking, the tantrums, the desperation continued.

On his side.

On my side.

Dambudzo's presence in our house became a burden. When I told him he had to leave on the 10th of December, when school holidays started and we would be going to the Vumba mountains, after which my brother and his family were coming on a visit, he broke down.

'How can you do this to me?' he cried. 'You want to expel me? Where should I go? Back to the streets?'

As always, he was a master of emotional manipulation, making everyone else feel guilty for the misery in his own life. I was exasperated.

'Why do you not do anything to stand on your own feet?' I said. 'You always depend on other people. You are a parasite, a bloodsucker. I do not want to see you again!'

'Okay, okay, I am leaving. Forget about me. Get yourself another lover who will tickle your pussy until you scream. I am going.' He got his backpack down from the cupboard, grabbed a few things and started cramming them into it, shouting at me over his shoulder. 'I am going to find someone to buy the copyright for *The House of Hunger* from me, and then I'll get a ticket to Europe!'

And with that he stomped out and off our property.

I sat on the veranda as he left, crouched into one of the wicker chairs. My mind was blank. It was too much to take. After a while the tears welled up and I cried and cried until I was exhausted and the tension began to ebb.

What was going on? What should I do? Why could I not just leave Dambudzo to his own way of destroying himself?

I did not have an answer. All I know is that I could not let go – not then and not for many more months to come.

After I had calmed myself, I got into the car and drove into town. It was already late at night. Victor was sleeping. The children were quiet. I went to all the bars I knew Dambudzo frequented – the Park Lane, the Oasis, the Ambassador – until I found him. He was happy to see me. 'For the first time in my life,' he said, 'there is someone who cares for me.'

He promised he would make an effort, change his habits, start courting me again, win my love all over again. A few happy peaceful days followed.

How much I could not have loved him.

In a tranquil mood we drove to Rusape – me, the children and Dambudzo. He had not visited his hometown since his return from England the year before.

The German volunteer who had invited us to visit the co-operative where he worked took us around. He showed us the carpentry, which he was helping to build up. Friendly faces looked up from their workbench, men in neat overalls; they seemed to like our young friend, who was unobtrusive in the way he instructed them. He told us how enthusiastic they were but also how difficult it was to establish a self-reliant administration where everyone, men and women, had equal say and responsibilities. In the large vegetable garden women were bent over rows of pumpkins and squash. With a curtsey, they gave us a basket full of vegetables for our supper.

The first day was peaceful. We were like a family, going for walks through the fields with the children, sharing a room. When the boys were asleep, we made love, quietly, so that they would not wake up. For the second time Dambudzo asked me whether I would not want to live with him, me and the children, all of us together.

That night when I slipped out of our room to go to the bathroom, I saw our volunteer friend through a basement window. He was lying on his mattress with a black woman, both of them naked, fondling each other. What was the difference, I wondered.

The next day Dambudzo was irritable. The ghosts of his childhood in Rusape had been reawakened. Being driven out of their house after his father died, living in a slum, the violence of his older brother, of men towards their wives, of his mother prostituting herself so that she could sustain nine children – these things haunted him.

'Oh, I don't know. I shouldn't have come here,' he said.

That night, needing a beer, he went to Vengere township, the place where he had grown up, and spent several hours at the local beer hall there. When he came back, his hand was bleeding. Later he would write: *The first ten-year-late handshake, from my knuckles drew red blood ...*

He did not say much, but I could see the terror in his eyes. He did not want to come here again. Ever.

He did not.

But I did.

I did not know he would bequeath me the legacy to revisit his life, to walk through the streets of Vengere, to see for myself the 'house of hunger'.

When we got home to Boscobel Drive, over supper together on the veranda we told Victor about the trip. Christmas beetles whirred around us, dropping down with a plop onto the terracotta tiles. Our two Doberman dogs were restless behind our chairs, dribbling, lusting for the meat – huge T-bone steaks from the rural butcher in Rusape – on the braai.

'Tamara, out!' Max shouted.

'Yango, out!' Franz echoed (he couldn't pronounce Django yet, our other dog's name).

Dambudzo was part of it. And he wasn't.

When I told him I wasn't going to sleep in his bed that night, he freaked out. The next morning, he told me he hadn't slept the whole night, that he had heard me scream.

'Scream?' I said. 'I did not scream. What are you hearing?'

Sometimes his intense jealousy made him hallucinate.

We were back to where we had been before the trip.

Every night it got worse.

Dambudzo would come home drunk, wake me up, harass me, insult me. It was exhausting.

The 10th of December approached. Point of crisis. On the morning before our departure Dambudzo came into the kitchen, where I was busy packing bags with provisions for the trip to the Vumba mountains.

'Hey,' he said, 'what are you doing?'

I looked up into his morning face, which I so loved because it was without defences.

'I am packing things for our trip,' I said.

'What trip? What are you talking about?'

I knew that look, the look of a hunted animal.

'Come on. You know,' I said. 'We have told you many times. We are going to the Vumba tomorrow.'

'What? And what about me?'

'You have to leave.'

'So you are expelling me.' His voice got louder. 'As always. As everyone.' He began retreating through the kitchen door.

I tried to say something – 'But look …' Again, that feeling of guilt.

'Don't worry, I am going! It is back to the streets. I am used to it. Back in London, the beggars under the bridge knew me, the watchmen in the park.'

Max came running from the playroom where he had been packing his books and toys.

'Why is Dambudzo shouting, Mum?'

'Because we are going away.'

'Can he not also come?'

'No, lovey, it is not possible.'

'Why?'

'Ah, Max, my friend,' Dambudzo said, now standing in the door of the cottage, 'your parents are chasing me away.'

'Oh, you shut up!' I yelled at him. I pulled Max to me and closed the kitchen door. From outside Dambudzo's curses followed us.

'I am going! Yes, I am going. You will never see me again!'

Five minutes later, he came in, slammed his keys down on the kitchen counter, and with rucksack on his back, left.

Relief. Anger. Worry.

I did not know what to feel. It had all been too much these last weeks. Better just look forward to a quiet week with the children and Victor.

'You know, there are horses where we are going,' I said to Max, trying to distract him. 'So you can have riding lessons every day.'

'Yippee!'

In the evening, when Victor was back from work and we were having supper, there was a knock on the back door. Franz ran into the kitchen to open it.

'It's Zambuzo,' he said.

Dambudzo stood there, head down, shoulders drooping. He looked like he was at the end of his tether. Pitiful. Without resistance.

He said simply: 'I did not find anywhere to go to.'

Victor, who in such situations tended to be more understanding and generous than me, looked at me.

'All right,' he said to Dambudzo. 'You may stay for one more week, while we are in the Vumba, on your own. Anna will be on leave.'

Dambudzo's head jerked up, his body straightened. Brightness came over him.

'Do not worry,' he said. 'I will look after the house. I will also have the dogs to keep me company. Everything will be spick and span when you come back.'

Vumba and the Grand Finale

THE YEARNING STARTED THE moment we set out from Harare on the eastward road towards Mutare. All the pain, the hurt, the desperation about a love which could not be lived shrank to tiny dots, like drops of blood which, once dried, you do not notice anymore. In their place my heart was filling with longing.

Passing through Marondera, with its huge mills and silos which in the years to come would be filled to the brim with maize, Zimbabwe becoming the granary of the SADAC region; shortly after, Malvatte, the farmhouse where you could have coffee and cake on the lawn, surrounded by orchards and grazing sheep, and fill up on fresh vegetables; an hour later, Rusape.

Remember, Dambudzo? Our two days there, the pain of your return, the passion of our embraces?

'It is an eagle, an elephant, a whale!' the children cried out at each picturesque rock formation we drove past in the grassland on our right.

After another hour's drive we had reached the crest of the road. Down below us the city of Mutare, glistening white, spreading far out onto the plain.

What is he doing? Does he feel lonely? How is he feeling all by himself?

Some miles past Mutare, the road began to climb again and we drove, up, up, up, in serpentine loops towards the heights of the Vumba, a cone-shaped mountain of about 1 900 metres at its peak. The higher we climbed, the more it felt like we were entering a jungle, a dense tapestry of foliage enclosing us, slings of lianas and braids of moss dangling down into the narrow bends. On either side vines, creepers and ferns made the forest appear impenetrable. It became so dark and misty we had to switch the headlights on.

'This is eerie,' Max whispered. 'Is this where the elves are hiding? Look, the road is all wet. Has it been raining?'

'Vumba means mist in Shona,' Victor explained. 'It is so humid here that the moisture remains on the road even if it is not raining.'

'Look – baboons!' Franz crowed as a mother with a babe on her back bobbed across the road in front of us, quickly vanishing into the thicket. 'Can we see more?'

From the main road we had another long drive ahead of us, this time on a bumpy gravel road, before our final destination: a cottage on the coffee farm where we would spend our holiday. It was slow going, up and down the hills, past terraces of coffee plants with their red berries against shiny green leaves, overtaking the occasional tractor or pick-up truck loading or off-loading its wares. We passed women walking along the road with babies on their backs and bundles of firewood on their heads. A few huts crouching at the foot of the slopes. Was that where the farm workers lived, we wondered.

The children were getting impatient.

'How far is it?'

'Just a few more minutes,' I said. 'Look up there, to your right. That must be the Leopard Rock Hotel.'

'Ooooh, leopards, can we see some?'

'I don't know. Maybe it has that name because the rock looks like a pouncing leopard. Don't you think so?'

'Nonsense, Mummy, there must be leopards. Can we go and ask?'

'The hotel is closed. But maybe we can climb up the hill ...'

A reminder of bygone times, the hotel, built to look like a castle, had once hosted royal guests and affluent holidaymakers. Sheltered by the overhanging rock and with a magnificent view into the far distance of valleys and hills, it had offered all the amenities of luxury holidays: golf course, tennis courts, swimming pool, and well-kept gardens. Partly damaged and closed during the war, it was now slowly decomposing, awaiting an investor to spruce it up for the newly rich.

Our cottage was on a ridge, just behind the house of the farm owner. The children loved rolling down the slope of lawn, the hardy grass a prickly carpet, while Victor and I were content to relax in the shade of the umbrella acacias, reading, writing or just drinking in the view. To all sides your gaze would glide over the green hills and trees and plains and fields and shimmering water until the horizon started swimming, blending in with what, on clear days, was the Mozambican coast.

Victor was preparing for Dambudzo's public reading, re-reading *The House of Hunger*, underlining, making notes. Now and then I would hear him murmur to himself, saying things like: 'That is really excellent. Way above the usual writing you get here.' 'You can see how steeped he is in James Joyce and many other world writers.' Victor was a great Joyce lover himself.

The farmer, Mr C.M., and his wife invited us over for sundowners. Their house was immense. Like a huge vessel, it was built onto the nib of the ridge reaching out in the valley below. The lounge filled out the half oval of that tip. Windows and glass panes from ceiling to floor made it look like an oversized cockpit. It was like being on an airship, with a view far beyond and below into the hills and the valleys. The sky with the orange ball of the sinking sun seemed to extend into the room.

Mr C.M. had the typical appearance of a Rhodesian farmer: bulbous belly protruding under an open shirt, shorts, hairy legs, flip-flops or veldskoen on the feet, and a spongy sunburned face under a floppy hat. Victor and I felt awed by the airiness of the place but we also felt slightly uncomfortable. This property seemed such a statement of wealth and of rulership, the house like the castle of a king built on the top of a mountain, his labourers living in little huts at the bottom of the coffee fields in squalor and poverty.

Our host took down a couple of books from a shelf above his well-stocked bar.

'Ah yes, the Rhodesiana series,' I said, recognising the leather-bound volumes I had consulted at the reading room of the National Archives in Harare when I was researching Rhodesian history.

'Yes, these were great men,' he said, 'the Selous and the Baden-Powells. Paving the way for our pioneer column. It is thanks to them that this country was able to flourish, that coffee could be grown and wheat and tobacco on a large scale. They shouldn't forget that, Mugabe and his cronies. That their granaries are now full, they can feed the whole region – that is thanks to us and our forefathers.'

My tummy was sore from all the wincing I was doing against this self-righteousness, but neither Victor nor I challenged him. Should we have argued with him, contradicted him, pointed at the unethical conditions under which his labourers lived? Probably – but what would have been the use? When we asked how the war had affected that area, the farmer got even more animated. He began telling us how the 'bleddy terrs' crossed over into Mozambique, where they had their base. 'Yes,' his wife chipped in, 'killing a bunch of people at a mission just nearby. It was awful.'

It was this kind of schizophrenia within ourselves we had to live with when holidaying at beautiful places in the country. But, of course, we also knew that those freedom fighters whom we had supported had some of the historical guilt on their side.

In the evenings, the four of us would sit in front of our cottage, the children in their pyjamas cuddled in our arms. The clouds hung low, brewing into thick dark clumps, interlaced with sharp stripes of orange and violet. There was almost no light left. The air was so thick you could hardly breathe. In the far distance, in total silence, an apocalyptic spectacle unfolded: bolts of lightning criss-crossed the black clouds, some just a short flicker, others unzipping the sky for several seconds.

Above our cottage, on top of the ridge, was a huge ficus tree, more than a hundred years old. It had so many wiry stems and aerial roots, it seemed like a dense forest in itself. 'That is where the spirits live,' the African groom, with whom Max had riding lessons, had told our boys. 'It is a sacred place.'

Franz was scared. 'Are these the ghosts, coming out of that tree?' he asked, snuggling deeper into his father's arms.

'It's a thunderstorm,' Victor said.

'But why do we not hear the thunder?' Max asked, logically.

'Because it is so far away. So far we cannot hear the sound.'

'How far? Is it in Mozambique?'

'Yes, very far over Mozambique,' I said. 'Some hundred miles away, there, where the ocean starts.'

And Dambudzo, what is he doing? How is he?

Amazingly, although I did not know it then, Dambudzo was responding to my yearning in his own way.

While I was feeling overwhelmed by the melancholy beauty of the Vumba mountains, letting my thoughts fly high into the ether crossing the distance to him, he was sitting in my house, in the green living room, listening to one LP of classical music after the other, the volume full blast, putting his own longing into verse.

Eaglets in Vumba
The week a pang of desire.

While I was watching with my children the lightning flash in Vumba, he, on 'this tempestuous of nights', was sensing how 'lightning flashes over Highlands'.

And the room around my loneliness
Belongs to her in Vumba
O eaglet sub-desires!

The synchronicity of our longing, our feelings, found its way into Dambudzo's long poetic sequence 'My Arms Vanished Mountains'. In the course of the year since my arrival in Zimbabwe, our orbits had moved towards each other until they had finally met.

Now his narrative and mine were intertwined.

The many times we went there, Vumba always did this to me: it stirred in me a deep yearning and bittersweet melancholia. Desire it was that first time; mourning four years later when, up there in the mountains, I would write my last letter to him, after he had just passed on to the world of the spirits.

Yet, in the pre-Christmas days of 1983, the melodramatic mood of my longing, so eerily echoed by his poem, would, at our return, find a hilarious coda: Dambudzo was staging Dambudzo at his very best in what can only be called a 'grand finale' of that period in our relationship.

'Oh, there you are,' he said nonchalantly, welcoming us back home. 'Everything is okay. The gardener came to feed the dogs. Because Anna went kumusha, yeah, home to the village.'

'Sure, we know, we told you she would be on leave,' I said, amused at how he was taking on the role of the one in charge of the house.

'I stayed home pretty much,' he continued. 'Writing away.'

'What did you write?'

'You'll have to listen to it. A long poetic sequence. I want to read it to you and Victor.'

'Okay. When would you want to do that?'

'Tonight. When the children are in bed. Can you both come to the living room?'

So we did. The green curtains were drawn, the green carpet beside the armchair showing a few holes where he must have dropped a cigarette when falling asleep.

'Please get your recorder,' Dambudzo said, 'and put the *Bolero* on in the background, on the hi-fi.'

He settled in a chair, a glass and a bottle of red wine on the table beside him. Sheets of papers in his hand, he began reading.

I cannot recall how much I grasped of the string of broken images Dambudzo unleashed on us that night. My memory is more of the physical, visual and sonic impact of his performance.

Why did he want it to be recorded, I wonder, and with the music as a backdrop? Did he want to re-enact his mood of inspiration, of inception, of him sitting alone in our living room, listening to the composers whose music entered, full force, into the rhythm and the sound of his lyrics? Tchaikovsky, Brahms, Beethoven, Smetana, Grieg – their names and works reappear in the poem interlaced with the staccato of images from his life and soul, as they emerged in his mind in that moment, in those days, when he was left alone in our house, with the dogs, while we were up in the Vumba mountains.

How ironically provident of him to make me record it, to have this momentous incarnation of his poetic persona sealed onto strips of magnetic tape.

Two nights later the typescript fell prey to one of Dambudzo's tantrums. As if he always had to re-enact the same pattern: extreme bathos followed by disaster. When I told him that I wanted to sleep in my own bed, he stomped off in a fit of anger. That same night he tore the manuscript up. But the tape survived. Had he intended that I would, posthumously, so to speak, sabotage his act of destruction, of self-annihilation, and use the recording to transcribe the poem and thus save it for posterity? Did it cross his mind, even unconsciously? Perhaps. But he could not have foreseen the digital age, which still lay far in the future, or have known that the recording would be stored on the worldwide web to be listened to by anyone in the world who cared to access it.

Be that as it may – what I do know is that thanks to that recording in our living room the night we returned from Vumba, I was able to transcribe his words. I can revisit that poetic incarnation of our history together ten weeks after it had started. I can read the printed poem and concurrently hear him reading it.

The listening feels tortuous. Dambudzo's voice sounds stilted, at times melodramatic, tearful. The reading takes 40 minutes, my music player tells me. The *Bolero* phases out after about fifteen minutes. I do not feel a connection between his voice and the music. Maybe it is the bad quality of my recording. The *Bolero* starting off lightly with the flutes intoning the melody, like garlands winding around the gruesome images of the poem, then repeated perpetually by clarinet, horn, saxophone, bassoon, until the strings set in, building the momentum up to the final crescendo with the full orchestra.

Maybe he was listening to the piece while writing the sequence? Maybe he felt impassioned in his yearning, the relentless repetition in the musical piece corresponding to the relentless aching in himself?

After the abrupt stop of the music only Dambudzo's voice is heard and from time to time the crackling of the sheets of paper in his hand as he shuffles one page onto the next.

And yet the poem itself, with its weighty title, itself a pose, a statement, has a great momentum. It reads like a personal manifesto, a baring of the wounds that turned him into the poetic persona reading it.

> *The story's left arm was missing*
> *It needed thick-lensed spectacles*
> *They watched him fall from the tenth floor,*
> *Chewing gum stuck to his dentures*
> *Such a sun*
> *Such a crying morning song*
> *Falling directly onto the railing's spikings.*
> *This is my body.*
> *That is my pencil.*

The first lines are perfectly pitched, so chilling and poignant as only

Dambudzo could write: the text is the body and the body is the text, and it is hurt, injured, impaired, butchered. A harrowing scene like a flash from a movie, the body-poem falling, or rather being watched as it falls, grotesquely made into a person with thick-lensed spectacles – himself – chewing gum, sarcastic and belittling at the same time. The rhythm mellows as 'sun' vacillates into 'song' but the song, contrasted with the harsh onomatopoeic sound of 'spectacles' and 'spikings' is crying – you can hear the crashing. The two last lines bring relief. They are simple and unambiguous, affirming the theme of the poem: the correlation between body and the writer's craft.

And yet, any analysis, any exercise in practical criticism will fail. You cannot in the end decipher what these words, line by line, 'mean'. They go beyond rational understanding. They open up vistas of another world. That is Dambudzo's art.

The poem is bombastic. It rants and rambles, yet you see the poetic persona wrestling with the forces that be, writing back:

To the girls tightening belts against unwanted pregnancies
To the mothers, whores out of grim necessity,
To the father losing skin each day on the factory floor

More than anything you see him wrestling with the 'boulder' that has always threatened to crush him. 'Father Boulder Mountain Man' towers over the whole sequence. The trauma of the violent death of his father does not leave him, as he as a young boy was forced to look at the disfigured corpse in the mortuary: 'Death had reduced his face to skilled butcher's task'.

All through the poem you also see him wrestling with our relationship – his and mine – gauging it, its tenderness, beauty and passion against the despondency of him remaining the outsider and me the one in charge.

She invited me to tea on the veranda
Told me I was a bastard
Told me to get out
My dirty underwear assumed menacing proportions.

The last line touchingly sweet, a typical Marecheran down-tuning of anything too dramatic.

The 'eaglet sub-desires' that dive in and out of the poem are followed by the flat-out recognition: 'I am the place she staked out, pegged, registered.'

The battle that was going inside me, I realise, the need for being close to him and the knowledge that it could not be, the same battle was winding its way through his long poem written while I was away from him in the Vumba mountains. It was the inner thread holding us together.

Dambudzo's longing to be part of me and my life materialises, ironically, in the images he must have found in the book on our shelves about Der Alte Kanal in Nurnberg.

Stephanie and I
In oil skins dirty as romance
Frolicking in a barge by Amsterdam pier
…
All my plans for us she denounced as illusion
And these three her country-men
Their blood in her veins
Their thoughts in her thoughts
Their certain tragedy her tragedy
How could I presume and assume
A bridegroom's shirt-front and tails
Page after page.

Strewn in between snippets of his lonesome week in our house, calls to the dogs, 'Out, Tamara, out!', a 'husk of cheese', 'the solitary meal', unexpectedly, like a refrain, he quotes from my mouth: 'I will love you forever,' 'For ever, she whispered fiercely'.

These words; hearing him reading them, seeing them on the page, makes me shudder. I will never forget how I uttered them in those blissful moments of oblivion, where your own body melts away, becomes limp, without any will, and your love seems so absolute that nothing will ever deny or defy it. And though after more than a year of passion and disaster I finally disentangled myself from this bodily abandon and we became 'just friends', this love was never defeated. As the narrative would move on, the script of Dambudzo's life and of mine stayed entangled after his early death and into my survival.

'I have loved you forever,' I whisper.

The fictional scenarios of 'My Arms Vanished Mountains' had, as it were, two codas in real life, ironic echoes of Dambudzo's poetic visions.

Freshmen photo, New College Oxford, 1974. Marechera is third from left in the second row from the top. [Courtesy New College Oxford]

Marechera and the author, wearing her playful dungarees, in the Wilds' garden in Harare, 1985. [photo: Lourdes Mugica Arruti]

Zimbabwe Publishing House poster, 1983.

Marechera with Lewis Nkosi at the Writers' Conference in Harare, August 1983. [photo: Tessa Colvin]

Marechera in the crowd during Mungoshi's reading.
[photo: FVW]

Marechera reading in the Mall during the Book Fair Harare, 1983.
[photo: FVW]

Marechera with Max and Franz Wild in their playroom, November 1983. [FVW family album]

Public reading, Harare's College of Music, February 1984. [photo: FVW]

Mugabe giving his condolences to Marechera at the site of the bomb blast that killed the writer's sister. [photo: FVW]

Marechera's mother (standing, left) with female relatives at her homestead in Inyanga, 29 July 1990. [photo: FVW]

Marechera with Charles Mungoshi, Harare, 1986. [photo: Ernst Schade https://www.ernstschade.com]

'Dambudzo Marechera: The Writer, the Man, the Myth' at the Dambudzo Marechera Celebration in Oxford, May 2009. Panelists from left: James Currey, Norman Vance, Robert Fraser, Alastair Niven, the author. [photo: Dobrota Pucherova]

Coda 1: The Accident

THE STORY/BODY THAT NEEDED 'thick-lensed spectacles' did not fall from the tenth floor but was hit by a car; the left arm was not missing but broken.

After the rumpus of our return, the reading and the subsequent tearing up of the poem, Victor and I were spared the unpleasantness of having to expel our guest-writer from our house so that we could have a quiet Christmas with our visitors, my brother and his family. This time Dambudzo 'expelled himself'.

I was sitting on the veranda, where he had just left me, saying he was going to town, when someone came running onto the property. 'Come quick – there has been an accident!' He was holding Dambudzo's press card in his hand.

I hurried to Enterprise Road, where Dambudzo usually tried to get a lift to the city, and found him lying on the roadside.

'What happened?'

'I tried to cross the road and did not see that car coming. You know, without spectacles, I am almost blind.'

Dambudzo was dreadfully myopic. When he first moved in with us, he had found a pair of Victor's old spectacles in a drawer and was happy to see properly again. When, sometime later, he lost the glasses, his wry comment, typical of his self-irony, was: 'I don't want to see this shitty world anyway.'

When the ambulance came, I went with him to Parirenyatwa Hospital. He had bruises on one side and a fractured arm. They kept him in hospital for the week over Christmas. He seemed subdued (no booze of course) but not unhappy. He asked me to bring him my tape recorder so that he could record a book review he was working on.

After he was discharged, I found him in the Park Lane Hotel. Marilyn Poole had given him a hundred dollars and Lord Acton, husband of Judith Todd, another well-wishing friend, had given him money for a night's accommodation there. As he was one-handed, with his fractured arm in a cast, I helped him transcribe the book review. I don't recall which review it was or why the *Herald*, where he submitted it, chose not to publish it (it might well have been his review of JM Coetzee's novel *Life & Times of Michael K*, which had just appeared) but I remember how impressed I was by his brilliance as a critic.

Re-reading the *Michael K* review now, which I was eventually able to publish in the *Source Book on his Life and Work*, the documentary biography I published not long after his death, I marvel at its astuteness. The review was full of literary references and yet informative. It makes me realise how ignorant I was within the literary universe in which Dambudzo moved so aptly. The insights into what, for him, real art was were astonishing: the disturbing mixture of nightmare and beauty. 'Nothing of the usual racial black/white situation ... this book is as wide as all the rainbow mankind out there,' he wrote. When many years later I would teach JM Coetzee's work, I would always remember *Michael K* as my favourite novel because Dambudzo had introduced me to its fantastically disturbing universe – thanks to an accident on Enterprise Road at Christmas time 1983.

Coda 2: I Hate Death

ON THE 31ST OF JANUARY, JUST as Victor and I were settling into bed, I received a phone call from my mother.

My father had died.

'I found him this morning in his dressing room,' my mother said, 'still in his pyjamas. He must have got up to get some water. It was a heart attack.'

When, after the shock of this news, I was finally dozing off, the phone rang again.

'Who is this now?' Victor moaned, covering his ears with the blanket. I bent over towards the telephone on my bedside table, hesitating. Should I pick it up? At that time of the night, it couldn't be anyone else but *him*. But then I did. Out of instinct? Routine? Longing? We had not let Dambudzo move in with us again in the new year but I still got together with him whenever I could.

'Hello,' I said, wearily.

'Hey, it's me,' I heard his drunken voice bellowing through the receiver. 'I am here, at the Terrescane Bar. There was this guy, I really would want you to …' and he went on and on.

'Please leave me alone. I just had the news that my father died.'

'Oh, my gawd. Your father? Dead? I hate death!'

Coda 2: I Hate Death

I hung up. Next time the phone rang I did not pick up.

So, there it was again. Although it was my father who, aged 85, had died a peaceful, orderly death in his own home, in Dambudzo the gruesome images of his own father's death were evoked once more.

'Death had reduced his face to skilled butcher's task.'

PART FOUR

HEAVEN'S TERRIBLE ECSTASY

A Reading and a Murder Charge

As many critics later pointed out, Marechera's life and writing intermingled constantly. It was as if in his life he was staging the scripts for his stories or, vice versa, he was acting out what he had written. Much of it was absurdist comedy or, as he would say in the splendid lecture he gave in 1986, it came close to 'Menippean Satire'.

> Heaven and hell are close and may be visited. Madness, dreams and daydreams, abnormal states of mind and all kinds of erratic inclinations are explored. The world of such novels is complex, unstable, comic, satirical, fantastic, poetical and committed to the pursuit of truth. The hero can travel anywhere in this world and beyond. Fantasy and symbolism are combined with low-life naturalism.

As I had the 'privilege' of travelling with the hero to some of such vantage points, looking back to them now they do indeed read 'complex, unstable, comic and satirical'. Even those of us who were made part of these stories acted strangely at times.

In hindsight the preparations for Dambudzo's public reading in February 1984 read like a caricature of the interaction that was taking place between the threesome that we were: Dambudzo, the ingenious writer and spoilt brat, Victor, his magnanimous sponsor and rival, and me, his lover and sponsor in one.

Much promotion had gone into this first public appearance by Dambudzo Marechera. It had been a long time since the heady days after his return from exile in 1982. We could not risk a fiasco. Eminent dignitaries had accepted our invitation: the German ambassador, representatives of the British Council and the Alliance Française, as well as the patron of the Zimbabwe German Society (ZGS), who was a well-known Zimbabwean businessman and who agreed to speak words of welcome. We were especially proud to have secured the Minister of Education and Culture, Dzingai Mutumbuka, to introduce the writer. He and Dambudzo had been contemporaries at the University of Rhodesia and were expelled together in the 1973 student unrest around the famous 'pots-and-pans demonstration'. While Marechera went on to Oxford, Mutumbuka had joined the armed struggle. After independence he became a minister in the first Mugabe cabinet.

With about two weeks to go before the reading, Victor and I deliberated what the best strategy might be to ensure that everything proceeded smoothly. We couldn't guarantee that Dambudzo wouldn't go astray and not appear for the lecture – 'and what a blunder that would be for all of us!' – and so we agreed that we should let him stay at the house until the reading.

Not concealing his delight, Dambudzo moved in with us again – not in the cottage this time but in our guest room in the main house, close to the other bedrooms.

All went on as usual.

Now and then I swapped beds.

Servants were mute, friends astounded, and the children only complained if there seemed to be real strife.

On the day before the event, Victor and I were still feeling nervous. Would Dambudzo turn up for the reading? And if so, would he be sober? As a result of such worries, we plotted with our friend Gabi, whom our protégé also considered a friend. Dambudzo would stay at her house during the hours before the function. She would keep him in good spirits, letting him have carefully measured quantities of alcohol – too sober he did not function well either – and then she would personally take him in her car to the reading.

Amazingly, Dambudzo agreed to this ludicrously patronising plan, whether he saw through our scheming or not.

And what was more – the plan worked.

I remember his tiny figure in suit and tie, his face hardly visible above and the massive wooden lectern in the recital hall of Harare's College of Music, his myopic eyes close to the sheets from which he read. His throat dry at first, his words coming haltingly, but then, after a few sips from the bottle of water beside him (which contained some gin – another ruse from our side), his tongue loosened.

Dambudzo read confidently and impressively – excerpts from *The House of Hunger*, *Mindblast* and also from his new manuscript, *Tony Fights Tonight*. He extemporised in between and, politely, answered questions at the end. All went well. He 'behaved'. Everybody congratulated us – maybe even more than they congratulated him – on the success of the event.

An ironic aside: in his introductory speech Mutumbuka praised the writer's work for giving 'illuminating insights into the struggle for sanity in a situation full of contradictions, where there was a severe dislocation of moral and social norms', yet, only four years later, in 1988, the eminent minister's own moral and social norms would be dislocated: He would be involved in the first major corruption scandal of the new political elite, 'Willowgate', and have to quit government. His former fellow student was dead by then, but his voice had taken on prophetic quality: 'Scandalous and eccentric behaviour disrupts the seemly course of human affairs. Society is unpredictable, roles can quickly change.'

Relieved as everyone was that the reading had gone so smoothly, we should have had a foreboding. Never would the eponymous troublemaker let such a day end in peace and harmony.

The big-bang backlash that whipped at us the next evening reads like an absurdist play at its best.

Around eight o'clock Dambudzo came back to our house, dead drunk, a bottle of vodka in his hand. He had obviously spent most of the money Victor had given him for the reading in bars.

'Yeah, now that I have done my job for you,' he yelled at Victor, 'you will of course expel me from your house.'

When, around ten, we wanted to go to bed and urged him to do so too, he stood in the passage outside our closed bedroom door and carried on shouting.

'Fuck you!' he bawled. 'Enjoy yourself with your husband, you slut! He is a good person, yeah, he pays money to your lover, that drunkard, that black bastard from the ghetto so that he can scratch your pussy whenever you feel like it, when that German chief of yours is not around.'

At such moments – and there were many of them as long as I knew Dambudzo – I felt completely detached from him. He was like a different person, not the man whose kisses and embraces I craved. He was just that irksome, galling scoundrel of a writer.

He stubbornly remained where he was in the passage, making a terrible racket. At first, we tried to ignore him, but the insults and curses grew louder and more obscene, and his tone became increasingly aggressive. Our silence made him even angrier. He wanted a reaction, a fight.

Suddenly there came a crash, an enormous bang. Victor jumped out of bed and opened the door. Dambudzo had hurled a heavy file containing his manuscripts against our bedroom door.

'That's enough, Dambudzo!' Victor said. 'You leave this house immediately!'

While I tried to comfort the children who, stirred by the commotion, were fearfully peering out of their own bedroom door, Victor tried to haul our guest to the door and push him out of the house. Dambudzo, resisting and tottering, drunk as he was, slipped, crashing heavily into the glass cabinet in the narrow hallway.

'Oh my God!' Dambudzo screamed. 'You see? He is really serious. He is trying to kill me! Slashing me with a sword. Look at all the blood. How I hate blood.'

The glass had splintered, causing serious cuts to his head and neck.

I can't recall all the details, but when I rushed outside I saw Dambudzo standing on the veranda, a puddle of blood gathering on the terracotta tiles – thick, black, gluey blood. His head was clenched between his shoulders, his face upright, rigid, his eyes staring into nowhere.

'Don't touch me,' he growled when I tried to put a towel on the cuts on his cheek and neck to soak up the blood. 'I will wait here until the police arrive. Your husband has tried to kill me. I will charge him for attempted murder.'

As he made it clear that he did not want us to touch his wounds, Victor and I took him to our neighbour, the doctor whom he had seen before, but he still refused to have his wounds dressed. Instead he insisted on phoning the police.

Nobody came.

Oh, another drunkard raising hell, the officers on duty at the Highlands police station most probably thought.

Dambudzo stood there, in the doctor's living room, blood dripping from his face, his neck, his shirt, his tie, with another big puddle of blood forming at his feet. We couldn't let him remain like that, in that state, any longer, so Victor and the doctor's husband finally went and fetched the police themselves.

'Well... well...' the two officers said after taking one look at the pitiful poet, who had by then begun to weep. 'You have to go to the hospital. Let your friends take you.'

When Dambudzo refused, they tried to drag him to their car, whereupon he cried, 'I am not a prisoner! I would rather bleed to death.' Then, pointing at Victor, he said dramatically: 'You should arrest *him*! He tried to murder me!'

Finally, Dambudzo was taken to the Parirenyatwa Hospital and Victor was allowed to drive home.

Anyone who might have thought this was the end of it did not know the kind of twists this Marecheran drama had in store. The final act was yet to come.

At 2 am someone knocked at our bedroom window. It was the police. They had our house guest in tow. Dambudzo had given our place as his residential address.

Victor shouted: 'I'd rather pay for a hotel room than let him in again!'

'What?' said Dambudzo. 'With all this blood?' He had been nicely bandaged at the hospital but his face and shirt were still covered with blood.

After lengthy negotiations through the locked door, Victor eventually let them inside so that Dambudzo could wash up. While one policeman assisted in the bathroom, the other proceeded to the guest bedroom, where he started browsing through Dambudzo's folder from the evening's reading, which contained the manuscript of *Mindblast,* all the while cautiously helping himself to the bottle of vodka on the bedside table.

As by now the tension was easing, Victor consented that our guest return to his bed, cleaner and more sober than a couple of hours before.

Final scene of the drama: The bandaged poet in his bed. Left and right of him two policemen reading to each other from the 'park bench journal', chuckling at the parts they found particularly amusing, sipping from their vodka glasses (which by then I had provided). In such convivial atmosphere, Dambudzo's paranoia and anger melted away. He officially withdrew his murder charge against Victor, signing a statement I had quickly typed, with the two police officers as witnesses.

Around 4 am the two constables, who surely must have enjoyed this special night shift, staggered back to their car.

Victor gave Dambudzo a sleeping pill and we went back to bed.

All strife resolved.

Curtain.

Yet, as I recall, there was also a coda to this event. Not too long afterwards, a squadron of heavily armoured police vehicles filled our driveway in the middle of the night. Someone had called them, they said, from this house, in connection with an imminent danger.

Victor reassured them. We were all fine, he said. It must have been an erroneous call.

The armoured vehicles left the scene.

What happened in the next days, weeks, months before Dambudzo finally got his own flat is difficult to recount in detail. Some notes and letters, some fragments of memory, provide a thin storyline of what seemed to be an endless repetition of one and the same pattern.

'You cannot stay here anymore. Go and look after yourself.'

Dambudzo could not and would not.

Like a revenant, he kept showing up, drenched, lonely, pitiful.

They Are Boiling My Bones in The Kitchen

WHAT A LINE. IT KEEPS RECURRING in my mind. I hear it in the booming voice of Albert Nyathi, who already as a student at UZ was a zealous Marechera follower. I see him, years later, stamping onstage, blasting that first line, anger and contempt driving him forward as he recites the poem.

It was 1992. A group of five of us staged a performance of poetry and music to celebrate the publication of *Cemetery of Mind*. Soon afterwards, Albert became an imbongi, a Ndebele praise-singer, strutting proudly in traditional garb, a leopard tail around his head, more leopard tails flapping around his hips, singing the praises of his Ndebele king, old Mzilikazi. No wonder that twenty years on, in 2012, when my essay 'Me and Dambudzo' was hitting the news in Zimbabwe, Albert told the Bulawayo *Chronicle* that he 'never suspected that Prof Veit-Wild had a sexual relationship with Marechera. She never at any time told us that the two were lovers. It's news to me.' How ironic that the article was written by someone called Lenin Ndebele, who seemed as exasperated as Albert by the revelation that 'they did it in motels, in a car and in her matrimonial home'.

Male traditionalists that you are, I can't help thinking, me, the 'professor-perpetrator': you can't hide your salaciousness – and rightly so, because that's how the poem continues:

They are boiling my bones in the kitchen
Between her thighs
They are criticising my poems in the newsroom
Between her lovely (so pink!) lips

The grotesque image, the strong rhythm. The doubling of the 'b' setting a stark, almost heroic tone, which right after – how it makes me smile – is dismantled, ridiculed by a typical Marecheran disclaimer: Don't think of cannibals sitting around a steaming pot at a fireplace in a Rider Haggard movie! It is just a kitchen …

A kitchen. In a flash I see myself lying in bed with Dambudzo under rough blankets in a dark room.

'I have this place,' he told me. 'There are other people too but they might move out soon.'

He was referring to the flat in Sloane Court – which was soon to become his own.

At the agreed time I knocked on the window, then snuck in through the French doors behind the hedge that shielded the ground floor flats from the street. Trying to close my nostrils against the stench of dirt, unwashed clothes and human bodies, I tiptoed to the heavy-framed bed.

'Are you sure it's all right?' I said as we fumbled beneath the blankets (there were no sheets, as far as I remember). I could see light behind the door on the other side of the room, where the kitchen was, and could hear a murmur of voices. There was a sour smell of food being cooked.

'Don't worry, there are people in the kitchen, but they will be leaving soon. They won't disturb us.'

So I tried to relax, happy to be in bed with him, touching him, arousing him, getting aroused. But then, suddenly, I can't say at which moment of our lovemaking, the door to the kitchen opened and the light was switched on. Terrified, I slid down under the blanket.

'Oh, you are here,' a male voice said.

'Uh … yeah,' Dambudzo stammered. 'Do you need anything?'

'No worries,' the voice said.

The light was switched off again and the door closed.

'Dear me, who was that?' I asked, resurfacing. 'How many people are staying here? Where do you sleep? And where do the others sleep?'

Dambudzo was evasive. 'Ah ... well ... we take turns,' he said, 'or some sleep in the kitchen. They usually let me sleep in the bed ...'

'On your own?'

'Sometimes. Sometimes with others.'

There are six people in the sinister room
And winter on the window clouds her breath with subdued passion
'I cannot come today,' she said.

'They Are Boiling My Bones in the Kitchen' became one of Dambudzo's series of poems which, with their flamboyantly erotic imagery, reflect that most benign period in our love relationship – when he had become the sole tenant of the flat.

8 Sloane Court

As often happened in his life, in his forays through the city bars, tired, starving, desolate, Dambudzo had bumped into a relative of a relative. 'Mukoma, you don't have a place to stay? No problem, come along, uncle, get some sleep in my flat.'

As it turned out, the tenants of the flat were in arrears with their rent and rates and were about to be evicted, so Dambudzo told us. Thus, what had looked like a temporary arrangement was able to become, by chance and with our help, a permanent one. We negotiated with the management of the building and after we had paid the outstanding debts, Dambudzo obtained a lease agreement. Sharing the rent as well as water and electricity bills between Victor and I and Marilyn Poole, our protégé writer was able to live in 8 Sloane Court until the time of his death.

Before he moved in, we had the flat thoroughly cleaned, fumigated and whitewashed. We put up a bookshelf and gave Dambudzo some odd pieces of furniture, pots, pans and crockery. I sewed curtains from a fabric we had brought from Germany and put them up at his window. The fabric had a kind of Scandinavian pattern, I remember – slanting stripes in bold red and white – you can see the curtains in the background of the photos taken of him in the flat. Sewing, like knitting, has a warm, caring side. I sewed the curtains for Dambudzo, hoping he would be happier, feel sheltered in this place of his. I was hoping for us, too, for our love to have a space to steady itself and expand. But would it?

It was mostly in the early afternoon that I knocked at his window, a couple of hours before my German classes at the nearby Zimbabwe German Society. It was also the best time to be with him. He would have spent the morning writing or reading, maybe got some food from the nearby shopping centre, and he tended to be in a placid mood; much better than in the evening, when he became restless because he wanted to go out and drink; or was drunk already.

I would often have a hip flask of sherry in my bag, from which we would take sips in between, to flavour our mouths and enhance the sensuousness in our limbs. The flask had belonged to my father, one of those gentleman's gadgets from early in that century, bound in leather. I still have a few such items of my father's – like the round leather box with a lid and a buckle in which I keep small bags for jewellery; at the time it must have been a collar box. Also of brown leather is a smaller oval-shaped case, which would have contained my father's shaving kit, just big enough to fit the brush and a bar of soap.

Was there a timeline from my father of half a decade before, he, the handsome 'man of the ladies'? What a gruesome note this image took on when a while ago I talked to the son of one of my father's lovers (who was also one of my mother's best friends). She came from a rich Jewish family. Her husband, an eminent cellist, declined to divorce his Jewish wife when he was put under pressure by the Nazis to do so, after which he was no longer allowed to perform. My mother recorded in her diary of 1940 how they organised clandestine recitals for him in friends' homes. In 1944 the Gestapo deported him to a forced labour camp in Leuna, where the Nazis tried to maintain an important industrial plant. He, the musician, with his delicate hands, was condemned to very heavy and humiliating manual work. The disastrous conditions in the camp ruined his health and he died, aged 58, two years after the war.

His wife, who was fully Jewish and had a J in her passport, would have ended in Theresienstadt, her son told me, if it had not been for her love affair with my father. One day there was the dreaded knock on their door. 'Where is C. B.?', several men in the black SS uniform barked. 'She was not at home,' her son told me. 'She was in bed with your father.' What dreadful, sarcastic irony. Now that the family had been warned, they were able to arrange that my parents' friend was not deported. The family had connections. Hitler at that point in history did not want to antagonise certain economically powerful groups, even if this implied protecting some Jews.

I did not, of course, know this at the time when I was offering sweet sherry to my Zimbabwean lover from my father's flask. Yet he would have seen a connection. As a black man under the Rhodesian police state, he had seen villagers disappear in what he called in one of his works, 'Concentration Camps'.

So many invisible threads when two lives interweave at a certain point in time, as Dambudzo's and mine did. So many similarities and inter-connections – of thought, of history – in a different space and time. I remember being particularly hurt when once, out of one of his unpredictable moods, Dambudzo yelled at me: 'You and the Nazis, you did with the Jews just what the Rhodesians did to us!'

Those weeks, perhaps it was two to three months, after Dambudzo had moved into Sloane Court, were for me the most pleasurable and most satisfying period in our time as lovers. 'Heaven's terrible ecstasy', the closing image of one of the series of beautiful, sensuous erotic poems he wrote at the time, encompasses it all.

> *Laughter's thief sours her sighs*
> *And conman Time draws the curtains*
> *Over our happiness.*
> *Conscience raises his gun*
> *Demands repentance –*
> *Is this eerie unease*
> *Appetite's sleeping partner?*

I feel my heart (and body) swelling with recollected delight. I feel the room around us tinged in warm red light, filtering through the drawn curtains. I taste on our tongues the sweet sherry. I feel my lover's lips clasping my nipples; the sweat gluing our bodies together; and then, the surrender, the eclipse, at that ever-astounding leap when he dipped into the dampness within me.

> *What rough night erased the bloom from ruby red lips?*

Coarse hand tempering her secret's petal blue eyes
Pelvic fury drastic intimacy joy of fistkisses
And O what surrender out of her out of me judders –

Wheels spinning at cliffedge – sky's immense tumult
Cannot halt desire's frenzy
Sweatsoaked sheets in the gloaming dark
Fingertip luminaries touch's traceries tongue to tongue
And Yes what surrender out of her out of me judders –

There was ecstasy, there was happiness, and desire's frenzy – also in him; yet was there not always an element of illusion, of wariness, of time bought and administered by me, behind the curtains I had sewn, when conman Time said I had to leave him? Then, on those afternoons before my German class, hurriedly I would put on my clothes, and with his taste in my mouth, his sweat on my skin, I would appear before my students. Did they notice that I was still drunk with passion? That I was glowing like an iron on fire?

For me, it was a phase in my life when 'I felt complete', to use a phrase I learned in California many years later.

In the mornings, when the children were at school, I would be at my desk, reading, writing, preparing activities. I helped organise cultural events for the ZGS. An event at the National Gallery on women's art (writing, drama, music and photographs) was my first initiative to promote women writers. At the time, an awareness among the women in Zimbabwe was beginning to grow. Although they had fought by the side of their men in the struggle for independence, after national liberation there was a feeling that they were being left behind. There had been a public outcry the year before when the government ordered police to round up women who were walking alone in the streets. 'Operation Clean-up', it was called, labelling independent women as prostitutes. It was out of that shock that the Women's Action Group was founded, fostering and promoting feminist thinking in Zimbabwe. In the years to come I would help organise readings and discussions for women who wanted to get out of the closet in their homes, where their husbands or fathers would burn their manuscripts or roll tobacco in the paper. It seemed like a great stream breaking loose. It culminated in the founding of the Zimbabwe Women Writers in 1990. For me, who, since my arrival in Zimbabwe, had begun to discover new potential as a woman in myself, it was very fulfilling to contribute to this movement.

The afternoons were mostly spent with my children. Once a week I ran a mime workshop with them and a few other children. We passed invisible objects around: an uncooked egg that had to be handled with care; a big heavy pumpkin; or a prickly fruit. Or – great laughter when it was an animal – a spiky hedgehog passed (or dropped!) from hand to hand, or a butterfly, light and fluttery, which might suddenly escape from the cupped little hands and fly away to settle on a flower.

Miming, which I had started in Nurnberg, was a way of recreating myself.

I had an affinity with the way the body becomes the medium to tell stories, to arouse the imagination, to let the world transcend from the real into the unreal. The vendor of balloons bending down to one little person after the other, tying the string with a balloon to one little hand after the other; until he is finally fed up and pops the whole bunch into one hand, and then you see that kid being lifted into the air, higher and higher, and you see him peering down anxiously as he – or she – sees the ground disappearing far below.

In much later years, the figures of the mime emerged again in me in the gestalt of my puppets. These fanciful creatures would help me to fight the 'Lady in Black', to turn the shadows of depression into something playful and light.

At the time it felt good to pass on some of the lightness and the creative energy I felt in the miming to the children. We staged little sketches and performed them at the Christmas Bazaar. In the first year, all the children mimed animals, crawling and prancing out of their den with leopard and lion masks. A year or two later, Max and Franz became quite professional: they created an invisible mirror, one boy cloning each little movement the other made through an empty picture frame. Or Max, a bit older again, with a devilish rubber mask I had acquired in England; I see him in front of a crowd of children, bent over, his posture gnome-like, speaking to them in a fairytale voice, luring, scary, carefree. Even at these small performances I could see the great stage presence he would later have as a grown-up musician.

Once, I think it was my birthday party in May 1986, we invited Dambudzo to a mime show I had rehearsed with my boys and two of their friends. They performed on the veranda, which was a great natural stage, the spectators, party guests, standing on the lawn.

There is a photo in my album where you see Dambudzo dancing wildly with the children. Max and Franz, the whities, are dressed in black, the two other dark-skinned boys in white. The photo captures the moment when, after the performance, while everyone is still applauding the boys for their magnificent performance, Dambudzo jumps onto the stage. He grabs Max and Franz by their hands and, as the music sets on, starts to dance with them, wildly, drawing other children into the circle.

'Hey, you,' I can imagine him saying, 'you *are* real artists. Your show … um … um, yeah, it was reaaaally brilliant.'

Now he is himself centre stage, he is one of the actors. With his light beige overalls and long-sleeve black shirt underneath, he is part of the show; he is dancing in a frenzy, upper body bent forward, gaze downward. His mouth, pulled wide open, exposes two rows of teeth, stunningly white against the gleaming brown skin. These teeth seem to outshine everything else in the picture, their brilliant white reflecting the faces of two of the boys, who are still wearing their white mimes' paint. All the children's faces are turned towards him, their eyes shining, their mouths open with glee. They seem mesmerised by the wizard, the shamanic dancer as, with some otherworldly force, he pulls them into his magic circle.

I rarely saw Dambudzo dance or be as he was in that moment. Free, without self-consciousness, without fear. Happy to be alive, amongst children.

Who would have thought that he had only fifteen months more to live?

The Ghost of Amelia

> The fear of abandonment phobia is characterized by extreme dependency on others. It is commonly seen in adults and children who are also diagnosed with Borderline Personality disorders. Such people live in the constant fear that their 'world will collapse' if their protectors or loved ones abandon them.

I LEAVE IT TO SPECIALISTS TO DECIDE whether the 'Borderline Personality' syndrome, to which the above quote from a medical handbook refers, might have applied to Dambudzo's psyche or not. What I am sure of, however, and what many examples in my narrative reflect, is that my friend was horrified at the prospect of being left alone.

When he could not accuse me of expelling him – because he had his own flat – he hissed the flag of abandonment.

In August 1984 my family and I went on our first visit home to Germany.

When I told Dambudzo that I would be away for a month, his world collapsed. He thought he would never see me again. Although his fear was utterly irrational and, for me, incomprehensible, for him this was reality. All through his life he seemed to re-enact the dejection he had lived through as a child: his father's violent death and his mother's turning to other men in order to make a living for him and his siblings.

The 'Amelia Sonnets', which he wrote in anticipation of my departure, talk about his fears of abandonment. The ordinary objects around him, the dust, the crockery, the cockroaches, turn into symbols of absence.

> *A band of near-molten steel tightens*
> *Around my iceblock head. The clock ticking*
> *Hurls loneliness' searing arrows. The dust*
> *In the neglected flat, glows like radioactive*
> *Particles under my bare feet. Though noon,*
> *I stand in my nightshirt grinning inanely,*
> *Afraid to draw the curtains on the bright*
> *Nightmare of daylight.*
> *...*
> *All that's left of Amelia is all this pottery*
> *Silent, soothing, yet eerily arranged around my memories.*

Absence, loneliness, abandonment become premonitions of death. In apocalyptic scenarios heaven and hell are invoked, ghosts and skeletons embrace each other in lecherous dances, foul flesh and rotten bones haunt the figure of Amelia.

> *On my seventh drink she appeared in strips*
> *Of rotting flesh and faintly gleaming bones – Her*
> *Hollow eye sockets instantly found me.*

She, who appears, 'in luminous white nightdress', as the figure of purity and innocence and the poet's inner longings, 'crazed visions of life's beauty', drowns; she becomes herself a phantom and can only be visited in dream and nightmare.

> *And she, my human hunger, grew pale, lost appetite, became haggard*
> *Shunned by her own kind. Outraged storms, as if fired from some*
> *Celestial cannon up there, day after day blew down upon us. Amelia*
> *Drowned. I shunned man and his daylight ways. I made the terrible pact*
> *And nightly may visit her in spite of her horns and forked tail.*

I remember the impact the poems had on me when Dambudzo first let me read them. I was struck by their poetic beauty, by their craft of the sonnet form, by the way they transformed all the passion, the hurt and the hopelessness of our love into visions beyond words. I was also terrified by their gothic scenarios, those allegories of imminent death.

As I realise now, re-reading them so many years later, the 'Amelia Sonnets' appear as ominous precursors of the last poems Dambudzo wrote, when 'death was knocking on his door'. Titles such as 'Cemetery of Mind', 'Phantoms of Delight', 'Her Hand My Eyes Closes' seem to reach out into the future to 'The Chair in Grief', 'Darkness a Bird of Prey' and 'Which One of You Bastards is Death?'

Did the Amelia poems even predict, I hardly dare ask myself, the ghastly outcome of our love affair? Did the viral ghosts capering around in Dambudzo's blood – and soon in mine – make an incognito appearance in Amelia's dance macabre?

In the meantime, our relationship as a 'literary couple' was taking on a pattern. As is often the case with poets writing about their loved ones, much of his poetry was inspired by us being together, by the beauty, the passion, the tensions, the hopes and the absences between me and him.

At the same time, in the course of that first year together, I developed my 'second persona' outside his poems as his interlocutor and critic. This in turn inspired him, at times, to develop his own ideas and concepts, to spell them out in that intellectually distinct way of his. He wasn't only an ingenious writer; he was also a great theorist.

The first interview I did with Dambudzo, in November 1983, about the language question, gave him the idea of writing his 'self-interview', a most witty and succinct source for understanding his literary persona as well as undoing common misconceptions on African writing. Since his death it has been published and referred to frequently.

In an interview on poetry I conducted with him in December 1984, he developed his own commentary on the 'Amelia Sonnets', and afterwards, inspired through this conversation, he wrote a short preface to them.

Different from the immediacy of carnal joy in the erotic poems ('My full-grown tree erupts ...'), the Amelia poems appear more removed from the real experience of passion. Though talking about our love affair, he chose a fictional name for the loved person. In the interview he explains that he came upon the name Amelia when reading Heinrich Heine's poems about his cousin, and describes the affinity he felt for the 'emotional chaos' Heine had gone through, the 'mystical, the nightmare element' in Heine's poems. 'To love is to discover terror, a very personal and intimate kind of terror: you are no longer yourself, you are no longer self-sufficient, you are the other person and the other person, of course, has got her own life.'

But the interview also explains that the feeling of loss and dejection was not only born out of my imminent departure to Germany, a temporary absence, but that they were always part of our relationship.

> Another part of the ambiguity of the Amelia-poems is that I know that Amelia will never be mine, wholly mine, my own. To love somebody is to want them all the time, to want to drown their identity in one's own identity, that everything they do or say or decide or think is centred on what I am. In other words, Amelia is not the record of a straightforward love affair, it is the record of a very tragic love affair.

Conversing with each other as lovers on one side and as writer and critic on the other had its own irony. There we were, in the writer's flat – the very place where, at other times, we would act out our passion, our hurt, our anger – he in his armchair, I opposite him, with tape recorder and microphone, talking about that very love affair as if it had nothing to do with us.

How peculiar the situation was!

When Dambudzo referenced Shakespeare's sonnets to the 'Dark Lady', which Shakespeare wrote to contain his bewildering emotions about what at the time was seen as a scandalous relationship, I bluntly asked the question: 'Are you hinting at a comparable situation you have experienced? Are you referring to love across the colour line?' Was there a tinge of humour in my voice, I now wonder. Was I enjoying being the one and the other?

But Dambudzo answered in all seriousness. Setting the personal aspect aside, his answer was thoughtful; the approach he took became part of my own stance on the issue of 'race', which, currently, is so controversial.

'Yes,' he said. 'For many people love across the colour line still is a taboo.'

> The whole thing demands total control: control of language, tightened syntax, and – if I may say so – a very rigorous knowledge

of myth and legend. Thus, one can enclose the most outrageous statement with some ancient myth.

Fearing that he might become evasive, I insisted: 'But why do you never mention explicitly that you are talking/writing about love between two people of different races?'

> Because for me, personally, it is not a problem. It is just another human relationship you can write about. I actually find love of people of the same race very much as an incest.

How typically and hilariously Marecheran!
He further elaborates – and the following quote stands lucidly for how the 'race question' was *embodied*, in the literal sense, in our relationship.

> Amelia is white, I am black. But I am the one full of digressions and frustrations. Amelia does not have any sense of race. In a very personal sense it does not matter at all what race Amelia is but there are times, especially when I have gone through some shitty incidents or I remember some of the things which were happening here before 1980, that's when I feel very violent towards Amelia. That's when this brutality from the township comes out and even when I am making love to her I find that I am actually with my whole self trying to fool myself that I am revenging myself against the whole white race. Afterwards, of course, one realises that it was simply an illusion that one can revenge oneself on history.

Obviously, for me, knowing him, talking to him, interviewing him, was an immense source of inspiration, of knowledge, of forming my own views on Africa and on African literature. I had never before met someone who had read so widely in the whole of world literature and could talk and write so succinctly and interestingly about it. His reading was, as much as he could make it possible, up to date with international literature. Dambudzo always made sure that friends who went overseas brought him the most recent literary publications. When we went to Germany again in 1986, he gave us a long list of books to bring for him.

Reflecting on it now, I feel ashamed of how little literary knowledge I had at the time and how inadequate I was as a literary interlocutor for

Dambudzo. I remember that at some point he was reading *Midnight's Children*, which had appeared not long before, and how engrossed he was. I had never heard about the Rushdie book, nor did I borrow it from him at the time.

When he was angry with me, he would actually spell out his scorn for my ignorance: 'I can't even talk to you about literature, about what interests me.'

Would he have believed that only ten years later I would become a professor of African literature? Again, how ironic.

The only mentionable inspiration I was able to offer from my side was Christa Wolf's work. Her short novel *Cassandra*, which appeared in 1983, excited me so much that I wanted to share it with Dambudzo. As soon as I could I got him the English translation. He loved it. It revived in him his inner connection with Greek mythology. Cassandra, Apollo, Dido, Ares and Hecuba, and many more figures from Greek mythology, turned up in his poems. In the preface to the Amelia Sonnets he grounds his concept of the universality of love on that mythology.

The Other Woman

DURING OUR HOLIDAY IN GERMANY, travelling here and there, seeing many different friends and family in various places, Dambudzo moved into the back of my mind. I was not worried about him, I was not yearning for him, I did not think much about him. Even when I heard from someone that a writer had been detained during Zimbabwe Book Fair and that apparently it had been him, I remained largely unaffected. I probably just shrugged my shoulders and made a comment like 'Oh, what kind of scene did he stage this time?'

However, already on our flight back from Frankfurt to Harare, the butterflies were starting to dance in my belly. I had told myself to wait for a while before going to see him. I wanted to keep the distance. I was afraid I would get sucked in again into the whirlpool of unresolved emotions, of a love that remained an illusion – that even, perhaps, was insincere?

My intent was useless. It did not take more than a day or two – in fact on my first drive to the shops to stock up our supplies – before I found myself making a detour to Dambudzo's flat.

'How are you?' I said, embracing him. 'We only got back yesterday. I cannot stay. But I am glad you are in. I just needed to see you. I have missed you so much.'

Dambudzo was strangely distant. My emotions flying out towards him, my desire that had flared up again, seemed to drop down to the floor where he was standing.

'So, you are back,' he said. 'I did not expect you.'

I asked what had happened at the book fair.

'Yes,' he confirmed, 'they detained me. I spent six days behind bars.'

A day before the fair had started, he said, he had been sitting in the lounge of the Meikles Hotel giving an interview to two Swedish women journalists. All of a sudden, two undercover policemen, CIO, walked up and arrested him. They confiscated the journalists' tape and camera.

There was less of the usual rage in Dambudzo's voice as he told me what had happened. What had hurt him most, it seemed, was that his fellow writers had not done anything to come to his rescue. 'None of them even came to visit me in detention,' he told Fiona Lloyd, a Zimbabwean journalist, in an interview sometime later. He was so angered that at a meeting of the Writers' Union a couple of weeks afterwards, he heckled throughout the evening. He asked each of the poets who read from their work the same questions: 'Why did you do nothing to get me out of jail? Is the Union toothless? Are we never going to protect our members?'

He seemed calm when he told me about the detention on that day after my return. Yet I sensed some subdued irritation in his voice which I could not place – it seemed directed towards me.

'And *Mindblast*? Has it been published?' I asked.

'Oh yes, here it is.'

He gave me a copy.

'But aren't you glad? Finally, it is out.'

'Well, sure, but I wasn't even there to talk about it at the book fair because they had put me into prison.'

'Will you autograph it for me?'

He did. 'With lots of love and tenderness,' he wrote.

Even this seemed without warmth to me. It did not contain anything particular or personal, not even my name. He had just obliged. I was disappointed. Even reproaches about being 'abandoned' would have been better than this uncommitted politeness.

When I went to visit Dambudzo again, this time at an arranged time, I realised why he had been so subdued. He was embarrassed. Whether or not he had really believed that I would not come back, or whether it was just out of loneliness – there was another woman.

It was not anything serious, he said, a young Canadian who was teaching somewhere in the rural areas. She was in Harare for the holidays but was leaving soon. I do not think I was particularly shocked or jealous. I knew Dambudzo could not stay on his own for long. And anyway, what claim did I have on him, me, with husband and family, for whom he was, he could rightly claim, a lover of convenience?

Also, I suppose – or maybe this was the main reason – I felt superior.

I was a strong presence in his life. Photos of me and of my children in his flat reflected that presence. In the years to come, the few that were left to him, once we had finally ended our sexual relationship, he used to say: 'They are all afraid of you, the other women, they know who you are for me …' It was like saying, 'You are the senior wife.'

As if to prove my superiority, it was me this time who set up my 'rival' in a jocular kind of duel. That was how I described my 'performance' in a letter to him afterwards, written like a film script.

> Dark-haired woman stopping with her car in front of a block of flats. Seeing the red curtains drawn at no. 8, she turns to her children: 'Oh, is he not in?' She gets out of the car and peeps in at a corner where the curtains are leaving a gap. Seeing that he is in, she raps gently at the window. At that moment she sees a tall blonde woman getting up from a chair and leaving the flat hurriedly on the other side. The woman outside remains still for some seconds in surprise and a slight fear, then she starts running around to the other side of the block, where the entrances are; on her way just getting a final glimpse of the blonde woman running across the street. She finds the Black Poet in his flat in utter confusion, looking desperately for his keys. 'Was that HER?' she says. 'Yes,' he mumbles, 'but I can't find this damned key. We wanted to run away, both of us, before you were coming, but we were looking for these keys.' 'So you wanted to run away,' the woman says, 'that's shit, running away. But anyway, let's go to the car, I have got the bookshelf for you and the saucepan and cleaning material.' So they go to the car and get the things, the Black Poet still confused and absent-minded and pale under his dark skin. The two blond boys, dressed-up as cowboys, are playing and shooting around with their plastic pistols. Back in the flat, the woman puts up the bookshelf, places a vase with bougainvillea on top of it that she has brought from her garden. 'She came last night,' the Poet says, 'after I had

phoned you. She left a note at the flat. And now she is waiting for me at the Park Lane Hotel, but I can't go, because I can't find these keys,' and he is still fumbling around looking for them. 'The keys are lost – how symbolic!' The woman leaves him and drives to the Park Lane Hotel. 'We'll have a Coke there,' she tells her boys.

The blonde woman is sitting at one of the tables in the garden bar. When she sees the other woman with her two boys entering, she gets up and disappears into the 'Ladies'. The dark-haired woman quietly takes a seat at the table where the blonde one had been sitting and orders three Cokes; her little boy complaining because he wants to sit at a different table. Finally the blonde woman comes back from the toilet and regains her seat. 'Hi,' says the dark one, 'I suppose you are Jane.' 'Yes, and you are Stephanie.' They smile at each other, stupidly. 'I only wanted to meet you, you shouldn't have run away.' They ask each other some questions about what they are doing in Zimbabwe. Then the conversation stops. 'We have to go now,' the dark one says, and gets up. 'He is still in the flat, looking for his keys. I wonder whether I should wait for him,' says the blonde one. With a smile they shake hands and say 'Goodbye'. 'Have a nice weekend,' the dark one adds.

There the scenario stopped. But in my letter to Dambudzo I went on talking about what was going on in my mind at that time. 'I see her as your mate, your drinking mate, bed-mate (though that still hurts me or rather I can't imagine it, I can only see you with her drinking, killing the time and so on).'

The strange encounter with the Canadian girl had made me think about my own relationship with the Black Poet. Was this love an illusion? This feeling of being so close to another person that one does not have to hide anything and does not have to pretend and 'feels like sparklings merging into each other', as I wrote – is it only fiction, a figure of imagination?

For him, Dambudzo often said, love was always a fiction. There was his mother who fought for him and his siblings by prostituting herself; there was his missionary education condemning sex as something filthy, vile and baneful, something you have to fight in yourself. There was his first horrid experience with sex in the township when his brother had given him money for a prostitute and he had caught a venereal disease.

After that he had believed he would never be able to love a woman.

Yet, he also said, at times, in loving me, fiction and reality had come close, as never before.

But what was happening to it now?

It was around this time, the last months of 1984, I remember, that the first intimations of depression came over me, the feeling of paralysis that would grip me, up to this day, at various points in my life.

I remember crouching on the steps of the veranda, hiding my head between my knees. The stark brightness of the African sun, the crying colours, all seemed to hit me, with violent force. I could not stand the obtrusive pink of the bougainvillea, the obscene red of the flamboyant, and the pool, always glittering blue, dragonflies flitting across its surface. I wanted to sink into the earth, into nothingness. I felt drained.

Projects and Rejects

WHEN DAMBUDZO AND I AT LAST had become close again, and the other woman had disappeared into the countryside, I made attempts to consolidate our relationship.

We jostled with the idea of writing letters to each other, exchanging views on literature, sharing experiences, talking about his life and mine; and then publish the correspondence in book form. He seemed enthusiastic. But when I mentioned it again and wanted to make it work, he did not respond.

In fact, Dambudzo never ever wrote a single letter to me. What he felt about us, it was all in his poems, in his writing.

Another project I suggested we tackle together was an anthology of poetry.

I had discussed the idea with Peter Ripken, the representative of the German booksellers at the Zimbabwe International Book Fair. We considered a collection of poetry to introduce Zimbabwean writing, which had started to flourish since the country's independence, to a German readership. Ripken had close ties to Zimbabwean writers and publishers. He knew Dambudzo – they had met some years before at the African Literature Festival in West Berlin in 1979.

'We could select the poems together and write an introduction,' I said to Dambudzo. 'Wouldn't it be good to have something to work on? Otherwise we will continue with these useless discussions …'

'No. Not with me. You do it, if you like. Why should I work for others if nobody is interested in supporting me?'

'You would not be working for others,' I pointed out. 'You could write about the poets and their poems. You do this so well. And I would just do the correspondence and organise it all.'

'No, you do your work. Don't try to exploit me. I do my writing, and if nobody wants to publish it, they should all go to hell.'

That was the crux of it. His frustration, his anger about being ignored, about local writers, readers, publishers being too illiterate to appreciate his work.

After he'd moved into his flat, Dambudzo wrote 'The Depth of Diamonds', a fairly short novel. He gave it to College Press, to his old friend Stanley Nyamfukudza, together with a bunch of his recent poetry. Nyamfukudza did not know what to do with the poems, whether they were meant as a part of the manuscript or not, and returned the material – all of it – without a comment. The readers' reports on the novel found the narrative too loose and concluded that the many literary cross-references would definitely discourage the general reader. Substantial rewriting was suggested.

Marechera never rewrote.

David Caute, a British writer and friend of Dambudzo, tried to have the manuscript published in the UK or the USA but also failed.

But the poems! The poems were brilliant – and yet they were also rejected.

When Dambudzo had submitted the Amelia poems and a bunch of others, altogether around 35 poems, it was Chenjerai Hove, yet another fellow writer, and editor with ZPH after Mungoshi left the publishing house, who returned them. He took issue with the many references to Greek mythology, which, he said, 'makes it very difficult for a reader in this part of the world'. Beyond that criticism, he also raised the usual prejudices against an 'anarchic vision without any commitment to the improvement of any aspect of society' and for what he saw as 'a deep sense of loss, bitterness and disgust at life and all its ingredients'.

When Dambudzo showed me the rejection letter, I was very angry. This was definitely a crime. It came from a cultural nationalist understanding of how Zimbabwean literature should be. Even more so I was alarmed by what Hove said about Marechera's 'derogatory references' to women:

> In his poetry, woman is the mother of 'bastards', the 'bitch' or the 'wench'. And woman is mainly a sexual object, nothing more. This portrayal betrays the struggle to improve woman's position in society.

How much on the surface such a statement remains.

Patterns of Poetry

THE ANTHOLOGY PROJECT WAS NEVER done. Yet, unwittingly, as is often the case with my endeavours, something else emerged from it: my first little book, *Patterns of Poetry in Zimbabwe*.

In view of the planned anthology, I had done a series of interviews with seven Zimbabwean poets (the interview with Dambudzo was one of them). I wanted to get a better understanding of the poems I had started to collect and know more about the background and motives of the poets. Once I had transcribed the interviews, I gave the transcripts to Dambudzo to read. His response was enthusiastic.

'Nothing like this has been done before,' he said. 'I have been trying to know my fellow writers since I came back here and have not succeeded. All these writers are writing isolated from each other.'

'So do you think I should get them published?'

'Oh yes. Give them to Stanley. College Press should be interested.'

His reaction of course spurred me on. And he was spurred on too. He developed his own ideas about the poets I had interviewed and their poetry. So, while we did not work on a project together, Dambudzo set out to speak to some of 'my' poets himself, when he found them sitting in a bar he frequented. In a sort of after- or meta-interview with me he raised the poems under discussion to a higher level of appreciation. In a way, my work, still unrefined and haphazard, triggered in him the most insightful and ingenious reflections. Whereas in the comments within my interview questions and the critical introduction I later wrote for the book, I criticised Chenjerai Hove's poems about human suffering during the war of liberation as 'sometimes overloaded with meaning, with images and metaphors changing all the time', and told Zimunya that I found some of his poems 'too intentional, too moralistic', Dambudzo placed them in the wider context of world literature. This, for me, opened a much more refined insight in those poems and their writers.

> Each of the poets you have interviewed faces the same struggle. There is Chenjerai Hove who is almost like the English novelist Graham Greene, who, like Hove, was a Roman Catholic and has dealt with violence in almost all the five continents and has managed to retain his humanity in the depiction of these societies, like in Haiti or in Bolivia or in Kenya or in the Congo and in Vietnam.
>
> The secret to Chenjerai Hove's poetry is that absolution is only through exposure, and exposure of that which degrades human beings.
>
> Musa Zimunya tries to walk where angels are afraid to tread. For me Zimunya is the Walt Whitman of Zimbabwean poetry at the moment. Hence his extended narrative, his long and gushing description, symbols, imagery. Where Chenjerai Hove has found himself in a Jesuitical approach to life, Zimunya has found himself in being the selective poetic historian of this nation. He dramatizes and epitomizes those moments in our history which have become public monuments like heroes' acre. But he is also capable of writing the most humorous poems.
>
> There is this acceptance of things – most of the poets have this same weakness. You have the feeling that each one of them starts from a position of surrender or of despair to circumstances, and that the only resources left to the individual are either those on personal terms or those, as with Zimunya, on political eulogy.

I had never published a book before. It was a long journey, exciting, hazardous and challenging, before I saw it in print and displayed in bookshop windows – and what a great moment that was. Working on the manuscript brought me friend and fiend. It launched me into the battlefield of views and voices fighting over the appraisal of Zimbabwean literature at that time in history. Lewis Nkosi became my mentor. Musaemura Zimunya my adversary.

In 1995, two years after I had left the country, eight years after Marechera had died, a public debate about my role in Zimbabwean literature in general and regarding Marechera in particular had started, in articles and magazines and also on the radio. Journalists had confronted me repeatedly with the quite prevalent opinion that I had made money and reputation out of my affiliation with Marechera.

Zimunya, who chipped in with a lengthy tirade, 'Flora Veit-Wild: A Black Insider's Testimony', serialised in two parts in the local magazine *Parade*, dates his antagonism back to my interview with him for *Patterns of Poetry*.

> Ever since that interview with her in 1984 whose truth she now half-tells, I am more than convinced that she has no respect for African–Shona traditions ... As soon as the interview started I realised I was in a trap. Flora had already arrived at a conclusion, she didn't like my poetry because it was borrowing too heavily on the Shona tradition, and it mattered little that she did not understand that tradition.
>
> My poetry did not, according to her discerning judgement, reflect modernistic tendencies in its spirit, form and style. Her attitude was, to say the least, condescending, presumptuous and downright insulting.

There were many more angry accusations.

Re-reading my interviews and my introduction to *Patterns of Poetry* today, I can see that Zimunya had his points. I did not know anything about Shona tradition. I had not learned the art of doing qualified interviews. My literary knowledge was quite limited but I still dared ask very outright questions and did not withhold my own personal views and judgements. I suppose it was a mixture of naivety and forthrightness that made me make those statements. I was anxious not to fall into the trap of what a German journalist had once called 'falsche Demut' – false humility – vis-à-vis a culture that is foreign to oneself. I saw it as my right, if not obligation, to speak with an African writer in the same way as with any other writer in Europe or anywhere else. Yet I realise now that my questions, which were often accompanied by my personal comments, lacked refinement and sensitivity.

Once I had the whole manuscript ready, introduction, interviews and around ten poems of each of the poets, I gave it to Nyamfukudza, who had indicated that College Press might be interested. He read it but then said, no, they were not interested. Whether he mumbled something else with his eyes remaining mute, his face silent, I do not remember.

The next publisher I tried was Zimbabwe Publishing House. They took a long time over the manuscript and when their letter of rejection arrived in the post it was quite a blow. Their main point was that my approach to the Zimbabwean poets and their work was too Eurocentric.

Then Lewis Nkosi came to my rescue.

I had met Lewis around 1984, in Dambudzo's flat. My imagination tells me it could have happened like this:

One afternoon, when I came to see Dambudzo and was about to fling my arms around his neck and kiss him after several days of yearning, I heard someone clear his throat. As I turned my head, I saw a handsome man sitting in the chair in the corner – I had not caught sight of him when I'd peeped through the French window before entering. He had his eyes fixed on me.

'Oh, you have a guest?' I looked at Dambudzo questioningly. He had not told me that we would not be alone.

'Yes, this is Lewis Nkosi,' he said, adding somewhat pompously: '*Professor* Lewis Nkosi. He teaches literature at the University of Zambia in Lusaka.'

'Oh, I see, so you have come to interview our famous rebel writer, professor?' I said as I turned round to greet the man.

'No need for that. I have known this scoundrel from his infancy, so to speak, at least from his literary infancy.'

'Lewis and I used to drink together at the Africa Centre in London. We were always the last ones to be thrown out when the bar was closing. By the way, my throat is getting dry, we should go out and –'

'Wait, man,' the visitor interrupted, 'you have not even introduced us properly. So is this beautiful lady, your German – well, you know what I mean, you have been telling me about her –' Then, winking at Dambudzo, he added in a lower voice, 'Isn't it cute, the way she blushes?'

'I am Flora Wild,' I said quickly, putting my hand out to greet him.

'And I remember you. Were you not here at the book fair last year, at that writers' conference?'

'Yes, I was, my lovely,' he said. He got up and, with a slight bow of his head, mimicked a hand kiss.

'Well,' I stammered, now flushing up to my ears. 'It was the first literary event I attended here in Africa. I was so excited to see all those famous writers. And then, of course, dearest Dambudzo started all that uproar, jumping up from his seat and shouting at the minister. I remember you walking over to him and patting him on his shoulder as you tried to calm him.'

'Yes, that's right,' he said with a broad smile. 'Our hothead can't keep his mouth shut.'

'That's not true, Lewis,' Dambudzo protested, his arm around my hip. He was obviously trying to mark his territory. 'But you know all those dumbheads in the government, some of them even poets, believe it or not, they will never listen if you don't shout.'

Trying to overcome my intimidation, I risked a compliment. 'You definitely looked very unshaken and serene,' I told Lewis.

'Thank you, my dear,' Lewis replied, in his mixture of grandeur and impishness, which I found both amusing and disconcerting.

After this first acquaintance, I met Lewis often when he came to Harare. We exchanged news and views about literature. He was an attentive listener. He took interest in my fledgling attempts at engaging with Zimbabwean writers and became instrumental in my bringing out my 'baby' book, *Patterns of Poetry*. When I had received the rejection letter from ZPH, shocked, perplexed and at a loss with their verdict, I phoned Lewis in Lusaka. I was in quite a state.

'Lewis,' I said, 'I don't understand. They have rejected my manuscript. They say it's Eurocentric.'

He replied: 'So what? You *are* European.'

This simple remark, down to earth, low keyed, liberated me from all chips on my shoulder as a European critic of African literature, then and for ever. Years later, when fate had destined me to become Professor of African Literature at Humboldt University in Berlin, and students expressed their inhibitions about imposing 'Eurocentric' views on the African world, I would quote that response: 'So what? You are European. There is nothing wrong with that.'

Lewis helped me improve my book. Caringly – and, as always,

flirtatiously – he showed me where I was wrong. After reading my manuscript, he returned it with numerous comments showing me how little I still knew and how awkward my expressions often were. Over a weekend at his home in Lusaka, where he was living with his Polish wife, we worked on revising and expanding my introductory essay. When, in 1988, the book was finally accepted for publication by Mambo Press he graced it with a most generous preface.

> Flora Wild is one of those rare Europeans we supposed had vanished after the European Renaissance, only to encounter them once again at the end of the 20th century. Free, independent of spirit, recognising no frontiers between themselves and the object of their contemplations, they wandered around Europe, around the world, among other cultures, exploring, comparing, evaluating.

There can be no doubting that the appreciation shown by such a prominent figure as Nkosi was my baptism as an upcoming literary critic. He gave me his blessing, hinting, in the preface, only mildly at my 'striking yet direct simplicity' and 'somewhat naïve formulation'. What an understatement! Re-reading my book today, 30 years later, I feel embarrassed by the truly naïve and presumptuous manner in which I commented on the poems at hand.

But I have been running ahead.

When *Patterns of Poetry* was finally published, as late as 1988, Dambudzo had passed on. All I could do was dedicate it to him.

Now I have to get back to him and me in my final attempts to hold onto our love.

Angry Notes

THE LETTERS PROJECT HAD not worked.

The anthology project had not worked.

We had productive moments together: He encouraged me with my book, my book made him reach out to others. But on the whole Dambudzo was lonely. He suffered from the ignorance he saw in people around him, in publishers who were not interested in his work.

He felt rejected.

And so, he rejected me.

Not openly, not consciously, but out of the mood of a child who refuses to be good when the world does not give him what he wants and instead throws a tantrum.

The last months of the year were fraught. There were times when Dambudzo and I would find each other again, but they were fewer and fewer and the tensions grew intolerable. I would scream with frustration. People in the block might have thought I was in physical pain, that he was beating me up. He did not. He hurt me with words.

There were many angry notes that I left at his bedside.

'Dambudzo, now it's enough, it's finished, it's out. Pain, anger, hate in my mind.'

'Have you ever loved me? I don't believe that you can love at all, women are just there for you as something one needs, interchangeable.'

'You say I am authoritarian? Just asking you not to drink too much before and when we meet?'

'Yesterday I really got the feeling you don't care for me at all, there was nothing, just indifference, cruel drunken indifference.'

And yet, I could not let go. I depended on him. The more indifferent he became, the more my urge to be close to him grew.

I was clinging to a chimera. I wanted to hold onto the moments of bliss, of being one in body and soul that we had had. But the more I tried, the more elusive such moments became.

I was too intense, expected too much.

He wouldn't 'deliver' what I wanted him to be.

It was always the same pattern – he resented the way I 'used' him, as he would claim; that I always determined when and for how long we would be together.

'What should we do?' I said one night towards the end of the year. 'How can we make it work again?'

'We never have enough time together,' he said. 'You will always go back to your family. You do not even stay the whole night. That is why it does not work.'

That was the cue. It got me going. I was inventive. If it was just a matter of more time together, I would create it.

What followed was the entrapment at Lake McIlwaine.

Even now, as I want to recreate those moments, I stumble. It is so hard to talk about it. So painful.

Did Dambudzo want to punish me?

Did I really think it could work? Was I that naïve?

Lake McIlwaine – The Entrapment

I CANNOT THINK OF LAKE MCLLWAINE without a shiver. It contained both the apex of sexual fulfilment and the deepest, the most radical descent into a fathomless despair. It was also, so I imagine in a mythical kind of way, the moment when the virus entered my body, after which my life would not ever be the same.

Lake McIlwaine is a big water reservoir about 30 kilometres west of Harare. You drive out of town in the direction of Bulawayo, first passing Heroes Acre with the gigantic monument in socialist-realist style created for the new government by their North Korean friends. Then comes Warren Hills Cemetery, the vast burial ground which, around the time Dambudzo would be put into the earth there in 1987, was growing at an unprecedented pace. Then the bird garden, the snake park and the lion and cheetah park, attractions I knew well from visits with my children. And then you come to the National Park, which at the time still bore the colonial name (it is now called Lake Chivero).

Sir Robert McIlwaine – obviously a Scotsman with a very Scottish spelling – had been some kind of civil engineer who did very useful things for the Rhodesian settlers by looking into water and soil conservation. The settlers of course needed a steady water supply; they couldn't just go with the seasons as the African population had done. So in the 1950s, when the cities were growing rapidly, dams were created to ensure a permanent water supply for the municipal water piping system. Most of the dams and the surrounding land also became national parks. Thus the settlers also had their recreational areas, where they could take their families and friends for game viewing, fishing and their beloved braais.

The national parks were very well organised and equipped. They had self-catering lodges and chalets and camping sites.

Needless to say, it fell to me to make a booking, and also to bring all the provisions we would need for the three days we planned to stay there, meat for the braai and beer and wine.

I booked one of the lodges near the water, which I knew because not long before I had spent a weekend there with my family. The park was not too far from Harare and the lodges, each named after one of the many species of birds that populated the banks of the lake, were beautiful, spacious and private – you wouldn't see or hear anyone from the next lodge.

And yet, taking Dambudzo into Fish Eagle Lodge was like taking a fish – to stay within the imagery of the lake – out of water. It was a mad idea.

Victor had agreed with my plan but we only had one car, and he needed it to drop the children at school in the mornings and then drive to his office. By then he had quit his job at the training workshop. The embassy had provided a paid position for him with the Zimbabwe German Society.

Dambudzo and I could not get to the place of our retreat without a car. Even if you hitchhiked to the park gate, it was another eight or ten kilometres to the site where the lodges were. And you were not allowed to walk because wild animals had been relocated into the savannah land of the park from other much larger wildlife areas. So, if not lions, there were giraffes, zebras, wildebeest, baboons and a few rhino; and certainly wild pigs, hyenas and jackals.

Ingenious as I was in organising all such things, I turned once again to my friend Gabi, who had helped keep our writer safe and reasonably sound before his public reading the year before. I asked her to drive me and my lover to the park, leave us there, and pick us up at an arranged time two days later.

That was the trap.

Once dropped, we could not get away.

It's hard to imagine such a situation today. Mobile phones did not exist.

Internet did not exist. And when, in despair, we wanted to communicate with Gabi and ask her to pick us up earlier than the arranged day and time, there was not even a traditional landline available. Even worse, because it was in the middle of the week, there were no other visitors staying in the lodges or at the camping site, whom we might have asked for a lift.

It was just us.

It was the third week of January 1985. The beginning of our third year in Zimbabwe. The beginning of a new school year for our sons. Max had started Grade 3, Franz was with the 'Lions', the bigger boys in his nursery school.

The day starts as always. I take the boys to school, Max on his own bike, Franz in a child's seat on mine – or is he riding his own already and I have to warn him to be careful on the steep slope leading down to the meadowy grounds where the riding school is. The nursery school is on the road behind it and, just two hundred metres on, Lewisam Primary School, where I leave Max.

It can also be that Victor drops the boys off by car and then drives on to his office at the ZGS; or does he go to the National Archives instead this morning, where he spends as much time as possible researching the history of Zimbabwean businessmen.

I spend the morning with my usual routine, working at my desk, transcribing interviews or typing notes. Or do I? Am I too excited at the prospect of a three-day excursion with my lover so I busy myself with preparations? Maybe it's me who takes the car to drop the boys off, and Victor his bike – it's an easy ride from our house down Enterprise Road to the ZGS building – and afterwards I go on to the nearby shopping centre to stock up on supplies for the family for the days I'll be away. I buy provisions for the trip with Dambudzo at the same time.

I am glowing. Three days and two nights just the two of us, without any interruptions, far away from the usual hubbub of daily life … Thinking of the pleasures ahead makes me feel weak in my legs. The butterflies in my tummy are having a ball.

I pick the children up from school and we have lunch together at home on the veranda. My bags are packed. I am ready.

'Gabi will be here just now,' I tell them. 'You remember, I'll be going away for two days?'

Did I tell them who I was going with?

There is a hoot from the driveway. 'Ah, that's her!' I kiss them goodbye and, rushing through the kitchen on my way out, I wave to Anna. 'I am off. Thank you, Anna!'

We collect Dambudzo from Sloane Court. He has a shoulder bag with books and an extra T-shirt or so.

He seems in a good mood. I think he starts talking to Gabi, about something completely unrelated to our trip. Maybe:

'How are your classes going?' (Gabi teaches German now too) or 'Oh yeah, I also like teaching, at least from time to time. I should find a new teaching job ... I have actually thought of putting all my papers together, you know, school certificates and so on, and what I have from Oxford, and register at the university, finally finish a degree.'

To which, laughing, I say from the back seat: 'Come on, Dambudzo, where will you find such papers? You haven't kept any documents anywhere with all your wandering around.'

(He did, at some point, though that might have been in the following year, when he started to feel his strength and stamina waning, talk seriously of wanting to finish a degree.)

'Imagine,' he chuckles, 'me with a degree and a paid job, finally becoming settled and self-content, leading a "regular" life, like all my compatriots there at UZ or in the ministries or the publishing houses! I would feel like a bloody sell-out.'

'Dambudzo,' Gabi laughs, shaking her curly hair, and glancing sideways at our friend. 'You? I won't believe it.'

The conversation distracts from the awkward situation, the embarrassment Dambudzo is surely feeling right now, being driven by his mistress's friend to a holiday resort for three days of pleasure.

We arrive at the gate of the national park. I flash my reservation sheet and register our names on the form we are handed: F.W. and D.M.

'What about yourself, madam?' the man at the gate asks Gabi. 'And the car?'

'Oh, I am not staying,' Gabi replies with a sideways smile full of meaning. 'I am only dropping my friends.'

'All right, but I still have to enter your vehicle registration number,' he says. He hands the key to the lodge to me, with a map of the park. 'Please drive slowly – there might be some game crossing the road – and do not get out of the car. Especially when it is getting dark. That's when the hippos come on land, and, bloody hell, they can run fast.'

The drive on the gravel road up to the lodges seems endless.

Conversation has stopped.

Thick clouds are gathering.

'You might get some rain,' Gabi says as the camping site comes into view. 'But anyway, would that matter? You are not here for wildlife viewing, are you?'

'Shut up, Gabi,' I say. 'Stop your stupid jokes. You are just jealous.'

Gabi loves to tease and I like her jokey tone, her voice with a slight lisp and a challenging look in her eyes.

'Be good, you two,' she says. She reverses her car and disappears back the way we came.

We take our bags and the basket with provisions and walk to the lodge.

Unlike the year before, it was an abundant rainy season. It had rained every day, sometimes non-stop. In our house in Highlands, the doors would not shut anymore because the timber had become spongy with all the moisture, and mould was creeping out of the corners.

It did not rain that afternoon but there were clouds, the light was milky.

We strolled around in the garden of the lodge, getting a feel for the place. The lawn was enclosed by a low wall and there were a few boulders here and there. Through the shrubs you could get a glimpse of the lake. The water was unruffled, without depth, of an indistinct grey.

I was full of gleeful anticipation. How good it was to be here with him. The time ahead stretched out before us, seeming endless.

'Let's take a walk down the path,' I said.

I took his arm, pressing him close to me.

Was it what he wanted?

We didn't walk far and soon we were back at the lodge.

'Oh wait, I know what we'll do now,' I said. 'Stay there!' I ran inside and came out with my camera. 'The light seems just right, not too bright but a bit of sun – let's take photos. You know I have wanted to get a good portrait of you, like I did with the other writers, for my book.'

The photos! If anything good came out of this venture, doomed as it was, it was the photos.

Dambudzo was very professional about it. Photos of the writer to be used in a publication were part of his public persona. Just as he granted interviews, he would grant that photos be taken of him. So, in a way at that moment, even in this most private time I had created for us, we slipped into the duality of writer and critic.

We walked around on the grass, talking, and I followed him with my camera. At one moment I called out to him and as he turned his head towards me, I snapped. He was frozen in the instance and in the movement. His head is turning towards the camera, first with a pout, then with knitted eyebrows. Was he angry, upset, nervous? Behind the camera I did not know what was going on in his mind right then, how he felt having arrived at this enclave he had longed for and I had arranged. He was not posing but quite natural about it, and yet aware of the camera as a recorder of his life, part of his trade. Pen or camera, both were instruments to look at the world from a certain angle. In *Black Sunlight*, the narrator is a photojournalist.

I took more photos of him sitting in a chair, his gaze downwards to the book he was reading. Though he was not looking at the camera, his face, even his skin, shows that he is self-conscious of the situation. As if he is thinking, 'Yes, you may snap away, I am your model, but you won't intrude into my inner thoughts.'

Those photos, taken on that day of imminent crisis, of highest delight followed by utmost annihilation, in black and white, with my Olympus reflex camera, solid and heavy, have outlasted it all. Dambudzo seen through my lens.

There he is on the cover of *The Black Insider*, looking out of the greyness of the lake into the camera, blurred outlines of thorny branches like ornaments behind his head, his brows slightly knitted; his lips, full, slightly parted, giving a glimpse of his lower teeth with one of them missing; his expression is serious, even angry; yet there is also a mute kind of sadness in his face. Looking at the photo now, which I took over 30 years ago and have since seen so many times, I want to drop the camera and rush over to him; I want to enclose him in my arms, hold him, soothe him.

In the second photo, which appeared on the cover of *Cemetery of Mind*, Dambudzo is looking sideways, lips closed into a pout; cheeky, challenging the onlooker, arresting.

It is the third photo that I love the most – I used it for *Patterns of Poetry*. Again, you only see his chest but his eyes are looking downwards;

he seems to be reading; his lips appear almost white; he seems calm, serene, within himself.

There are two more photos in that pose, taken from different angles, all so tender, inward, touching the heart. His skin, tenuous, a threadbare fabric, blends with the paleness around so that the contours of his face dissolve; it leaves him unprotected, the pain underneath lying bare. Only his hair, a dark matted cap with little stubs of dreads, gives the downward bent skull some firmness and closure.

> *But first, to found the bone in lemonbright sunlight*
> *A pause ...*
> *To gain, under destiny's lampshade, a permanent intensity, dare I hesitate?*
> *To cry, what no scream ever whispered, to shrill, to howl*
> *what no dread bombardment ever shuddered!*
> *Fear is no small thing under the microscope. Fear is the flesh, the gorgeous dress my skeleton wears.*

Later we grilled meat on the braai. We had salad and vegetables and a few drinks. Then we sank into bed.

It was that moment of sinking down from the heights of utmost exaltation, when your body and soul tighten and stretch out in yearning, and the peak you are reaching out for seems to elude you the more you want it; when you hold your breath and are numb with the vastness around you; you don't feel the body beside or above or inside you; and then, after what seems like an eternity, you hear the scream bursting out of your throat, like a long-lasting, plaintive howl, an animal succumbing to its hunter. You are a creature without will. There is lightning under your eyelids, electrical shock waves make you quiver; and the contractions suck it all into the pool inside you, you feel the gripping, the ripples set in motion by the crest of desire, ebbing, fading; and you crumple and whimper, and finally sink back beside the other body; and you feel so grateful and fulfilled, stammering, knowing: I will never need that again.

All craving seemed stilled. Now and for ever.

I remember that moment with absolute clarity.

I have only felt like that once.

It was the moment of conceiving the virus, as my mythical tale tells me now.

Lake McIlwaine – The Entrapment

The next day everything was different.

It was over. The dream was shattered, crushed, ridiculed.

From the utmost height of fulfilment, I fell into the deepest hole.

Dambudzo did not say much. He was sullen, morose, hostile.

'When is Gabi coming?'

'Tomorrow afternoon.'

'Oh.'

'What?'

'Can she come earlier?'

'Why?'

'I have to get away.'

I do not remember any details. I did not argue. We did not fight. He did not even come up with one of his usual fictions of a plot against him.

'How should we reach her? There is no one around.'

'Do they not have a telephone here?'

'We can ask the warden when he comes round again.'

Silence.

What was it that caused his sudden change of mood? Did the falseness of the whole set-up only dawn upon him now? The shame of being here, the penniless poet hosted by his white mistress at a place that was utterly alien to him?

'Oh yeah, the warden,' he might have said. 'You don't even speak his language. You won't know where he comes from, some shithole in the ghetto, just like me. And now he is here to tidy up the bed where I slept with you and the kitchen where you prepared your white people's food.'

Maybe he did not say it. But did I realise that such thoughts were in his mind? That he would always strike back when he felt at my mercy?

I did not. I felt hurt, utterly hurt and betrayed.

When the warden came back with firewood and coal to prepare the braai for the next evening, we asked him.

No, there was no phone anywhere near.

We had to succumb. We had to play along in the bleakest of black comedies. Pure Beckett. The Black Poet and his Lover Trapped at Lake McIlwaine.

Dambudzo did not speak to me. He did not touch me.

He sat apart somewhere, a book in his hands. Smoking. Drinking. Completely closed up in himself.

I feel my stomach tighten thinking about it. The anger, the pain, the frustration.

Inside I was screaming, How can you do this to me?

It was like a grander version of what he had done to me those many times when I left angry notes at his flat – emotional annihilation. Those other times, though, I had been able to get away. Now I could not. And he could not.

We were trapped in our own illusion.

How did I pass the day, the endless hours until night? I don't know.

Time crept along; a mutilated snake, about to die. A nightmare from which you try to wake up but cannot; shock frozen, a scream stuck in your throat.

Barefoot, I climbed one of the boulders at the fringe of the enclosure, thinking how pleasant the previous evening had been, trying to make sense of it all. After sunset, we had sat peaceably side by side, sundowners in our hands, the meat roasting on the open fire. Now and then I took a puff from his cigarette. We did not speak but I felt calm and at ease. On the low wall that surrounded the lawn we could see rock dassies, those weird creatures without tails, scurrying about, their grey fur hardly visible against the stones in the dimming light. It had been so peaceful, no sounds but the twitter and chirping of the birds and now and then the muffled moo of far-away cattle.

Now there was the same stillness but it felt opaque and suffocating, a buffer around my lover's sullen mood and my cries for help.

Or was it just that I was wearing 'unsexy clothes', as Dambudzo would say, when many weeks ahead we could speak to each other again and laugh about the absurd situation we had created for ourselves at the lake.

'You know,' he chuckled, 'I even checked the wardrobe, when you were not looking, to see whether you had not brought any other clothes.'

I had come in a short cotton dress, but at the lodge I wore baggy grey shorts and a black and white striped T-shirt, comfortable outdoor clothes. I would never have guessed that he found them hideous and that my outfit made a difference. He had always liked the way I dressed – sometimes he would even 'steal' an item from my wardrobe – and anyway, had I not imagined myself most of the time without clothes?

How silly this remark made it all seem. Trivial, unnecessary. How happy 'we could not have been'.

But there we were, within the walls of our entrapment, and there was no way out. We had to stick it out, through a whole day, and a night, and another half day, in mutual distaste, until Gabi came and relieved us.

What would the warden have been thinking when he came to tidy the beds on the second morning and realised that the guests had slept in separate rooms?

Coda 1: Seroconversion

When the HI-virus first enters your body, you may experience a short 'flu-like' illness.

This is known as the 'seroconversion illness,' and it occurs because your blood is being converted from HIV negative to HIV positive by the production of antibodies.

Everybody infected with HIV will seroconvert at some stage, but only about 80% of patients will notice any symptoms.

Seroconversion usually occurs 1–3 weeks after infection, but could take up to 6 months.

The most common early signs are flu-like symptoms that you'd expect from most 24-hour bugs.

You'll probably start with a high fever, chills and sweats which may be accompanied by a sore throat and mouth ulcers.

Swollen lymph nodes can appear early on in seroconversion and last for a few weeks or more. After disappearing, they will probably return later on in infection and last for 3 months or more.

Many people experience a 'maculopapular rash' (a flat, red skin rash that's covered in raised bumps) in the early stages of HIV infection.

You are 20 times more contagious during acute HIV

infection than you are during long-term infection.

This is because the viral load in your blood is far higher during seroconversion than it is at any other stage.[1]

IN EARLY APRIL THAT YEAR OF 1985 I had a flu-like illness with fever, a rash, sore throat and swollen glands. Ten days later Victor came down with very similar symptoms. Doctors could not identify the cause for our illness. They suspected Pfeiffer glandular fever but we both tested negative for it. The cause for our condition remained undetected.

I was not aware of that post-operation crisis. He only told me later. I only knew that I paid the costs for his stay and treatment at Montagu Clinic. A receipt for over a couple of hundred dollars from that time emerged among my papers.

---

1 (https://www.dred.com/uk/early-symptoms-of-hiv.html)

Coda 2: Conception

IN MY PRIVATE TALE, THE 'confinement' at Lake McIlwaine was the time I received the deadly virus. On that first night at the lake, at the peak of sexual satisfaction. Only then was my body ready for the 'gift'.

Dambudzo might have been carrying the virus for a long time already.

He could have passed it on to me on that first night at the Seven Miles Hotel.

And apparently did not.

I cannot prove that it happened that night. I cannot prove anything.

When many weeks later the chagrin of my steep downfall had passed, I knocked at his window again. Though I knew the end had come and we could not be a loving couple anymore, I lay in his arms once or twice more after our trip to Lake McIlwaine.

In April came the illness. The virus had settled.

My tale had found its closure.

PART FIVE

BASTARD DEATH

The Great Scare

IN 1987, THE ASSOCIATION for the German Language selects 'AIDS' as word of the year, together with 'condom'. The two words win out over Perestroika, Glasnost, Waterkantgate, and Ozonloch (Ozone hole).

If AIDS for the past years has been a faint rumbling on the horizon, a mysterious disease going round in far-away gay communities, it is now at the centre of media attention and general concern.

The first major waves of mass hysteria about AIDS are sweeping through Germany, kindled by the boulevard press.

In a letter dated 13.2.1987 a friend from Germany writes: 'Almost every day there is something about AIDS in the media. ... More and more people are affected.'

In the US, the death toll rises to 4 135. The AIDS quilt is started in San Francisco. Each three-by-six-foot panel commemorates someone who has died of AIDS.

During February 1987 not a single issue of the leading German tabloid *BILD* misses the opportunity to invoke an apocalyptic scenario caused by what is called the 'lust plague' (Lustseuche). Disease and death are decried as punishment for exorbitant sexual appetite; medieval images of 'black death' are resuscitated. An A to Z of AIDS risks starts with 'anal intercourse' and ends with 'French kiss' (Zungenkuss). Photos show an American mortician in full scrubs, including eye, mouth and hair protection and double latex gloves.

The magazine *STERN* touts for readers with cover headlines like: 'AIDS. Sternreport. The plague that changes our lives'.

Concurrently, the Bavarian secretary of Home Affairs, Peter Gauweiler, stipulates that HIV-infected persons be reported, isolated and, if necessary, imprisoned. He implements mandatory blood tests for prostitutes, drug addicts, prison inmates, applicants for civil service jobs and non-Europeans seeking residence.

Equally, in February 1987, the British media run an AIDS advertising campaign. The motto is: 'Anyone can get it, gay or straight, male or female. Already 30,000 people are infected'. The 'tombstone' advert, with its creepy and scary imagery and sound, is aired on national TV. Under a darkened sky a volcano erupts. Cascading lava rocks are followed by shots of a tombstone being chiselled. Offside, the gloomy voice of actor John Hurt intones a dire warning: 'There is now a danger that has become a threat to us all. It is a deadly disease and there is no known cure.' Church bells and a low humming are heard, while the inscription etched into the tombstone becomes visible: 'AIDS'. With a thump the tombstone topples over backwards and lies flat on the ground. From off-stage a bunch of white lilies is thrown on top of it, while the voiceover repeats: 'Don't die of ignorance.'

Media analysts have confirmed that AIDS fulfilled all the criteria for sensationalist tabloid headlines:

It was transmitted through sex.

It spread quickly. It spread indiscriminately.

It disfigured the famous and the beautiful through its gruesome symptoms: wasting, Kaposi, herpes, thrush on the tongue and in the throat, pneumonia, toxoplasmosis of the brain.

One did not know where it came from.

One did not know who was carrying it.

One did not know how contagious it was.

One did not know how long people could live with it.

An overall feeling was generated: AIDS is a plague caused by sexual lust.

Apocalyptic visions are invoked: Man will be punished for sins of the flesh.

By February 1987, the World Health Organization has been notified of 43 880 cases of AIDS in 91 countries.

In Africa the perception of the disease is still almost nil. The first prominent death is Zambia's president Kenneth Kaunda's son, who dies of AIDS in December 1986.

'The president announced the death to the world, becoming one of the first high-profile leaders to do so on a continent where people largely talk about HIV/AIDS in whispers,' Reuters reports.

On the 25th of February 1987 my husband and I receive the diagnosis that we are both infected with the Human Immunodeficiency Virus.

The Hourglass

THE FIRST WEEKS AND MONTHS OF 1987 are sealed off in my memory like in a glass cabinet with little porcelain figurines that have been taken out by some invisible hand, moved about and put back inside – up to now they are stuck in that very moment.

Can I open it and go through the motions again?

I will try.

The doctor's phone call set us in a state of panic.

'Could you and Victor come to see me? It is about Dambudzo.'

This was a couple of days after I had found Dambudzo in his flat in a frightful state. He was running a high temperature, coughing blood, emaciated. Open books between dirty sheets, a half-eaten pie on a table. I had dragged him into my car and driven him to the doctor's rooms around the corner in The Avenues.

'You are not looking so good today, Dambudzo,' Nick C., our family GP, said, and after a brief consultation, to me: 'Here is a referral. Take him straight into Parirenyatwa Hospital.'

Visiting our GP was always an uplifting experience. He would usually see you off with the prescription: 'All you need is TLC!' On the phone he had seemed concerned, which got us worried. We wracked our minds. What was wrong with Dambudzo? Why had Nick not wanted to tell us over the phone? Was it cancer? Or – what if it was AIDS?

'I have no contact details for any of Dambudzo's relatives,' Nick said when we had settled in his office. 'He was always very dismissive when I asked him to name someone –'

'Yes,' I confirmed, in order to calm my nerves '– he wouldn't want his family interfering with his life.'

Nick nodded. 'So for me you are his closest kin,' he said.

Victor and I waited.

'The news is not good. I have been phoned by Parirenyatwa. Dambudzo has a far advanced pneumonia which is caused – as a test has proved – by AIDS.'

Nick must have seen our faces freeze, but he did not know our story yet. I only told him after we had received our own test results.

'So … what does this mean?' I stammered. 'How are they treating him?'

'With antibiotics, which will bring some ease to his lungs. But otherwise? What do we know? His illness is apparently at quite a progressed state. There is no treatment.'

'For how long do you think will it last?'

'Who knows?' Nick shrugged. He looked sorrowful. 'I really cannot tell you.'

'Life changes fast. Life changes in the instant.'

This is how Joan Didion starts her account of a *Year of Magical Thinking* after her husband dropped dead at the dinner table and their only daughter was lying in intensive care in a coma.

Our life changed in slow motion.

The figurines were cast to act in a thriller and there was no way out. You could not reject your role. You were under contract.

Again and again we went through the same set of questions: When did Dambudzo contract the virus? Was it before I got sexually involved with him? If so, might he have passed it on to me? And – the last possible option – might I have passed it on to my husband?

Over and over I went through all the instances, looking for one that might give a clue.

My mind hit on the surgery Dambudzo had undergone the year before.

One day, when I stopped by his flat, as I used to after our sexual relationship had ended, bringing him some vegetables from the garden or taking him to see friends or go to an event, he said he needed to see a doctor.

'You know,' he said, trying to laugh off his embarrassment, 'sometimes when I am lonely … ahem … ahem, well, you know … then I do it myself, and, wow, all of a sudden there was so much blood in my sperm.'

'Okay,' I said, 'I'll make an appointment with Nick C., our GP. He is around the corner and he is really nice.'

Nick transferred him to the Montagu Clinic, a small private surgery nearby.

'It was quite hilarious,' Dambudzo chuckled, when he related his visit to the clinic to me. 'They needed a specimen of my sperm. So the nurses gave me a vial and said, "Mr Marechera, would you mind going into that little room and, well, fill that. Take your time, there is no rush." They were so embarrassed, giggling among themselves, not knowing where to look. Our famous writer – here for a sperm test …'

A testicular abscess was diagnosed and subsequently surgically removed. After two days in the clinic Dambudzo was sent home. The real drama started a day or two afterwards, as he reported in an interview later that year:

> I thought I was going to die actually, you know. I had to go for this operation and then the doctor discharged me less than 24 hours after the operation and just told me to go home. And so I came back in here and I was trying to sleep and I woke up around midnight, you know, I was haemorrhaging and for fuck's sake, it was really, really painful! I mean physical pain. I was haemorrhaging in bed; I have had to throw away some of the sheets and blankets and I had to clean it up in the bathroom fairly well – it was disgusting. But you see, that kind of pain, physical pain, you cannot reason away. I mean, that was the first time I'd ever had an operation or been in hospital, and when I came out of hospital I started writing a series of more or less surrealist poems. One of them is entitled 'Execute an Anarchist and See what Happens'. In other words, I really got into this physical feeling of protest, not mental feeling of protest

but just a physical revulsion against the way the body can betray one into such a condition; as well as, you know, just suddenly realising one's own mortality, that, Jesus Christ, I've been living as if life is one happy hippie condition where you have your own way. That's when I almost gave up the stands I had taken in my published books so far.

Dambudzo managed to get himself to Parirenyatwa.

I was not aware of that post-operation crisis. He only told me later. I only remember that I paid the costs for his stay and treatment at the Montagu Clinic.

That was in early 1986. Did they not do an HIV test, I now wondered. If they did, did they not tell him about the results? Or if they did, did he not want to acknowledge it and let it slip from his mind?

For Victor and me it was obvious that we needed to be tested. But where? If we got tested locally the information might leak out. The Harare community was so small – gallery openings, theatre performances, lectures, readings – you always met the same people. At the Italian Bakery in Avondale you could be sure to find familiar faces over coffee and cake. At Bonmarché supermarket I might bump into the ambassador's wife who, across our trolleys with milk, cheese and wine, would be sure to put on her polite smile and enquire sweetly, 'How are you, my dear, and how is your husband?'

It was all so shameful, so unthinkable, we could only share our situation with a very few people, those whom we trusted.

After consultations with my brother and his wife, both medical doctors with their own practice in Germany, we decided to have our blood taken by a German doctor who worked at a hospital in Masvingo, and then send the serum (which is durable) to Germany and have the test done there. Without telling anyone at home, we drove the 250 kilometres down south. The whole way there, Victor and I hardly spoke. Lead seemed to fix our feet to the earth and our tongues to the back of our mouths. The doctor, a woman, was full of empathy. We told her our story while she took samples of our blood and then we stood in front of the centrifuge staring at the liquid spinning in there as the blood was converted into serum.

What did it contain? What would the verdict be?

How did we get through the three weeks between the doctor's call and our test results?

I saw the world as if through frosted glass.

In the mornings I got the boys ready for school. Max, now nine years old, would already be sitting at his desk drawing or writing, fully dressed in his school uniform, his tie neat, satchel packed. Franz had just started Grade 2 and was testing my nerves with his rituals of dithering; endless admonitions to 'please get dressed now – I don't want to say it again', countered by a 'just have to do another wee'. A few drops squeezed out, and finally he got on his bicycle and followed his brother to school.

When I settled at my desk, my usual morning routine, my thoughts would trail back to the first days I had sat at that very spot. 'This is paradise, it is just paradise,' I remembered telling myself over and over again, as I looked through the window into the large garden with the huge old trees, the wide expanse of lawn, lush green from the recent rains, and the bougainvillea cascading from high up into the flowerbed below. 'It is so unbelievably beautiful.'

Now the same view made my heart cramp. The trees seemed overpowering, the lawn impertinently green and the pink of the bougainvillea hurt my eyes.

People were distant schemes to which I could not relate. A niece was staying with us at the time, together with a friend. I remember how glad I was, in the afternoon, to see the children having fun with the two young women, diving from their shoulders into the pool, splashing, bouncing, screaming. It meant I could stay inside and they would not feel my gloom.

But in the evening, when I came to kiss them goodnight, did they notice the veil over my eyes?

When my brother phoned, Victor and I were out. My mother, who was visiting us, was standing in the doorway when we got home, reproach on her face. 'Here you are at last! Stefan phoned. He wanted to speak to you but wouldn't tell me what it was about. He said you must phone him immediately. What is the matter?'

After my father's death my mother spent several weeks with us every year. In her early seventies, she was still youthful and a great sport for her grandsons, doing all sorts of nonsense with them, playing cards for hours or telling them stories from her life – like the time that she had spent in India when she was 20 and her brother bought her a horse fitting to her rather small stature, and how fast she went on it, going on hunts, racing and jumping.

She was full of admiration for our life in Zimbabwe, liked our circle of friends and loved the garden – she was a passionate gardener herself. She also tried to be discreet and was quite self-sufficient; if she wasn't doing something with the boys, she would just sit on the veranda with her knitting or a book. 'What a great mother you have,' my friends used to say. Some of my women friends would come and sit with her and get advice on their marital problems. 'She is so open and practical and understanding.'

'I will never forget,' Gabi told me, many times, with a big smile, 'now that I am getting to that age myself, something your mother said. "When I entered a room and men's eyes were not anymore turning to me, I knew I was getting old. It was devastating – being regarded a neuter."'

I knew that I could share anything with my mother, and had done so, in delicate matters, in the past. And yet, having her in my home for several weeks was a challenge. She had such a strong presence. Even if she did not say anything, I could just feel that she wanted to be involved in every little detail of our family life, trivial as it might be. And something as serious as what was at stake now? How could I keep this from her?

One thing I knew was that she would not be judgemental.

Much later, when she knew about our medical condition and my affair with Dambudzo, she once said to me: 'You know that I could not ever blame you, having never been monogamous myself. But with that one?!'

She had met our friend once or twice, at one of our parties, where, on seeing her, he immediately put on his posh accent. 'Hello Vic-to-ri-a, it is so good to see you again. My gawd, frankly, I am amazed, you are always knitting. For whom will this lo-ve-ly blue jum-m-m-per be?'

My poor mother. What she would have seen and heard was a strange creature of a man, one tooth missing, skinny to his bones, a mug of beer in his hand, mouthing something in her direction of which she would only catch a discomforting sound. Her English was very good but she was hard of hearing and even had difficulties following conversations with our other friends, with their Rhodesian accents, let alone Dambudzo's drawling, drunken voice, his stilted pronunciation of an Oxford boy but with the 'r' rolling from his tongue into his throat.

The image of me in bed with Dambudzo would have been beyond her grasp. Her own flirtations would have been with well-tanned skiing instructors or silver-haired medical doctors, not a creepy dark fellow such as she would have regarded Dambudzo.

There was no way I could talk to her about this now.

The next hours of that night, the most terrifying night of my whole life, were probably almost as bad for her as they were for us. Hundreds of thoughts would have been coursing through her brain. Why did Stefan need to talk to us to urgently? Why couldn't he tell her? Had something happened to someone close to her? One of her brothers? Had someone died? Did Stefan have a problem with his wife? With his children? Was he himself in a crisis again?

My brother had gone through childhood in the shadow of his big sister. Unlike me, the poor boy had been sent to a classical grammar school with Latin and Greek as main languages. My mother swotted Latin vocabulary with him and for practising Greek she sent him to the learned mother of a classmate. Our father's expectations, unspoken but looming, and our mother's coaxing him on through school meant that Stefan's was not an easy lot.

Once he finished school, he cracked.

In Paris, where he spent some weeks after finishing high school, he wanted to throw himself into the Seine.

When he started university in Germany with a vague interest in the humanities, he was completely lost. After slashing his wrists twice, he spent several months in a psychiatric hospital.

Extended periods of psychotherapy and various forms of medication did not cure him. Throughout his adult life he went through long phases of severe depression. His handsome face lost all movement. With his classical features and full dark hair, he had the good looks of a film star, but depression turned him into stone. He did not move. He did not speak. He seemed not from this world.

The manic phases which occurred in between only made the next depression worse.

'It is a family curse,' my father used to say, resignation in his voice. 'The poor lad has inherited the bad genes from my mother's family.' My father was alluding to the predicament of his mother and his only sister and there was great sadness in his voice, but he never gave any details. Only when, a long time after his death, I started researching our family history, did I learn that my grandmother had suffered from depressive anorexia and my aunt had committed suicide. I had met neither of them. Like my maternal grandmother, my father's mother was a Jew in Nazi terms. This made her leave Germany before I was born.

It was during his first psychiatric ward experience that my brother decided to become a medical doctor. He wanted to turn his own suffering into knowledge. At medical school he met his future wife, who, coming from a completely different social background, a working-class family, had great stamina and a clear perspective on life. With her help, he managed to pass all his medical exams and eventually they opened their own practice together.

That was where he had now received our HIV test results.

I brush my mother aside and pull Victor into my bedroom, where the telephone is. I lock the door.

'Please – you phone.'

I watch his index finger dial the numbers. I hear the tone in the line, faint, far away.

Then Stefan answers. A pause. Then his voice, toneless: 'Positive. You both tested positive.'

Positive. How I hate the mockery of that term.

Was it my brother's fate to be the harbinger of our impending death? Was it his own depressive inclination or his medical experience, or both brought together, that in the time to come made him so pessimistic? Until a decade later, when effective anti-viral medication came onto the market, he did not believe in our survival.

But then, come the new millennium, he himself walked down into the valley of death.

I almost followed him.

What follows are hours of Victor and me lying on our bed, clinging to each other, whimpering, shivering, muttering.

'What shall we do?'

'How can it be?'

'What does this mean?'

And, above all: 'The children. What will happen to the children?'

Hours pass. I know my mother is waiting, sitting in her bedroom down the corridor, thinking, What is going on? Why are they not telling me?

'I can't,' I say. 'I just cannot tell her.'

The roosters in the bougainvillea bush outside the window begin their wake-up crowing. Victor pulls away from me. 'We have to tell her. I'll go.' When he comes back the first light is filtering through the trees, flickering over our bodies. A few hours of slumber, then it is time to get

the boys ready for school.
Life changes in an instant.

During the days that followed, I kept looking down at my body, touching my arms, my legs, my belly, asking myself: How can it be? *Nothing* has changed. I am as I was a couple of hours ago and yet, *all* has changed.

Victor shielded his body and mind against further damage by resigning from his job; he wanted to devote all his – remaining – time and strength to things of his own choosing, his research. He grew a beard. He put on weight. And he mellowed. The children noticed it.

What did he feel? Did he not blame you? friends would ask me.

Victor's answer was simple: 'It could have happened to me too. Nobody is to blame. No one knew about AIDS at the time.'

I spoke to a friend. 'See it as a chance,' she said. 'Life feels more precious when awareness of death sets in. You do not know what will happen. Any of us can die or lose someone close at any time. Feel the intensity of life.'

Her advice worked. I started to feel alive again, more alive than before.

I will always remember her words of encouragement and their tragic irony because only six months later, out of the blue, her 21-year-old son died. Less than 24 hours before Dambudzo succumbed to AIDS.

Back in February 1987, there was more to come.

In the first weeks after our diagnosis, the idea of sex seemed shrouded. How could one ever enjoy it again? It appeared as the great taboo, a close mate of death. A month might have passed before our bodies found each other again.

And then, after another few weeks, the miracle: I was pregnant.

News that was shockingly sad at that moment.

Two years before, in that entrapment of Lake McIlwaine, I had conceived the virus. Now that I had conceived a child, the virus lifted his head. A spitting cobra, it hissed vindictively: 'There is not room for two. You have to go.'

It would be decades before doctors would know how to prevent the transmission of the disease from mother to child. So I could not risk to have that baby of mine. And yet, when I went to see our doctor again to tell him that now I had tested positive with child, he said: 'Look at it like this. Even if you cannot keep the child, new life has sprung up between yourself and Victor. Your body is alive. Isn't that good news?'

In April we went to Germany for further tests and consultations at one of the first HIV/AIDS research centres in Germany at Frankfurt University. The gynaecologist I saw there for the abortion and sterilisation, was incredibly moved by my story. I had never seen such empathy and human feeling in a doctor for a patient he had never seen before. He would not believe that nothing could be done to prevent us dying.

He became one of our best friends. He and his wife, and later also their children, visited us in Zimbabwe.

Another sign of life, of growing.

Not all doctors were like this, however.

The last image I took with me before we went back to Zimbabwe was my visit to Professor Helm, head of the HIV/AIDS research centre in Frankfurt. I wanted to discuss perspectives of living with the virus with her.

It was like meeting the Grim Reaper with the hourglass.

All she said was: 'Whoever comes into my room will see a continuous decrease of their helper cells. Nothing can stop it.'

The sand in her glass got stuck many years ago. Otherwise I could not have written this story.

How to Live On

AT THAT POINT, IN 1987, medical knowledge about the development of the illness was still rudimentary. Assumptions of the general public, those who were infected and those who were not, had little foundation. One theory was that among those who tested HIV positive some were only carriers of the virus whereas, in others, it might take between one and ten years until they would have full-blown AIDS. The most significant indicator was the number of helper cells in your blood in relation to the killer cells. If the helper cells dropped below 200, opportunistic diseases would normally begin, we were told; from 100 downwards to zero you were on the trip to full-blown AIDS.

Blood needed to be monitored every three months and so we continued to send samples of serum to Germany; if we were visiting, we had the tests done there in person. The period of waiting for the results was the most harrowing time. Would the number of helper cells have dropped again?

You felt on a downward slope, hoping only that the slide would not be too fast, or that a miracle would happen before you reached the bottom. You would also continuously be checking your body for possible symptoms, feeling for swollen glands, being alarmed by minor changes on your tongue, on your skin, or by night sweats. While there was no cure in sight, doctors advised us on prophylactic methods which might prevent certain forms of the illness, first of all the most dreaded one, Pneumocystis pneumonia (PCP), a typical AIDS-related killer disease.

It was what Dambudzo would die from, in August that year.

Once a month we had to inhale a certain substance using an electrical inhalator. There was the hassle of making sure we always had a sufficient supply of the substance and of the tubes needed for the inhalations. The procedure took one hour. The children kept asking why we were doing this. I hated it.

Our children. They were nine and six years old when we had received our diagnosis.

My brother, in his pessimistic outlook, urged us to tell them and also to have them tested. In the time before we knew, they might have had blood contact with one of us, he said.

I could not.

Seeing them grow up in all their charm and liveliness and insouciance, the knowledge that both their parents were at risk of dying was the heaviest weight on my heart. Having them tested on top of that – that was out of the question for me. Unbearable to think that they, too, could be hosting the virus. We were told that this was unlikely, so why then?

We told Max and Franz about our condition five years later. The knowledge became part of their young lives. They had to deal with it in their own way.

Shadows of Death

Death wears, from within all faces,
a secretive smile;
from within all gesture
an incomprehensible movement;
From within all voices
a sound beyond all hearing.

DAMBUDZO KNEW THAT DEATH was coming. In 1986, the surgery and haemorrhaging. In 1987, pneumonia and a diagnosis. He was in constant conversation with 'Bastard Death', as he called him. But there seemed no reprieve. His strength to withstand was waning.

Darkness a Bird of Prey

What are the things, bright-winged
That within me no longer move
No longer 'bruptly leap clear to soar
Towards the stars above this dead-weight night?

Where is that ecstatic turmoil

Which once fired my youth into desperate acts
Visions beyond any known to the hideous devil?
Where! that demented force that hurls Death
'Get thee behind me'?

The hundred knocks on the door
To my thirties-old life
And th'impatient question 'Is anyone in there?' – I have
No strength to shudder, to utter, to
Scream YES or painfully mutter 'Go away'.

We did not talk much after I knew his diagnosis, not about what was on his mind nor about what was on mine. I could not and would not believe that he was dying because would that not mean that I would follow, not now but maybe in a year, or two, or whenever? I was not able to tell him that the Bastard was hovering over my life too, and that of my husband. That my children might become orphans. The thought was too horrifying to be uttered.

He never asked the question: What about you? And Victor? The children? I never asked him if he knew that he had AIDS. He only mentioned that they had found 'some kind of virus'.

Our conversations clung to daily necessities.

His knees ached, he told me; could I get him another prescription for the pills to relieve the pain?

After Dambudzo was discharged from hospital Victor and I gathered some friends inside and outside Zimbabwe to contribute to a fund from which he received monthly payments to buy food. Then, to make sure he would actually eat, we arranged for him to have lunch and dinner at a nearby restaurant. He did so for a while.

His last public appearance was in April that year at a literature colloquium at the University of Zimbabwe. It ran over two days. I picked him up in the mornings and we drove to the venue together.

He attended all sessions, looking frail but attentive and smoking throughout. During the breaks he was surrounded by a crowd of student admirers asking him questions. He was not as aggressive and disruptive as he used to be at such occasions in earlier years. He seemed in a serene, somewhat subdued mood. Now and then he threw in one of his witty remarks or asked a question, such as after the paper by Emmanuel Ngara, the stalwart of socialist realism, whom I had already witnessed at the first ZIBF in 1983. As usual Ngara stressed the need for the writer to serve the masses and such like.

'Marechera stood up carefully,' remembers one of the participants, 'adjusted his glasses, passed a hand over his dreadlocks, seemed to collect himself and asked with artless simplicity: "Why shouldn't we be allowed to celebrate our uselessness?"'

1987. What a tragic year it became for the Marechera family.

While the 'Bird of Prey' was already circling above Dambudzo's head, some cruelty of fate made it first swoop down on two of his siblings.

In April his eldest brother Lovemore died of liver cirrhosis. I only knew Lovemore from *The House of Hunger*, where he appeared as Peter who was beating up his girlfriend and mocking his 'bookshit' brother.

After receiving the news, Dambudzo went to Marondera, an hour's drive from Harare, where Lovemore and his family had been living. I think he had been asked by Michael, the brother who came after Lovemore, to help with the funeral arrangements. Dambudzo was back the next day, and in distress.

'What happened?' I enquired, when I saw his irritation. 'Why are you back already?'

'Oh, I don't know,' he said. 'They did not want me there. So I left before the funeral.' He was vague and it was difficult for me to understand what had been going on. Had they rejected him because he was ill?

On the whole, Dambudzo's relationship with his family stayed nebulous to me. I only knew that he did not want to have much to do with them; that he did not share their beliefs, abhorred the rituals that would have meant him going home to be 'cleansed' after being overseas; and that 'they', according to him, were 'only after my money'. This was what he had said to me when some female relatives had come to see him in hospital.

Only a month later, a much greater family tragedy occurred.

One morning in May, I collected *The Herald* from our letterbox as usual. The news right on the front page was utterly shocking: Tsitsi, Dambudzo's sister, the only one in the family to whom he had felt close, had been killed in a bomb blast in her flat in Harare's Avenues. She had turned on a TV set which her husband, who was an ANC activist, had brought from Maputo. A powerful explosive device, intended for him, had been hidden in the TV and it went off, tearing Tsitsi to pieces and destroying the flat and part of the whole block. Her two children and her brother Michael, who happened to be there, survived. Her husband was not at home at the time.

This time Dambudzo's family did not even inform him. He only learned about the disastrous event and Tsitsi's horrific death the day after it happened, when it was public headlines.

I had only just read the news when he phoned me. I drove down to his flat to fetch him and together we went to the site of the devastated building. There were lots of onlookers outside and police and officials inside the grounds. Michael came by at some point, only greeting briefly. Then Mugabe arrived on the scene with some ministers. When he was told that Dambudzo was there, he came and offered his condolences. A photo of that moment appeared in the magazine *Parade*. Mugabe in the centre, bowing slightly, his right hand in front of his stomach, flanked by two of his ministers. Dambudzo, seen from the side, a lone figure, marked already by death, his arms hanging down, his face with the heavy glasses expressionless.

Tsitsi had been a freedom fighter. The government celebrated her as a hero. Dambudzo refused to attend her funeral. 'It is the government celebrating her as a hero, I am not part of it,' he said.

In his poetry, the blood that she had shed in that act of political crime by the South African apartheid regime, mixed with his own blood, the blood that he was coughing out of his lungs.

I Used to Like Tomatoes

I get tired of the blood
And the coughing
and more blood
I get out of that flat real fast
to some cool quarrelling bar
and talk big to the bigger comrades
washing down the blood with Castle an' Label
shaking hands about Tsitsi bombed to heaven ...
It's back at the flat on my back
swallowing it all read back hard down
I wake up too tired to break out so bright red a bubble.

Five years later, when we performed his poems on stage, that was one of the poems I recited. I stood by his side again, in his pain and his loss and his angst.

Dambudzo died a couple of days before the 1987 Zimbabwe International Book Fair.

Its theme that year was 'Literature for Children'. How fitting for him.

He had wanted to contribute and had started a story: 'Fuzzy Goo's Guide to the Earth'. He wrote it by hand into a new notebook, starting on the last page. 'Turn the adult world upside down, backside front', was what he wanted to tell the children. The title page was carefully graphed. It looked beautiful.

On one of my last rounds to his flat before I found him so ill that I had to take him to hospital, he showed me the story and made me read it. In my usual schoolmasterly way I said that I liked it but suggested it should have a bit more of a real plot, children would prefer that.

He did not look at the story again. It stayed incomplete. A year later, after I had sorted all his papers and notebooks, I gave Max, who was then ten years old, the story to read. He scolded me. 'Why did you mess up Dambudzo's story? You don't understand it. You are an adult. We children like it.'

It was the last writing Dambudzo did. And I made him stop. It was my last blunder, meddling with his work, while he was still on earth. Did others follow when he was underneath and could not make Fuzzy Goo continue his 'guide to the earth'?

> Society is the secret club of big human beings. The job of this secret society is to make little human beings grow up. Growing up means giving up all things you like to do. Growing up means not saying your favourite words. Growing up means turning into a monster just like your father and your mother. Growing up is to become blah. Very, very blah.

He is Dead

MY MEMORY OF THE DAYS AND weeks after Dambudzo's death is hazy. There was inner turmoil but also tranquillity. Time seemed to stand still.
But there are the letters and the dreams.
'Dambudzo,' I wrote, on 21 August, three days after he had gone …

… Now you are under the soil. Gone. For ever. And still so close, so alive. Your voice on the cassette, your photographs, your face a few days ago only, so gentle and sad and yet peaceful. I embraced you to say farewell and to tell you that we are with you, that we won't leave you alone. And you held me back with your skinny arms, you held me and wouldn't let me go. Then I went, waving back at you.

The next day I came with the letter inviting you to the INTER-LIT conference 1988 in Erlangen – you couldn't recognize me anymore. Your body was still alive but your mind had gone. You were struggling. You didn't want to leave us.

And then there was my friend's grief who had lost her son the very same morning. And I came back to sit with you, I just sat there watching you, breathing heavily, fighting, fighting for this precious life which had treated you badly; this body whose strength was going to betray you, which you had hated, had refused to accept as the fragile, transitory physical side of yourself.

Now I am sitting here on the veranda in the morning sun, where you loved to sit, and listening to Mozart's requiem, which you loved to hear. You loved beauty and peacefulness and yet could never hold it for long.

And then the burial. Your family, your mother, who had lost the third child within a few months. She seemed to be almost with no tears left.

And your family unable to relate to you.

Your father's brother in his speech in the funeral chapel (on Rhodes Avenue, so close to your flat): This child was very gifted, learnt very well, knew English. Went to university, then had to leave the country, went to England. We did not hear from him anymore, only sometimes in the press. Then he came back. He was writing his books. At least he made a living. He did not marry. He had friends who helped him.

And your brother Michael at the grave (who had treated you so badly at Lovemore's and Tsitsi's death): Honouring and envying you at the same time, as the famous one in the family.

And then Musa Zimunya paying tribute in Shona.

And I said: 'On behalf of Dambudzo's international friends I would like to say that we all admired and respected him as an extraordinary writer and a sincere friend. We love him a lot and will miss him a lot.'

And there they all were, really grieving the loss of you: Ama Ata, Stanley, Mungoshi, and so on. Ama Ata saying how boring it will be without you, being able to conduct conferences without your scenes and disruptions.

I miss you. But you are not gone.

It was the last week of school holidays. We went to the eeriness of the Vumba mountains again, where the serenity of the hills soothes your eyes and stills your heart, where loss and longing, melancholy and mourning melt into one. And my thoughts could again fly far and high and linger on the images of the past weeks.

The next letter I wrote was to Lewis Nkosi, dated 4 September.

Dear Lewis,

The four of us are spending a week's holiday, very quietly, in the Vumba Mountains. Have you ever been here? It seems so heavenly, beautiful, peaceful – unreal. No worry or harm seems to reach you up here. And Victor and I need some rest after two very disturbing, restless, heavy weeks after Dambudzo's death.

I still can't believe it, thinking of him as being alive, seeing and hearing him – unreal again that he should not be there anymore.

I then told Lewis the details about how I had taken Dambudzo to hospital, that he wanted to make a will but I found him already unconscious the next day.

I did not get hold of the doctor and did not know about the critical state. I stayed with him till almost midnight, then went home to catch a few hours of sleep. At 1.30 a.m. the sister phoned me and told me that he had passed away. Alone. Lonely, as he had been in his life. I went straight back and found him still warm in his bed.

The following morning, Victor and I went to see Marilyn Poole who telexed you. We wrote an advert text with her which we had in the paper already on Wednesday [19th]. I include a copy for you as well as some newspaper articles.

Thursday already was the funeral at Warren Hill where only a few months before his sister had been buried.

I continued relating details of the funeral.

A lot of acknowledgement for him and his work has been shown since his death. Why couldn't they give him some more of that while he was still alive? If only he could hear a little of what is now being said about him and his writing! It is weird to see how people who couldn't cope with his personality at all now declare themselves his closest friends.

The next week the Book Fair took place, with a memorial for Dambudzo at the Monomotapa on Thursday night. I wished so much you would have been there to pay tribute to this extraordinary writer, in the way he would have deserved it. It was well meant but not up to his 'standards'. And I expected him, any minute, to walk in and wish everybody to hell.

So far very briefly. I thought you would like to know and I don't know whether anybody else informed you.

Of course, the important question regards his unpublished work.

> There is quite a lot and it is secured. Things have to get sorted out, how to proceed with it, legally and otherwise.
>
> What is sure: Dambudzo Marechera will not be forgotten and certainly some of his works will come out, posthumously.
>
> My book [Patterns of Poetry] was due for the book fair but then delayed again. The first proofs were rather a mess. But we made a very nice hand-out by which it was promoted at the fair. The cover design is by a local artist, Richard Jack. It looks really lovely, the back cover, with the seven photographs, as well. I just got the second proofs and it will definitely be out soon. Dambudzo would have loved to see it finally published. Now all I can do is dedicate it to him.

In a letter to a close friend in Germany I wrote, on 5 September:

> After D's death there has been so much going on: interviews, funeral, book fair. V. and I are making progress with our dissertations.
>
> If you think of it, life is better, more beautiful than it was ever before. It is of a haunting intensity and painful beauty. One is very much aware of the transience of life. It is not threatening but cuts deep wounds.

It was in the Vumba mountains that the dreams started.

30. 8. 1987
I am in a room with many people. Suddenly I realise that there are some out to shoot me. The moment I am aware of it and want to protect myself, it is already too late: I have been shot. I slump and fall down into a room beneath that room (like underneath a spectators' stand), all the while thinking: So that's how it feels when you are being shot, when you are dying. Then I notice that it was only a grazing shot along my eye and that I am not dead. But I know they are after me and I try to flee. Yet right then the gunmen are again near me. I am wrestling with one of them and plead not to shoot me because I have two small children. He lets go of me and I have also got hold of his MP. Thus armed I manage to pursue my flight, the others not daring to take aim at me. I secure a few more weapons from them and continue running. Now outside the room, I am running up a long, slanted rock escarpment. At the top there are, at the back of the rock's peak, crater-

like holes, with some spikes in between. I find a hole in which I can hide the guns. I try to remember it so that I will be able to retrieve them. While hiding them I am still terrified that I might be being watched and still pursued. But then I have made it and, relieved, I slide, on my bum, down the slope. Once at the bottom, I meet Victor and am happy to be with him.

4. 9. 87
I am in Wiesbaden, on Schöne Aussicht [a street near my home]. At first, I am together with others, at the corner to Prinzessin-Elisabeth-Strasse. Then I walk away on my own in the direction of Abeggstrasse [where my home was]. I think I have been warned that somewhere around here some loony guy is on the loose. When I am on the pavement across from the Verwilderter Garten ['a ragged garden'; that is how we, as children, called a terrain surrounded by an iron fence, with some trees and shrubs, and hidden under grass and leaves, one or two iron doors leading to a bunker; it was always very scary to go into that garden] I see him sauntering towards me, he assaults me, jabbing into himself and me some kind of quills, tiny arrows, filled with poison. I am not really alarmed. He wants to kill himself with the poison. He pulls the spikes out again from my arm and leg. Other people come. I just do not know whether enough of the poison has gone into my body or not so that I will die. But this again does not really worry me. I rather tend to think that I shall get off safely. There is some talk about driving to a doctor to examine how much of the poison has entered my body and what kind of poison it is. Then the dream gets fuzzy.

8. 9. 87
I was doing some errands with G. S., the new Secretary [of the ZGS]. All of a sudden, I had to leave quickly, had to attend a function, a funeral service, and somehow it became clear that it was for me. But then I had apparently missed it, because later on I asked others what had been said. Then I went to the venue (chapel) where it had taken place, there were still some sheets with notes lying around, from the pastor or who else had spoken, and I wanted to read what had been said about me.

Then I was talking to people who asked me how many children we had, and I said: *'We* had *two.'* Startled by that slip of my tongue, I *ran upstairs, where the children were supposed to be sleeping, together with other children. I found them. Max was already asleep; Franz was still romping about. I was relieved.*

PART SIX

ENTANGLED LEGACIES

Execution

YOU WERE DEAD. YOU HAD not written a will.

What should I do? All I knew was that your work had to be preserved.

And I knew your family had to be kept out of this. I had the key to your flat and I made sure to secure all your papers.

Many questions have been asked about my role as literary executor of the famous writer's work. Many myths evolved.

Q: Whenever Dambudzo Marechera's name is mentioned, your name comes up almost simultaneously. Some people insinuate that you have appropriated him and have used his name for your own personal benefits. Others commend you for consecrating most of your life to his legacy, a labour of love, as it were.

A: Yes, wherever I am introduced to someone in Zimbabwe or in African studies generally, the moment my name is mentioned, an air of recognition lights the face of the one I am being introduced to, followed by, 'Oh, is she the one ...?' Which is an insult, really, as if I did not have an identity of my own. So in a way I am being swallowed by the great reputation he has. Though sometimes it is really sweet. Like when I am in Zimbabwe, in the Book Café in

Harare, where many of the young poets hang out, and there is this youngster, skimpy, dreadlocked, and someone sitting with him, talking, points in my direction, and he gets up and walks over to me, his eyes wide open, gasping, 'Is this really you? No, it cannot be, I thought …' 'You thought I was something like a goddess?' I laugh. 'Well, here I am, an ordinary human being,' and he grabs my hand with both of his, shaking and squeezing it, his eyes glazed over as if he was seeing an apparition.

And yet, whatever people think or say with whatever subtext – envy, anger, admiration or curiosity – the assumption that once Marechera was in his grave I grabbed his unpublished work and set out to make it known to the world, is wrong.

Q: But is it not correct that you became Marechera's literary executor and biographer?

A: Yes, apparently it is so. But I do not feel that I chose that role, it rather chose me. I was very reluctant.

Q: Tell us what happened and why you were reluctant.

A: After I had roughly sorted the papers I had secured from his flat, I handed the whole pile of manuscripts, single sheets, notebooks, etc. over to College Press. It seemed the most natural move, because with *Mindblast* they had been his last publisher. As I can reconstruct from correspondence, at the end of September that year (1987) I had a meeting with Stanley Nyamfukudza, editor, and Margo Bedingfield, managing director of College Press. They said they were looking at the material but wanted to deal with – here comes the word – an executor. I had, in the meantime, found out the address of Michael Marechera, Dambudzo's brother, who was at the time the eldest male member of the immediate family. All through I had been consulting with Hugh Lewin, who together with Irene Staunton was just founding a new publishing house in Harare, Baobab Books. Their first book was a tribute collection with photos of Dambudzo and snippets from his unpublished work.

Hugh contacted a lawyer and, after consultations with him, Michael Marechera, Hugh Lewin and myself were officially instituted as executors.

The next step was to clarify the publishing rights. After further consultations, Michael agreed that a trust would be established with him, Hugh and myself as trustees, and he, the founder, would donate all the rights to his brother's works to the trust.

On 29 March 1988, in the presence of Harry Kantor, 'Notary Public by lawful authority', of the Harare law firm Kantor and Immerman, the deed of the Dambudzo Marechera Trust was signed. It stated as its first and foremost objective, 'to republish, reprint, distribute, grant rights of copyright in all media, translate, edit and generally promote the published and unpublished works, writings, books, manuscripts and poems of the late Dambudzo MARECHERA in Zimbabwe and worldwide'. It further stated that the Trust had 'to ensure that the net income from the works of the late Dambudzo MARECHERA published prior to his death are used exclusively for the support and welfare of the Founder and his blood relatives and at least 50 per cent of the net income from any works not previously published, for the same purpose'.

Q: So not even half a year after the writer had passed away, you already had established a sound basis from which to handle his work. Were you pleased?

A: I was relieved. The load of what to do with Dambudzo's work was taken off my shoulders.

Q: But the family, in the form of brother Michael, was also on board.

A: Yes, as he had not left a will, this had been unavoidable. Though all the time, I had been hearing Dambudzo's voice, 'nothing to the family'.

Q: How was it for you to deal with Michael?

A: Michael was difficult. He was unpredictable. There also seemed a streak of madness in him. When I looked into his face, I saw features of Dambudzo, but a different version of him, mouse-like, the skin over the skull not soft and sensuous but tightly spanned. The expression of someone who wanted to be important but did not know why and how. The figure, always in suit and tie, even tinier than that of his younger brother. Contrived.

I did not know what his intentions were. Did he want to shine in the light of his brother? Did he feel ashamed of him, who had caused so many scandals? Did he feel remorse that they had quarrelled over the graves of their brother and their sister? Did he think there was lots of money? Did he resent that foreigners, white people, seemed on top of things? I could often not decipher his face nor his words. They seemed so roundabout.

Q: How did he act within the Trust? Did he want to take influence on the work?

A: No, not really. That was the good thing. He was 'gated' by the Trust. He could not feel excluded. For him what seemed important was that he was the chairman of the Trust. That gave him importance. He left decisions about the manuscripts to Hugh and myself.

Q: ... and they were with College Press.

A: Not for long. They soon returned them. I cannot recall any specific reasons. I think they could not handle the amorphous mass of various bits and pieces, half-finished novels, fragments, essays, notes and poems.

Hugh and I held meetings with other publishers and writers. Baobab Books said they were interested in publishing posthumous editions. But someone was needed to sort the manuscripts and do the editing. And also search for other manuscripts that might be somewhere in the world.

Q: And the obvious person was yourself.

A: Some people thought so but not me.

Q: Why not?

A: It was 1988. I was in the middle of my PhD research. And also, I did not feel sufficiently qualified. I had no editing experience.

Q: Were there any other reasons?

A: Yes, possibly the most pertinent reason for my reluctance – I was not talking about it openly, maybe I was not even fully aware of it myself – was that I felt too close to Dambudzo. I did not want to split myself into two.

Q: But in the end you did.

A: Yes. Nobody else was found who would have had the time or inclination to take the task on. Then, in a final meeting, someone said: 'Flora, you are the one who has to do it.'

Q: So you picked up the baton.

A: Yes, with a sigh. I think it was the conviction, the clarity with which this role was assigned to me that made me take it on. Reflecting on this moment now, over 30 years later, I feel that the trust my friends and consultants put into me arose from the very same reason that had caused me to hesitate: that the writer whose work had to be preserved had been close to my heart.

Q: Had you, at this point, already read all that you had found in his flat, in the wardrobe among his clothes, beside his typewriter, on his bookshelf? Was there anything you were particularly excited about?

A: Of course, I knew quite a bit of the material already. All the poems, prose manuscripts and children's stories he had assembled and submitted to publishers in the last years of his life, which all had been rejected.

There were other pieces which he had mentioned he was writing but I had not seen, they were mostly left unfinished, like 'Prince Street', and 'The Concentration Camp'. I don't remember that he had mentioned that title but he had told me that he was going around researching about the so-called 'Keeps', detention camps the Rhodesian army had erected during the Chimurenga to keep the peasant families away from the guerrillas.

What stood out were a number of poems I had never seen before. Obviously written in the last months of his life, they contained haunting visions of death. Those poems moved me immensely. They evoked the months not long before when I had known that he had AIDS and would probably not live much longer, and I knew that I was also infected but did not speak to him about it. As I now read lines such as 'I have / No strength to shudder, to utter, to / Scream YES or painfully mutter "Go away"', I felt so much with him – I wished we had talked, wished I had been there to hold him, and wished he was there now as I was reading these poems.

Q: Did you find anything that surprised or shocked you, something very personal that might have compromised you as his former lover? Any letters?

A: This question brings back to my mind that I of course will have read, or at least looked through, everything before I handed the material over to College Press. And indeed, it was my prerogative as the one 'who had the key' to eliminate possible surprises or disclosures to others. In fact, I tore up one poem – ha, I have never mentioned this 'deed of execution' before. Though my name was not mentioned it was much too personal in an irritating way (and also it wasn't good – pretext from my side?).

I found my own notes and letters to him, angry ones, loving ones. And I found quite a few letters to him by friends, including girlfriends, which I did not peruse in detail; still haven't, partly out of discretion, partly because they bored me. There was not a single letter by him or a draft of a letter. He never wrote letters as long as I knew him.

There was one big surprise. An enigma. The poem 'The Declaration'. It puzzled me deeply.

Q: Why do you call it an enigma?

A: Since it was published in *Cemetery of Mind*, critics have read it as a clearly stated avowal of his medical status as HIV positive. I am not surprised that they do, I would have done so as well, would have attributed it to the phase in his life in early 1987 after he had been diagnosed with AIDS.

Q: What was the problem?

A: I recognised that it was typed with the keys of the typewriter he owned when I met him, the portable one with an orange lid, famous through the park-bench diary, belonging to the legendary image of the writer tramp, the city poet, sleeping on park benches and in driveways, the typewriter in one hand and a plastic bag with all his belongings in the other.

Q: And so? What is so curious about that?

A: He had lost that typewriter. It must have been in 1984 or 1985, when we were still lovers. He came back to his flat drunk and left the typewriter somewhere outside. He had told me vaguely about it. Then Stanley Nyamfukudza had brought him another one, an old-fashioned one, more 'desktop', not portable. He had that one on his desk until the end.

It was the eye of a detective that let me conclude that he must have written 'The Declaration' much earlier than the poems foreshadowing his death. I could clearly recognise the keys of the portable typewriter.

Q: And so?

A: This means, if 'The Declaration' does in fact entail that he knew he was HIV positive, he knew it already when we were still lovers.

Q: And did not tell you …

A: Yes. When I learned that he had AIDS and I was also diagnosed HIV positive, I often asked myself, when did he attract the virus? Did he already know about it long before the diagnosis in Parirenyatwa in January 1987? But how could he have known? Knowledge about that virus had been scarcely there.

Q: Did you have any clue when and how he will have got infected? And if he infected others besides yourself?

A: No. Though of course I pondered a lot about these questions. I was particularly intrigued, for many years, to know about the medical status of 'Olga', his lover before me, who appears in his park-bench journal.

Q: Did you find out?

A: Yes, I did. It took me a very long time until my curiosity finally impelled me to track her down.

Q: Wow. You did?

A: It was in 2010. I managed to get her phone number. As it turned out, she also lived in Berlin. I phoned her and we agreed to meet. It was the strangest meeting one can imagine.

She suggested Café Einstein, a well-known place with a long history, dating from the wild 1920s in Berlin. A mixture of avant-garde and tradition. 'I'll wear a hat,' I had said, 'brown, with a large rim.' How else should we have recognised each other, fleeting as our acquaintance had been more than 25 years before? When I arrived, I did not look at the sumptuous display of Sachertorte and apple pie and pastries of all sorts but looked for a place which would be central enough for her to find me and yet secluded. I sat with my back to a wood-panelled dividing wall, a cup of coffee in front of me on the art décor coffee table. It was afternoon, an animated chatter around me. My head was turning with each new person entering the café. What would she look like?

Finally, a lady entered, looked around hesitantly, then, spotting my large-brimmed hat, slowly approached my table. No! This could not be her. I had to conceal my astonishment – this matron with a plump figure and spongy face should be Olga, once a sprightly, slender girl, her dark hair bobbing around her vivacious face? Did I look like that?

It was her. She sat down opposite me. Ordered coffee. No cake, thank you. We were both fumbling for words. 'How we have changed.' 'How strange to meet now, here, after such a long time …' 'What do you do?' Finally: 'Are you …?' 'Yes. (Pause) And you? You too?' 'Yes.'

Like two widows meeting over the grave of a man they both once loved. Who have both survived him though they both could have died.

Q: So, did meeting 'Olga' give you more certainty regarding the 'travel history' of your virus?

A: Only in so far as to presume – though of course there was no proof – that Dambudzo had been infected already before I met him. When he was with her. For how long and how, of course, I still did not know.

Q: So the enigma of 'The Declaration' remained?

A: Yes. And though of course I pondered a lot about all these unsolvable questions as to the when and how and with whom, in the end I told myself that they were of no consequence for what had happened.

Yet in terms of a conclusive narrative the enigma somehow matters. It leaves a lacuna, an 'absence' or a 'spectre' as Roland Barthes might have called it. Free of fears as I have been now for many years, thanks to the medication that prevents the virus to make me ill and die and even to infect other people, I can say, laughingly, Good for you, Dambudzo, that you left me with this mystery. So, my hands as your executor and biographer are bound at least at that point, and I have to hand you over into the department of shamanism, which some critics have opened for you.

'Executor' – what a word. I only learned it by becoming one, doomed to become yours, Dambudzo. It always makes me feel like a hangman. Have I put you to the gallows, my love, by taking on this other persona, the Marechera Authority and Executor of his Estate?

How removed this feels from what happened between us in those years when we were united in passion, friendship and altercation.

Nevertheless, that is how your afterlife started, dear Dambudzo. You, the utmost anti-institutionalist, who was 'against whatever diminishes th'individual's blind impulse', as you famously stated, were encased in a trust. But do not frown. You were a master of oxymora. The Dambudzo Marechera Trust – doesn't this almost sound like *Black Sunlight*? Besides, I needed that institution to let your spirit fly and spread to all quarters of this world.

I also needed money to fulfil my task.

Being a single-minded person – as a local reviewer of one of my books once called me – I took advantage of an historical coincidence that came my way, the arrival of a new German ambassador to Zimbabwe. I had heard that he was quite culturally minded and was said to be not so much a diplomat in the usual sense than a man of culture. So I made an appointment and introduced myself to Dr Kilian.

Again, I do not need your sneer, Dambudzo, just wait and hear. Even men in formal positions can be amiable and open-minded – think of both your wardens at varsity, Knottenbelt at Manfred Hodson Hall, at the University of Rhodesia, and William Hayter at Oxford. They spoke of you with much affection when I interviewed them a year later. And I was only able to do that thanks to the money the German ambassador made available to the Trust.

It was June 1988 when I entered the reception room. Momentarily blinded by the rays of the winter sun pressing through the shutters, I heard a full voice saying, 'Do make yourself feel comfortable. I am so glad you have come. I have heard a lot about you.' Some sparkles of light were caught in the ambassador's silver-white hair, which was combed back from a face in which I sensed a glint of playfulness. He looked respectable but not at all intimidating. He did not have the bland diplomat's look behind the polite façade I had seen in some of his predecessors.

I think you would have liked him, dear troublemaker. At least he spoke an impeccable Queen's English without so much as a hint of a German accent. You would have approved.

'I am so glad to be posted here,' he said, 'after some years of mere desk work in the ministry in Bonn. Zimbabwe seems such a lively place. But of course, I have only arrived recently. Please tell me what is going on in the cultural sphere. I believe you are quite involved as a board member of the Zimbabwe German Society?'

After Victor had resigned as secretary of ZGS, I let myself be elected on its board. Thus I was able to initiate, as Victor had done before, activities that promoted Zimbabwean culture. I told Kilian about the broad movement of women writers that had emerged from panel discussions we had organised; the International Book Fair which was developing into a major meeting point of the African book world; and I emphasised how much Zimbabwean literature was flourishing. This of course was my bridge to advancing my quest.

'I am glad you are so interested in cultural affairs,' I said, 'because I have also come as an ambassadress of sorts.'

'I am all ears,' he said, with a warm smile and a slightly teasing twinkle in his eyes.

I outlined how Zimbabwean literature had developed since 1980 and then focused on your special role and place in it. 'Many people here know that his voice was prophetic,' I said. 'Already in the early 1980s, when everyone was enthusiastic about the new Zimbabwe, he decried the hypocrisy of politicians who were enriching themselves while those who had fought in the war were left in poverty. And his style of writing, it was so different from everything readers in Africa were used to. He had a huge fan community among students and young writers. He still has. It is actually growing by the day.

'You, Mr Ambassador, might not always have liked the invectives he might hurl at all kinds of authorities –' you will forgive me that comment, Dambudzo '– but you would have certainly admired his intellect and his literary horizon – honestly, I have never met anyone who had such a vast and distinct knowledge of literature from all parts of the world.'

I proceeded to tell him about the Trust and the tasks that lay ahead which I had been commissioned to pursue.

'Well, my dear,' he said, 'I definitely admire your stamina in promoting the cause of what, if I understand correctly, was quite a rebellious spirit, not always easy to handle. If you were coming to ask me to sponsor an economic venture, it would be easy to procure German money ... In the cultural sphere, however, the money is scarce. But let me see. A genius who died young, an inspiration for many – his work seems to deserve our attention. Do write a little proposal for me, make a list of what has to be undertaken and a budget of the costs you foresee. If it is not excessive, I might be able help.'

He was.

He convinced the German Foreign Office that Dambudzo Marechera's work was worthy of being collected and preserved. The Trust was given a grant allowing me to undertake the editorial and biographical research that was envisioned. It included a stipend for me for two years and travelling expenses. Later it was extended for another nine months.

Confess it, Dambudzo. You always had sympathies for Germany and West Berlin was one place you would have liked to return to. In this way, you had at least some posthumous German gratification.

That's another word I dislike – posthumous.

It reeks too much of the soil in which you are buried.

The Tracking

AND SO MY JOURNEY INTO YOUR life and work started.

I followed your traces, searched for your scattered left-behinds of works and of deeds. I ordered and structured, compiled, edited and published. I had to think for you and about you, had to act in your stead, whether you liked it or not.

All the while I could feel you somewhere close by, watching me, listening, smiling at times or smirking, howling out loud or just nudging me gently from the side, grinning: 'Serves him right – don't trust that one!'

Full of pride you were with every text that saw the light of day in the world, with every researcher who delved into the richness of your universe, with every critic who applauded your ingenuity. Full of spite at those who belittled you. Definitely throwing tantrums at me, your mighty 'executor', when you felt I was mishandling your precious imaginative offspring.

My search was like a jigsaw puzzle, or a detective story – more or less the same thing – as I followed clues, picked up traces, hunted for names and addresses.

To my surprise, wherever I knocked on people's doors, they reacted as if I was the tax collector. A shock of guilt and disbelief was in their faces.

The Tracking

What do you want? Have I not …? Oh, I am so sorry, I will certainly … They immediately thought that they had not done enough to help the poor genius – a genius he had certainly been, they agreed – and I had now come to hold them responsible for their omissions.

Some answered my questions with long-winded defences, others with self-irony, some guiltily but with affection. For others, you had been their alter ego, the person they would have wanted to be but did not have the courage, the stamina, the unperturbed mind to stand up to.

'People talk about themselves when they talk about him,' Peter H., one of my interlocutors, said. You had been together with him at the University of Rhodesia. Both of you had been Best Student in your year. 'I suspect that there are many who, in their regret for the loss of Dambudzo, find themselves facing the atrocious truth that his death made it easier to love him safely, without fear of abuse or rejection. Myths are easier than men.' For Peter you were 'the other option'. While you decided to become a writer, no matter what, Peter ended up as a lawyer.

I started my search in Oxford. 'Oxford Black Oxford' you had called it in a short story – I found it in the archives of *West Africa Magazine* in London. What a fitting title – cynical, ironic, perky – for what was the epitome of whiteness. I could feel, as I followed your tracks through the Oxford scenario, how bleakly black it must have been for you.

On the New College freshmen's photo of 1974, which the Dean's office only handed out to me after much hesitation – actually, it was only sent to me several years after my visit – you have to search for the two black faces among the rows of about 100 white students, most of them with the wild long hair of the 1970s, but all in gowns, the dress code of their trade. The warden, whom I would meet, is in the middle in the front row. Straining my eyes, I find you, in one of the top rows on the left, short against the tall white student next to you, who has a long mane of curly blond hair and a pleasant smile. Cramped into the white collar underneath your gown, you appear neckless; your hair is cropped short, your lips closed, your mien desultory. I think you were needing a drink.

After some scrutiny I find one other black face, right in the middle of the crowd, bespectacled, chin thrust forward, lips parted, looking straight ahead: Here is my chance. I have made it to Oxford, is what I read in that face.

'My skin sticks out a mile in all the crowds around here,' you start your story 'Black Skin What Mask' in *The House of Hunger*, the story that focuses on two black students at Oxford. While the one student, who tries to be whiter than white, slashes his wrists, the other drowns his anger in drink until he gets sent down from the college. I have often read the story with my students; the allusion to Fanon is so easy for them to grasp. Your freshmen's group photograph – an exact illustration of that story.

I stayed in Oxford for two months, May and June 1989, together with Max, who was eleven years old. He attended Dragon School, a great luxury for him, as the school had a reputation for enhancing the creative potential of its pupils. Victor stayed in a small place in Germany during that time, together with Franz, who attended the local village school and, in the afternoons, could roam the surroundings on a rickety bicycle. Victor was busy with research seminars and consultations with his PhD supervisor at the University of Giessen.

My academic host was Terence Ranger, head of African Studies at St Anthony's College. Though I don't suppose you ever met him in person, there is a link between him, the renowned Zimbabwe historian, and your own history. And, as I would find out, he also appears in your writing. Ranger first came to your country, then Southern Rhodesia, as a young lecturer at the recently founded University College. Marxist in outlook and full of youthful enthusiasm, he tried to be true to the idea behind that venture, the 'non-racial island of learning' in the middle of a white suburb in Salisbury. The University College, brainchild of the liberal government under Garfield Todd and installed in 1957, utterly failed once the racist settler regime took over in the 1960s. By the time you entered the very same institution, in the early 1970s – by then it was called the University of Rhodesia – it was starkly divided along racial lines. This in turn led to the black students' uprising which was brutally quelled by the racist regime. You, as many others, had to leave the country.

It was to Oxford you came, the same institution where I was now trying to find a footing at the grace of the said historian. Ranger, as is well known, in his book *Peasant Consciousness and Guerrilla War in Zimbabwe*, had given a strong theoretical backing to the struggles of your generation. In later years, that is, after independence, he lost faith in Mugabe and his ZANU-PF, revised some of his earlier views and henceforth focused on Ndebele history. At St Anthony's, he always had a crowd of young scholars from Zimbabwe around him; they also attended his weekly research seminar, in one of which I presented my current work on your doings in and around Oxford.

But, Dambudzo, the web of connections between your life and work is so dense that I can never tell my story in a straight line. There is always another thread. There is not only a historical line from my Oxford host back to your generation's struggles in the 1970s. Back in Harare, I found, in the archives of the university on the erstwhile whites-only Mount Pleasant hill (where we tried to find some quiet space in the first nights of our romantic entanglement and got rudely interrupted by the night watchman) a play of yours, serialised in the student magazine *Focus* in 1983/84. The play is set when the University College was first established, 'the late 1950s and early sixties', and it features our 'hero' of the time, Hudson (alias Ranger). The play makes us witnesses of Hudson/Ranger at his famous anti-colour bar demonstration in Salisbury's municipal swimming pool. Your stage directions announced the moment:

> Enter Hudson flanked by other anti-racist protesters. They are pushing through a line of enraged white citizens. The anti-racist protesters include a few blacks.

Very close to what really happened, Hudson demands access to the pool for blacks.
'Charlie is no black. Charlie is my guest. And I don't like people who insult my guests.'
'He's a nigger, ain't he?' the superintendent hits back. 'He's just another kaffir.'
A moment later one of the irate 'citizens' pushes the fully clothed Hudson into the pool.
'Deport him!' shouts the journalist from the 'Sunday Mule'.
Terence Ranger was deported not long after the swimming pool incident.

Oxford, for me, was a strange experience.
After undergoing various formalities and seeing various gatekeepers – the secretary, the librarian, the bursar, the warden – the latter being a countryman, Sir Ralph Dahrendorf, who in his aloof politeness seemed more British than the British – I was finally recognised as a SAM (Senior Associate Member). As a SAM I had a status. I was acknowledged as a legitimate member of the respectable setting – doors opened for me;

various library tickets filled my wallet.

Particularly intimidating and strange for me, a German who is not used to such rituals, was the admission to the famous old Bodleian Library. You have to swear, usually in your academic gown, and read a text of good conduct. Not having any such thing, I was allowed to perform the ritual in my street clothes.

'Oh dear,' I later noted in my diary, 'the English – they are still soooo English! Polite, withdrawn, friendly, inhibited, unerotic, hypocritical. Poor Charles Dambudzo! Among Sirs, Fellows, Gowns, High Tables.'

Still, it was useful to have the status and the college (with office space) as a base.

My first target, of course, was to see New College, but, as Ranger had advised me, before I could do that, there was protocol to be followed. I had to write a letter to the Dean explaining who I was, what I wanted, and that I had authorisation through the Trust and the Marechera family. After I had done this, Ranger wrote a supporting letter.

'He seems quite conceited with his role as my sponsor, and in dealing with me, acts as much controversial as he can,' I recorded. 'Emphasises that "even the outright Marxist and lefty" can be fitted in this system here (more easily than in Germany), as long as the system stays intact.'

Of course, he also had his views on you and your work. He disliked the violence in your writing, he told me. He compared this to the violence in corporal punishment in Zimbabwean schools, which I had brought up at an African Studies seminar as an example of colonial habits being continued. How ludicrous.

While waiting for things to move on in Oxford, I undertook my first trip to London.

It was the 18th of May, my birthday. At 6:30 I was on the bus to London; at 8:40 at Victoria. Crowds in the station. Where to find the ticket, the train? A jungle. I somehow managed, arriving at Crystal Palace, a south-eastern suburb, where Robert Fraser was expecting me. Do you remember, Dambudzo? I told you that I met Robert in 1986 at a conference in southern Germany, my very first international conference, where I gave a paper on Zimbabwean women's literature. We soon discovered our mutual connection with you. Interviewing Robert now, he told me how, ten years before, he, Ben Okri and you would spend hours bandying words about at the Africa Centre in Covent Garden. Okri, trying to find his unsteady feet on this brazen, bohemian sea, determined

The Tracking

not to sink, and Fraser swaying between the shore and craziness. In his obituary for you in the *Independent* he expresses this longing for different areas of mind and spirit very lucidly and melancholically. Now here I was, sitting with him in his suburban home, where he lived with his wife and their young son in a kind of happy family muddle, reminiscing about the star that had shone so brightly and disappeared so abruptly.

After battling again with London transport – the train to Victoria was cancelled (partial strike of British Rail) – I finally arrived at my next destination: David Caute's house. Journalist and writer, he was a friend of yours. On his last visit to Harare, you had entrusted him with two unpublished manuscripts, 'The Black Insider' and 'Portrait of the Black Artist in London'. You had written them in your London years and submitted them to Heinemann – both were rejected.

'David,' I can imagine you saying, 'you will get them published over there, won't you?'

But David failed. He sent the manuscripts on to Peter Ripken of the Frankfurt Book Fair, who discovered them gathering dust on a shelf in his office when, after your death, I was asking around for 'lost writings'.

David was friendly, open, warm. We talked about you and your work and possibilities of having these texts and others you had left behind published. What did you mean for him, I wondered. Also another version of himself? He seemed to be most impressed by your sex life (as the long essay he later wrote also testified). Was he jealous? What attracted all those women to you, he wanted to find out from me.

I don't know, I really don't know. I only know what I felt for you – I can't speak for 'all those women'. So I could not help him.

At 20:30 I was back home, utterly exhausted. Max, very sweetly, had put up a beautiful mobile for me as a birthday present. He had also made the beds and washed the dishes. 'He is so loving, relaxed. I am so happy that he can feel so secure in his young life,' I wrote in my diary.

Finally, the next day, I got permission to visit New College. Before my appointment with the Dean, I strolled through the college grounds – 'like a fort, a castle it seems to me, with the overtowering "Chapel", cathedral-like at its centre. I get lost in dark steep staircases, peep into the hall – wooden tables – like a medieval king's dining hall'. Oh, Dambudzo, how oppressive. How lost you must have felt! The setting, the gardens, meticulous, beautiful, the green squares surrounded by walls, cloister-like. Everything set, nothing to ask for, just to study, to get a degree, to obtain your degree – Oxford University – what a reputation. I marvelled, took some photographs … The grinning gargoyles were my favourites; I could see you in them, the mockery in their expression, the laughter, the sardonic wit.

I found the Dean in his comfortable, stylish office. Very friendly, very reserved. He did not remember much about you – could be bad memories, the guilt complex: 'I am sorry, what else should we have done?' But one thing he said was: 'He obviously had a chip on his shoulder about being black.'

Hah! that was the clue for me. 'I ain't got my balls on the chip on my shoulder' you had the chorus chant in 'Portrait of the Black Artist'. Just the day before I had asked David what 'chip on his shoulder' meant. Now here I was with the Dean of New College and out came the very same words. Now I see why you tried to smash everything with your violent language. Serves them right, the hypocrites.

Years later, when we were launching *Cemetery of Mind*, your collected poetry, and a group of us staged a performance of prose, poetry and music, I was one of those chanting the chorus line – 'I ain't got my balls on the chip on my shoulder' – and in my mind instantly I had flashes of the monstrous college buildings and you, the lone figure, with your rickety gait, a heavy chip on your shoulder pressing you down.

Some days later, I paid a visit to the former warden of New College, *your* warden, Sir William Hayter. Long since retired, he now lived with his wife at Stanton St John, a hamlet ten kilometres outside Oxford. After a pleasant bus ride through the countryside I arrived at their old country house, pretty, picturesque, flowers creeping up the walls outside, inside full of collector's items. Both very friendly old people. Very open-minded, trusting me and finding my research project important. A wonderful lunch with excellent home-cooked food. They talked about 'Charles' with lots of affection. Lady Iris said she had kept a diary which she would have to go through to see if she had made notes on you.

She had. Her entries about your arrival in Oxford are quite as charmingly quaint as her demeanour. On 3 October 1974 she notes: 'I answered the telephone instead of W[William] and found myself ordering a taxi from London airport for a Rhodesian. Luckily I think the College will pay or the British Council.' And on 4 October: 'I was much taken up with trying to help Mr Marechera. I asked him to lunch and instead he went to sleep. He has no clothes or possessions. I lent him this and that.'

How I wished at that moment you could have seen this, and her later entries. She gave them all to me to photocopy together with your student photo, a letter from you to her and some correspondence of hers. Well, all of this is now in that book of mine, the *Source Book*, which is full of such treasures. Let me close with two entries from 1975: 'Charles Marechera is giving great trouble – he is nocturnal.' (26 February) 'Charles Marechera and Owen Kibel appeared, Charles very neat in good form but as usual wanting money, but for the nice reason of going to stay at Romney with Owen's friend.' (18 September)

Have you ever had someone speak with so much grace and benevolence about your wilful habits? All other people I know reacted with great annoyance.

Owen Kibel was a fellow student from Rhodesia, whom you seemed to have befriended. He was studying psychology. Following the Hayters' clue, I managed to get in touch with him and he wrote me a long, very insightful letter with memories of you. He was particularly impressed by your verbal prowess.

> He had the reverse of a verbal deficit and he seemed to want to find the very best terminology. All this was new for me at the time; encountering an African whose precision and erudition in speaking surpassed nearly anyone I knew ...
>
> He explored language with the delight of a child, often seeming to have internalised a thesaurus if not an encyclopaedia. At certain words, when they were appropriate, he would suddenly light up with mirth or deliver the new-found expression with the disguise of solemnity.

A couple of days later, on the 24th of May, I travelled to London again. I took my bicycle on the train because this time the underground was on strike. I felt enterprising and courageous pedalling along in the 'jungle' of London, among buses, lorries, taxis.

My first interlocutor was James Currey, a key figure in your life in London. His stories are full of you arriving in different disguises at the Heinemann offices in Bedford Square, demanding another advance. The Heinemann files, which I would later have access to in their archives in Reading, were full of letters of complaint to him because you had scrounged books or food or whatever else you found handy in people's households; or from a policeman you had punched.

James was a real father figure for you, always supportive, always helping out, enduring your tantrums. He talked about you with much affection. He told me about the time, in 1979, he lent you shoes when the two of you flew to the African Writers Festival in West Berlin; and how, shortly before the plane's departure, you mentioned that you didn't have a passport. I don't know how he did not freak out.

'When you were with Marechera,' he explained, 'all your ordinary middle-class training had to be suspended. So we went into passport control and I showed my passport and said, "Look, this friend of mine wants to get to Berlin." And this chap was quite happy to let him out because, after all, one less black face in these islands, the better ... So we got on our plane and as soon as we were airborne Dambudzo began to knock back the miniature drinks.'

Heinemann was your next of kin in London. When Chris Austin was filming you in your London squat for that eventually aborted *House of Hunger* film, you told him how you had once been picked up on vagrancy charges and had had to fill in a form. On the line that required that you put down your next of kin, you stopped and, as you did not have family in the UK, you asked the officer at the charge office who you should put down.

'Whoever you want informed when you die,' he said.

'Will my publishers do?'

'That's fine.'

That was when you made one of my favourite quips, and James confirmed the story.

Looking straight into the camera with your impish grin, you said: 'Imagine being buried by Heinemann's.'

From Currey I moved on to see Chris Austin. It was rush hour, between 4 and 5, when I found myself cycling through Soho looking for Indigo Productions in Wardour Street, where I was supposed to meet him. Long queues at taxi ranks and bus stops. I felt independent on my bike but inhaling the exhaust fumes from so much traffic was not pleasant. At times, when I was not able to pass the jammed buses, I had to push the bike on the pavement. Those crowds! How can one live here, I wondered.

When I finally found Chris, he was in the middle of editing a film on a singer from Mali and he found it hard to concentrate on his memories of his time with you. For him I was definitely the tax collector – the bad conscience of the white liberal South African. How did it all go wrong in the end, he frowned. He felt that he had failed; regretted that he had not made another attempt, later, to pick up the threads with you and try to complete the film.

After some cool days, we had clear warm weather again. Max and I went on a boat on the Thames and the next day cycled along the river. I had bought him a BMX, after much pleading from his side, and a skateboard, which he and a friend he'd made quickly learned to ride. The riverside was crowded with people watching the finish of a regatta with eights. That night I wrote: 'The English crowds are terrible, and very ugly. And all this sportiness. A strange place.'

Having heard that I was at St Anthony's, a Zimbabwean named George Shire came to attend a seminar I was giving. He claimed to have been a close friend of yours and gave the impression that he had been at Oxford at the same time as you. It turned out that he had left already in 1972. I thought him a real show-off, actually: trying to impress Ranger, calling him out for having no Gramsci in his library, and so on. Conceited too, thinking every woman will go for him. He seemed to assume that I would entertain him, and even that he might spend the night with me. I sidestepped that suggestion, maintaining that I had no spare bed. He said that his publisher, Lawrence and Wishart (had he published anything yet?), was interested in publishing your work. L&W were the Communist Party publisher – they had the rights to Marx and Lenin in England – and were now on the side of the New Left. I must concede that Shire was true to his word on that. He did put me in touch with L&W and I had a meeting with them, and they eventually did their own edition of the *Black Insider*, after we had published it in Zimbabwe. But it remained a one-off, difficult to place in the London literary world of the time. They gave the book a strange postmodern cover.

Yet another trip to London, again with tube strike, again with bicycle. This time my route took me through Hyde Park to Piccadilly Circus, where I was seeing Alastair Niven at the Arts Council. He had been the director of the Africa Centre near Covent Garden where you used to hang out (with Okri and Fraser, among others), and sometimes spent the night. Niven talked very concisely into my Dictaphone recounting his precise memories of you and expressing his great esteem. Regrettably, he said, he had eventually had to ban you from the premises after you had smashed the front windows with some bricks. He seemed less doubtful about the role he had played than some of my other interviewees.

The following Monday I went to see Hans Zell, the Oxford-based publisher of a wide range of information resources on Africa. He talked like sparkling water, his accent revealing his Southern German roots. My visit with him was fruitful. He told me that he had just started a new book series called *Documentary Research in African Literatures*. The first volume was on Ngugi wa Thiong'o, subtitled *A Source Book in Kenyan Literature and Resistance*. Zell thought the results of my tracking your life down would fit perfectly into the series. I was thrilled. So far, I had not even thought of publishing what I was collecting. I found the idea of that type of *Source Book* particularly appealing because I did not want to streamline my findings into the conclusive narrative of a biography. So, I could collate all the various sources I was collecting and unearthing in the form of a documentary biography. It seemed an ideal option, and it had opened up before me quite unexpectedly. So many prospects! So much work – how should I cope with it?

In my remaining time in England, until the end of June, I saw a number of other people, communicated by phone and letter with various others, and did a few more trips outside Oxford. I went to Sussex University to interview Norman Vance. You will remember him, Dambudzo, he was your tutor at Oxford. He was very eager to talk about you, had done so already for half an hour on the phone, and very fondly.

I also went to Reading, where the Heinemann archives were kept. The two files related to your work, *The House of Hunger* and *Black Sunlight*, were an incredible source for 'finding you out', my dear. Your letters from prison in Wales! Superbly written, very funny. Do not growl, I know the time was not funny for you. And the letters shedding some light on your time as writer-in-residence in Sheffield – including the letter from that irate citizen who had let you stay at his flat but then sold your typewriter to buy his books back from the second-hand shop where you had sold them.

And what a wealth of information about works you had written of which I had never heard, and there were readers' reports for these – some very insightful ones – that Heinemann had commissioned: *The Black Heretic*, *A Bowl of Shadows*, and also *The Black Insider*. The tenor of the reports was mostly: This is brilliant work but it needs some revision. But, of course, you never revised. When asked to do so, you wrote a new text. But nothing really seemed to fit into what Heinemann's (or, rather, James Currey's) preconception of what a 'proper novel' should be. In the end

Currey decided to publish the last version of four, *Black Sunlight*.

I was allowed to make photocopies of everything in the files and take them home, so that when I was back in Harare I could reconstruct your writing and publishing history in those years in England after *The House of Hunger*. I used all that information to write my lengthy introduction to *The Black Insider,* which Baobab Books published in 1990 as the first of the three volumes that subsequently appeared without you being able to receive the honours – or the blame. All my attempts to unearth the manuscripts mentioned in the readers' reports were in vain. Where did you leave them, Dambudzo? How did you dispose of them? Or did you tear them up?

I also spent one whole weekend in London. I browsed the *West Africa* volumes of the years you were in London and found some of your pieces. I later published them together with *The Black Insider*.

I saw Peter Harvey, the white Rhodesian who was at University of Rhodesia with you. He saw you again in England but your friendship ended when you blamed him for what his family had done to the blacks in Rhodesia. That's an altercation that sounds familiar. One has to be very broad-minded to accept that you have to say such things, which you do not really mean.

I also strolled around with my camera, taking photos of places that you had known, tracking your traces as the black artist in London. I first went to Tolmer's Square. Tears came into my eyes when I saw the street sign. Dambudzo! That was where your squat was, where you wrote *The Black Insider*. Then to Dillons, your bookshop haunt, and probably where you coaxed many books to leave their shelves and wander away with you. I saw The Marlborough Arms, the pub in which you and many other exiles used to sit, drinking and wallowing in your misery of exile, all of which is expressed in *The Black Insider*.

> Emigrés in a racially colour-conscious country, artificiality came quite easily to both of us. We were talking in English, feeling like hippopotami that have been doped with injections of English culture.

I tried to see Ben Okri. I spoke to him on the phone several times, but he stayed elusive.

My last diary entry, 28th June 1989: 'I am just very exhausted from this work, looking forward to the end.'

Oxford and London gave me insight into the loneliness of the 'black insider' surrounded by hundreds of years of white elitism and into the constant battles of the writer tramp in a city under Thatcherism and violent racism.

In the months that followed, I moved back on the timeline of your life, your childhood in the 'ghetto', your schooling at what was for you the 'haven of St Augustine's' up to the student protests at the University of Rhodesia: your solo demonstration from campus into town, you as one of the ringleaders of the 'pots-and-pans' demonstration who were sent down and had to go into hiding.

Starting from names your brother Michael gave me, I followed clue after clue after clue. I spoke to former classmates, neighbours, teachers and university lecturers, and corresponded with those who had left the country. I found your report cards at St Augustine's, and your richly filled files in the archives of the University of Zimbabwe. Happy coincidences came my way, too, such as my interview with a professor of education at UZ which I did for my PhD research, who, when I mentioned your name, said: 'Wait a minute – what year did he pass his A-levels?' As it turned out she had conducted a questionnaire survey in 1971 – the year you passed your exams – among all secondary school leavers in Rhodesia. When I went to see her a second time, she had found the questionnaire you had filled in and which became a jewel in the mosaic of piecing your life together. I am pretty sure you'll remember it – the typically impertinent responses to some of the questions your admirers have loved you for. Each question gave options, boxes to be ticked and space for answers to be expanded on:

'How does the future look to you?'
'Very dull.'
'Why does the future look that way to you?'
'You ought to know yourself.'

To the question, 'Which person has influenced you most in deciding the kind of life you want?' your answer (*'Nobody'*), again so typical of your rejection of all outside influences on the person you became, flashes my narrative forward to the self-interview you wrote when you were staying with us in 1983. You start the interview with the question: 'Which writers influenced you?' Your answer: 'I find the question oblique, not to the point. It assumes a writer *has* to be influenced by other writers …'

Three years later, when you filled in my own questionnaire which I sent to a great number of Zimbabwean writers for my PhD research, one of my questions was: 'Which teachers influenced you most?' Your – obvious – answer: 'None.' Followed by the comment: 'School teachers had no influences on the writer I now am. Indeed, most of them would be indignant or embarrassed if anyone suggested this.'

Talking to people who had grown up with you, who had seen the kind of life you had lived in your home, your family, your 'house of hunger', was a very different experience from talking to those who had known you in the UK. There were none of the apologetic gestures of those who thought they were treating you as equal but never stopped patronising you.

'We grew up with Charles in Rusape. Charles was one of us,' the Makombe twins, Washington and Wattington, told me. You'd often mentioned the twins. I found them sitting at their desks in the office of the large insurance company they both worked for in Harare, facing each other, both dressed the same and looking very contained. They were happy to talk to me. They told me how, in the slum, the three of you played 'office', made from cardboard boxes.

> We had an old typewriter which we had picked up from the junk heap. And books – from comic strips right up to novels. Our parents were so poor that we had to go around scavenging: to the suburb where the Europeans used to live, to their bins and pick up their trash novels, which we would then read.

The many other childhood friends and neighbours I talked to remembered the pitiful circumstances in which your family lived, especially after your father's horrible death. They noticed how you were shamed by it all, how your moods would change. They let you come and eat at their table; they gave you some warmth and shelter. Once, your best friend's sister told me, you spent the whole of your school holiday at their house.

For all those who knew you then, there was no resentment, no feelings of guilt, only a deep empathy and brotherhood.

'He was one of us.'

The big challenge I still had to face was your family.

What mandate did I have to probe into a family history that seemed veiled in shame?

I did not have yours. I know that. You kept away from your family. You would have warned me against the despondency, the sinister beliefs, the general feeling of abjectness you had shunned after you came back from exile.

But I went. As much as I had to think and speak for you after you kicked the bucket, I am not you, Dambudzo. I have to carry that bucket. I have had to look into its depths.

Michael was the gatekeeper. If I wanted to get to your family, to your roots in the township, I had to go through him. I knew there had been strife between you and so I felt awkward and unsure. As Michael surely felt towards me.

Michael sat beside me on the passenger seat on our long drive to your mother's homestead in Inyanga. 'I am a scientist,' was how he started one of his many roundabout attempts to explain his frame of mind to me. 'I believe in genes, in biological facts. Not in witchcraft.'

I had not even asked a question. What did he think I thought?

He was a natural sciences teacher at Saint Mary Magdalene's Mission School at the far end of the Inyanga mountains. Our plan was to drive there after the visit to your mother.

'But … you know … you are not from here; you don't know our culture … how should I explain …'

Now and then I would turn my head and glance at him. I saw how his facial muscles were straining as he tried to extricate words from somewhere deep in his chest – strings of words, turning and twisting them, swallowing them back down again, gulping at them, chewing on them like on a thick cord, making him gag and splutter.

'How can I put it to you?' was your favourite phrase when you were trying to explain something difficult, and what followed was always lucid and very succinct.

Not so with your brother. It was hard for me to follow his train of thought. It made me think of an injured snake kicking and curling itself around its wounds.

Did he fear I would misunderstand him, that I would underestimate the brilliance of his mind, the rationality of the Natural Sciences teacher?

I stared ahead at the road in front of me, trying to make sense of what he was trying to convey to me about the family curse your mother had

The Tracking

passed on to you.

Stones clinked against the car from underneath as we approached your mother's homestead in the Nyanga district. The sky was clear, the air was dry. It was winter; the 28th of July 1990. To our sides, granite rocks piling up amidst white flecks of earth, shrubs, the occasional tree, leaves dry, goats here and there pulling the last tufts of grass out from the rubble. The road climbed, then dipped, then climbed again. In the distance I could see the ridge of the high mountains rising steeply from the plateau below. How tranquil it all seemed. How serene.

'Turn into there,' Michael motioned to me with this left thumb. Had he already been sipping from a bottle during our drive? His movements seemed rather contorted.

As we branched off onto a stony track more suitable for donkeys or an oxcart than a car, the engine started to stutter.

'You can park here,' Michael said. 'It is not far; we can walk the last couple of metres.'

I don't know what I expected. A village? A compound with several houses, stables, a well? What I found were two small, round, thatched huts, one for cooking, one for sleeping; a shed; a grid for pots. Flattened dry earth around them. A ragged fence made of rough sticks.

I was led into one of the huts. Men were not allowed into that hut, so Michael stayed outside. It was dark inside. In the dimness I could make out Mai Marechera, who was seated on the ground, and four other women. There were a couple of children and some babies. Everyone stared solemnly at the visitor. I was given a stool and invited to sit at one end of the row of women, Amai on the other end.

Your mother agreed to talk to me. Speaking in Shona, her voice low but steady, she would pause every so often so that one of the younger women could interpret. She also agreed that I could record the interview.

We began at the beginning, with her difficult pregnancy and your difficult birth. Finally, at 1 am on the 4th of June 1952, you came into the world. You were still, quiet. At last your mother's pain ebbed away.

There was pride in her eyes, too, when she talked about you, Dambudzo – not only sorrow for the son she had lost. She talked about your desire to learn from as young as five years old, your love of books, how you were chased away from school at first because you were too little, but the mistress gave you the books, because you always wanted books, you always wanted to write – panguva yega yega achingonyora.

She waited while her niece translated in her soft voice and then she said: 'If only my children would learn, if only they would do something which is right.' She was thankful for it, but (asi) then, without lowering or raising her voice, without transition, grief took hold of her words again: asi nhamo – affliction, misfortune, calamity, distress, woe – so deep is the despair in that word. Nhamo. That was what they called your younger brother. 'Hapana … there was nothing.'

Why did I never speak to you about these words, these names which in your language carry so much weight, so much fate?

Asi nhamo ichibva yangozouyawo vachindichengeta vaita vanhu vakura zvino vachibva vangondisiyawo.

Poverty came; when you, her children, had grown into adult men who could have looked after her, just then you abandoned her.

Did she mean that you died? Or was she thinking of the time you left for England and did not even go to bid her farewell? And when you came back, as you had often told me, you did not go to greet her?

Ndakazomuona paakanga akurwara.

She only saw you again when you were ill.

Yes, I know, you often told me that you did not go kumusha after you had come back from exile – I can still hear the contempt in your voice pronouncing that Shona word – going home to the village for ritual cleansing. You loathed it all, their witchcraft, their *tradition*.

'Why did you even go to see her,' I hear you shouting out of your grave. 'She was a slut! Did you want to shame me? Did you want to pose as some kind of Mother Teresa, kneeling down in the dust, venerating their poverty? How obscene!' And again: 'I hope you did not give them any money – that's all they were after.'

In the evening we arrived at Saint Mary Magdalene's, where Michael's wife was expecting us. I felt I was at the furthest end of the country. It was a very long drive on a sandy road, the gravel sparkling red from the setting sun against the range of mountains; a massive glistening ridge, a natural wall stretching along the border to Mozambique. Within minutes, just before we arrived at Michael's house, darkness had fallen.

The next day I drove on, on my own, to meet Nhamo and to see Vengere township, where you had grown up.

I find it hard to evoke a distinct image of your younger brother. In my visual memory I see a cagey animal in front of his burrow, all defence and attack at the same time, ready to run or to hiss and hit.

You did not talk about Nhamo much. Maybe that is why my memory of meeting him remains patchy, blended over by the photos I took on that day, by my notes and what he told me. I do not remember what the arrangement had been. Was he expecting me? And where? My notes of that day at the end of July 1990 tell me that it was an arduous undertaking to track him down.

When I arrived in Vengere township, which seemed very lively, it was a Saturday afternoon, a big Jairos Jiri Fête was taking place at the stadium. Shops were busy, I could see tailors and other tradesmen in dark small rooms. Women were washing clothes in the open at the communal taps. A few market stalls in the main square. Groups of people sitting on the ground, drinking.

As I was looking for your brother and asking around, someone rose from one of the groups and offered to take me to Nhamo's place. He was a constable with the Rusape Police. He joined me in my car and we drove past St Joseph's Mission, along the Lesapi Dam. We arrived at a small place, hardly a village, called Chidukuru, its centre the bottle store. Nhamo had just been there, people told us, and directed us to a road which led further up the hills. The road was so bad that my Passat could hardly make it and every now and then the constable had to get out to guide me over rocks and ridges. Luckily, we made it to the top of the hill where we were rewarded with a replenishing view far onto a plain, a lake glistening in the distance.

My skin is the map
Of a country beyond thought.
These scars results of a broken heart
Whose blood and muscle are the rivers
The valleys, the mountains of Lesapi.

I could feel how in your inner heart you were attached to that landscape, the river, the rocks, the trees, the view from the hills down onto the plain. I can feel the beauty of it in your poems and that magical tale of Protista the Manfish. Your longing for it when 'the scarred hand of exile was dry and deathlike' and you were dreaming of the Lesapi River, where you 'had learned to swim and to lie back into the soft green grass and relax, with my eyes closed and my head ringing with the cawing of the crows and the leisurely moo of cows ...'

But I could also feel the loneliness of the place, the desolation. I could see a few homesteads strewn across the plain, far apart. Dry grass, stones, some cattle. It was here that your family had withdrawn to around 1975, when you were already in the UK; it was here that your younger brother still lived. Surely you could not have lived here when you returned.

By now my quest started to feel almost absurd, like from one of your stories. Where was Nhamo? Yet my guide seemed unperturbed and, indeed, we then met a man on a bicycle, acquainted to the constable. He seemed to know exactly where we had to go and he preceded us on his bicycle. Eventually he motioned us to leave the car by the wall of a farm and another guide, our last, as it turned out, appeared. This was a young boy and it was he who showed us the way to Nhamo's place.

My heart constricted. The boy pointed at a kind of shed hidden behind a rock, with baboons jumping around, looking for something edible in the rubbish. There, he motioned – that is where Nhamo lives. A low brick construction with a corrugated-iron sheet, so small that it could hardly fit more than one person, a door and a window, dark shutters, all closed. The habitat of a recluse. But the recluse was not there.

I felt myself tensing up, distressed by the desolate feel of the place and the elusiveness of your brother. Would I ever find him? But I did. At the bottle store. In *House of Hunger* the bottle store is where the protagonist finds an anchor amidst the despondency around him and in his heart. When we started the steep and cumbersome drive back down the road people kept waving at us, indicating that Nhamo was at the bottle store. They had told him that we were looking for him and there he was, waiting for us. I saw a short man, his expression stern, dressed in a long beige trench-coat with marks of black grease on it. Your little brother. I felt unsure about how to approach him.

I bought him a bucket of chibuku, that frothy opaque local beer that people drink from those huge plastic containers, and he seemed to lose some of his tension. He got into the car beside me and we drove back up the hill.

I can still see him standing there, Dambudzo, in front of his burrow, in front of this poor habitation, a floppy hat shielding parts of his face from view, two front teeth missing, giving him something of a sinister look. His short body crooked, an invalid, an ex-combatant full of resentment against the world that had treated him badly.

And yet he seemed pleased that I had come to meet him and let me talk to him. He told me how you, eight years his senior, had been a tyrant regarding schoolwork, had beaten him several times when he had not worked hard enough or done something wrong.

A disciplinarian to your younger siblings, that is also what your youngest sister Florence would mention years later. You wanted them to get out of the bleakness of their childhood, as you had done.

Yet Nhamo's life narrative was different from yours. So much younger than you, he was a small child when your father died and your mother and her children were evicted from their house in the township. Nhamo grew up in the slum, in the real shanty town. He was still a schoolboy when he joined the guerrillas; he was wounded, and then he was at the front again. In 1980 he joined the National Army but was demobilised after two years; the allowance he got as a veteran was intermittent and very small. Since then he had been mostly unemployed, sharing the bitterness and poverty of so many other ex-combatants of the time.

Nhamo your parents had named him – tribulation, severe affliction. Was he the underdog, the shameful existence which in yourself you had always hated? Which in your writing you had fought against and tried so hard, again and again, to vanquish?

In the remaining years of our stay in Harare I divided my time between editing two more volumes of your work – always in consultation with my co-trustee Hugh Lewin – completing the biographical research, and completing my PhD thesis, which I defended in Frankfurt in May 1991. In 1992, I published and launched it in Harare: *Teachers, Preachers, Non-Believers – A Social History of Zimbabwean Literature.* In later years one of the professors at the English Department of UZ reported to me, with some glee, that students had been discredited from an exam because they had plagiarised my book. With all the flaws it certainly had, it was still regarded as canonical; there was just so little critical work in the field yet.

In the same year, Hans Zell published your, let me call it, mausoleum, my *Source Book* on your life and work. It was so heavy in weight (and in British pounds) that we had a much cheaper local edition done by the University of Zimbabwe Publications Office. The 1 000 copies sold out within one year, so eager was everyone to know more about the scandal-maker who had died so young.

The *Source Book* does contain real treasures. I enjoyed putting all the sources together; it was fun letting you shine and whine through all the extraordinary eyewitness accounts, letters, photographs and numerous other documents. It has become the 'bible' of all Marechera research.

Also in that year we launched *Cemetery of Mind*, which was followed two years later, when I had already left the country, by *Scrapiron Blues*. All three were published by Baobab Books, each carrying one of my portraits of you on its cover, the pictures I had taken during that ill-fated excursion to Lake MacIlwaine.

So, in a way, I could say: Mission accomplished. I had fulfilled my task. Three volumes more of your work were now out in the world, and many aspects of your life were also there for readers to peruse. Had I manhandled you – or, in proper gendered language: woman-handled you?

My efforts received much praise.

You would have been exalted to know that in 1996 Soyinka chose *Scrapiron Blues* as his 'book of the year'. While hailing you as 'a profound even if exaggeratedly self-aware writer ... in constant quest for his real self', he commended me, your executor, for preserving and publishing your work – 'an invaluable service to African literature'.

There were also objections and misgivings. Some of these were expressed in the open, but most of them silently. Why had I published some pieces but left out others? Was that not a form of editorial censorship? Was my way of putting various pieces of your creative remains together, taking apart others, introducing each volume with editorial and biographical comments – who was I to do this? Would my work as your biographer, editor and literary executor proscribe how you would henceforth be seen, be looked at, understood?

Others accused me of making money and a name out of appropriating you – to which I can only quote your words in that short poem 'Pub Conversation':

> *My name is not money*
>   *But Mind.*

The truth is, I did it all as best I could, with all the flaws and biases I, as a person, certainly have.

More importantly, however: When I had finished my work, I handed over all your original unedited manuscripts and all other complete unedited versions of all interviews and other sources I had collected, sorted neatly into 20 pink folders, to the National Archives of Zimbabwe.

A notice in *Horizon Magazine* of February 1993 wrote about the ceremony of donation:

> It was a curiously formal occasion. The German Ambassador was there, so were bespectacled academics and earnest research students. But when Flora Veit-Wild handed over the Dambudzo Marechera Archive, an extensive collection of the writer's original manuscripts, letters, taped interviews and videos, to the Director of the National Archive of Zimbabwe she acknowledged the irony.
>
> 'Dambudzo would vehemently protest against this mummification,' she said. 'But for the sake of future research it is important that primary and secondary sources on his life and work are deposited here.'
>
> The Marechera Archive ... is an intriguing chronicle of a man whose life was as contradictory as his fiction. Now members of the public will have the chance to see for themselves the writer's letters to his long-suffering friends and publishers and the scruffy notebooks where he jotted down observations about Harare's shebeens.

Immersing myself, over the years, in your writings, as editor, scholar, teacher; visiting places where you had been, tracking down people you had known, I think I got closer to you, Dambudzo, than I ever was while you were here in person. I understood much more the ghosts that haunted you, the eerie beauty of each of your images, lines, sentences, and the intellectual and political depth in the way you laid bare the farcical faces of those in power, showing the emperor without clothes.

It was an exciting and a daunting journey into the life and work of the 'black heretic'. At times I felt overwhelmed by the effort of it, at others thrilled by the miracles I unearthed. I felt so many things, Dambudzo: grateful, gratified, inadequate and, indeed, full of love.

Yet I had a price to pay.

The Moment of Terror

WHEN I WAKE UP IN THE MORNING, there is this moment of terror. That is what I call it. Terror of another day that has to be lived, to be lived up to.

It is like molten lead is sprawling through my veins. The crisis of the in-between. The anxiety, the angst of the living creature. I am alive, hence I must stand up for myself, must act, I must – There is no way back into the sheltering womb.

This is how I have felt many times.

The feeling has no name. But it has a colour and a texture.

It is a thick foil of fog clinging around me, tight, suffocating. Sticky foggy grey, black-spotted hyenas howling from afar. Opaque.

Sometimes it is a crow with large wings and a terrible croak circling above me, its shadow noiseless but haunting. At other times there is an iron ring around my heart. I am stuck. I can't move. The brain is cramped, the heart yells for help.

Or it is a Kraken, threatening to strangle me. Like the hovering crow. I try to duck away but its tentacles are too large, I can't escape. Trapped. Forever. No fire escape. The trauma of my youth, my childhood – the boa constrictor of my father around my neck: Don't talk if it is not meaningful. Children are not yet human beings. They have to listen and only speak when they are asked.

He is long dead. But the ugly Kraken remains, crawling out of his grave. Grabbing me, crawling over my body, my soul. Creepily. Kraken – crow – Krähe. The kr-sound – clenching your teeth to go on, no rest, to soldier on, no matter what, unseeing, not minding the cold, the heat.

Carnival and Cockroaches – The Appointment

A CIVIL SERVANT OF THE GERMAN state not only has to be a loyal citizen but also a citizen in good health. Hence before my appointment as a professor at Humboldt University I had to testify, in a personal details form, that I was politically and medically worthy and fit to become a civil servant for life.

The one part I could answer truthfully; for the other I had to lie.

Ironically, I did not have to lie about my political past. The Berlin senate, almost identical to the former senate of West Berlin, did not care about former Maoists or other 'enemies of the state' of West German provenance – all they were paranoid about were the 'communists' of the former GDR. No problem with that for me. The type of Marxist-Leninist organisations to which I had belonged were anti-authoritarian in their origins and as opposed to the authoritarian regime of the GDR as to 'Western capitalism and its state lackeys'. While the West German authorities had spied on us in the 1970s and barred us from their civil service as so-called 'radicals', this was of no interest anymore in the 1990s. The main enemy now was the former Stasi.

I had to lie on the medical side, or rather, tick a 'no' instead of a 'yes' where asked if I was suffering from any infectious diseases such as HIV.

When years later I enquired from the Berlin AIDS council if this false reply might have been reason to dismiss me, I was told: No, the question itself was illegitimate. And the status of being HIV positive is not an illness.

Indeed, I was not ill and did not feel ill at the time. And yet it was unfathomable on that day, when I sat at that desk at Human Resources of HU, this awe-inspiring institution, filling in that ominous questionnaire, that I would last the eighteen years to my retirement.

There was another twist of historical irony on my way to becoming a Humboldt professor. I was initially number two on the shortlist for the position. Number one was a colleague from the East, who had been for many years professor of African literature at the University of Leipzig. He was a renowned scholar among East European Africanists and a specialist in Swahili literature. He must have been the obvious choice for the committee, which consisted in the majority of staff from the old Humboldt University department.

My own presentation at the short hearing before the committee to which I had been invited in 1992, when we still resided in Harare, in which I delved into questions of hybridity in post-colonial literature, had apparently not impressed most committee members.

'Do you speak an African language?' I was asked.

'No,' I replied, not disputing, as I would do in later years, whether English and French were not also to be considered, by now, languages of Africa.

The fact of the matter was that I was a no-name. I had no university experience. I came straight 'from the bush', so to speak.

Yet historical luck was on my side. Eventually, after a long time of uncertainty and waiting, I heard that the Berlin government had not appointed the colleague from Leipzig. He had been sacked from his post there shortly after German unification, when all East German university staff were screened for their former political alliances and functions. He had, or so I heard, 'dirt under his carpet'; he was somehow politically implicated.

So the question arose: Would they now appoint me, the number two on the shortlist?

The problem was that I did not have what was normally required as prerequisite for becoming a professor at a German university, a *habilitation*. This is a kind of second doctoral degree based on a book publication in a different thematic area from your first PhD thesis. I, of course, did not have such higher academic anointment; I had just passed my PhD three years before, had never planned on joining the ranks of professorship and really felt hardly equipped to fill a position that seemed so much charged with scholarly grandiosity.

Yet it was a time where miracles happened; a time of eruptions, of quick changes, of turns of history nobody would have expected.

Victor and I spent a hiking holiday in September of 1989 in the Steiermark, a south-eastern province of Austria, bordering on what was then Yugoslavia. As we were sitting in a garden restaurant in the golden rays of a beautiful Indian summer, eating Apfelstrudel or tasting the exquisite wine of the region – our hikes had taken us through vineyards bursting with delicious grapes – within this setting of serene tranquillity we heard that not far from us there were 'leaks', holes, in the borders. Borders which for decades had been known as the Iron Curtain, closing the East from the West, were slowly being dismantled, bit by bit, step by step in the literal sense: People from Yugoslavia were cutting holes in fences and crossing over into neighbouring Hungary and from there into Austria. A few weeks before, the Hungarian government had officially opened the border. The pressure was mounting rapidly. More and more Germans from the GDR fled into Hungary and demanded to be let into the West.

We could hardly believe it. Two months later, in Harare, ears glued to a small transistor radio, we heard the news: The Wall is down.

It was in that climate of walls crumbling, of borders dissolving, that the iron walls within institutions began to slacken as well. Humboldt University, situated in Berlin's historical centre, close to the Brandenburg Gate, on its Eastern side, was rumbling with trenchant change. Many of the Old Guard had to go; many new heads were seen. A member of the Green Party, a woman, became university president.

In this crucible that was Humboldt in the early 1990s an unconventional decision was taken, allowing me, an academic outsider, entry into the venerable institution. Two external reviewers were asked to consider the body of my academic work in order to assess if it was equivalent to the degree of *habilitation*. They did and they agreed that it was. It was my comprehensive work on Dambudzo Marechera, the 'Black Insider' who called himself 'an outsider in my own biography, in my country's history' that allowed them to acknowledge me as a fully fledged academic persona.

I had almost given up hope, had started looking for other options of employment, when, in late April 1994, the letter of my appointment for September that year arrived.

Had it not been for you, Dambudzo, my irreverent, spiteful friend and mentor, had you not appointed me to execute your unwritten will, it would not have happened. I would not have become a person of such reverence as was the Humboldt professor of African literature.

On 27 September 1994 I was ordained. On 1 October my service started and lasted until 30 September 2012, the official date for my retirement.

'Karneval und Kakerlaken'– 'Carnival and Cockroaches' – I entitled my inaugural lecture. I dedicated the lecture to you, Dambudzo Marechera, 'who taught me that nothing is whole or holy, least of all African literature'.

The Lady in Black

'Depression is like a lady in black. If she turns up, don't shoo her away. Invite her in, offer her a seat, treat her like a guest and listen to what she wants to say.'

CG Jung

A YEAR AFTER I HAD STARTED MY position and work as a professor I cracked.

I had my first bout of clinical depression.

The Lady in Black made her appearance.

It was August 1995. I was sitting at my desk, notes from a recent trip to Johannesburg in front of me. I wanted to prepare a course on South African literature for the next semester. I also wanted to write an essay with my impressions of the new voices on the literary scene after the end of apartheid.

I could not concentrate. I could not read. I could not write. I could not think. Everything was blurred. With every day, with every hour, it got worse. I found myself sinking deeper and deeper into a void. It was unstoppable. It was frightening. It was like shooting down into a bottomless hole, in an elevator whose cables have snapped.

I paced around my room. I beat my fists against the wall. I felt besieged by a hammering inside me driving me mad. At night I could hardly sleep.

I woke up at four or five, feeling clamped in a vice, a jackhammer inside me going 'bumpbumpbump'.

'Help me!' I screamed. 'I cannot go on like this.'

Victor was by my side. But what could he do?

The Kraken had me in his claws.

That is how I remember the beginning. The helplessness, the agitation, the drowning. And not knowing why.

Six weeks in a psychiatric hospital.

Where does it come from, I wanted to know.

What makes you feel like this, the doctors asked. Is it your medical condition with HIV? Are you afraid of getting ill, of dying?

No, I am not. I have lived with the virus for many years. I have been well; I have felt strong. I am not afraid. I am a fighter. But it has all been too much. I am exhausted.

My life needed a pause, a time of stillness and mourning. It all had been too fast. Our return to Germany two years before. Then, another blow and loss: my mother fell into a coma after a hip operation. She lived on for five months. I was with her, looked after her until she died. She had just turned 80. She had been youthful and full of life.

Not even a year later, our move to Berlin, my appointment, my inauguration.

It had been intense. It had been fast. After years of striving and strife, life had propelled me forward to a position that seemed overpowering.

'The only thing I am afraid of,' I whimpered when the doctors asked me, 'is that I won't be able to do my job.'

Years of psychotherapy and of medication followed. I learned to do my job. I learned to be a professor. I learned to plan courses, to teach, to lecture, to be 'an authority'. I learned to give seminars on Dambudzo Marechera, to take on my public persona as expert on this unusual, 'un-African' writer, and inwardly wink at my other self, the woman who had loved him, had seen him die and had been threatened by death herself.

I also learned to live with the visits from the Lady in Black. And learned to listen to her. At some point I gave her a body I could talk to or scold or throw against the wall: a gestalt, made of fabric, cardboard, wire, ribbons and beads. She is still there by my bedside, the black now faded. She became the first, the ur-mutter of my puppets which from then on I made with my hands.

'Each book I write is part of myself,' is how I opened my book *Writing Madness – Borderlines of the Body in African Literature*, published many years later. And so are the dolls, the puppets – different effigies of my own self.

Lucy in the Sky came to life when a colleague of mine was dying.

We had been close allies in rebuilding the Department of African Studies at HU, he as the professor of African history, me in literature. Shaped by the same movements of our generation, he in Switzerland, I in West Germany, the marches against the Vietnam war, against apartheid, for peace, for a wholesome world, free spirits who would pronounce what they were thinking, we were eyed with some wariness if not resentment by colleagues and staff from the old GDR university.

'Ah, you are bringing yourself,' he said, when in March 2003 I came to bid him farewell. Preparing himself for death, he and his wife had returned to their flat near Zurich.

Lucy in the Sky – as with all her companions, she only made her name known to me once she had emerged from my hands – floated along by my side as I entered the flat. She was wearing a floral gown, a leftover of the same dress I was wearing on that day. Her hair, frizzy, a shrill pink around her white face with red beaded eyes, gave her a facetious air.

It was a beautifully mild early spring day, serene, as was my colleague himself, who knew he had only a few weeks to live. We sat on the balcony looking down on Lake Zurich, a shimmering grey-blue. I could see his spirit putting on wings and together with Lucy floating upwards ever so lightly into the sky. Was it a piece of my own life that was vanishing into the ether? I was left behind, alive.

When, a couple of weeks later, in Berlin, we held a memorial for our departed colleague, I put the Beatles song on. Cheerful and mournful, it had also been part of his youth.

'But she looks just like you!' Max exclaimed on the phone from New York.

He had just unpacked the airmail parcel I had sent him for his 30th birthday. It was elf-like Eliza, in pastel colours, light as a feather, a lacy scarf around her head, beads around her neck, a golden brooch on her breast; a free-floating cloak, multi-coloured, translucent, a touch of glamour. I had felt as light-hearted and joyous when, in a small plane above Madagascar, Max made me listen to his first composition, 'Zambezi Sunset'. Eliza – it was the sound that signalled her name.

Once I had started my fairytale puppets, I became a scavenger. I collected scraps of fabric from tailors, fashion designers and African markets; beads, pins, buttons, ribbons, trash jewellery, from wherever I was. A box with 'trick objects', squibs and miniature toys surviving from my sons' childhood years were a rich source. Some years on, after a visit to the Paul Klee Centre in Berne and seeing the bulbs and burned-out fuses Klee had used for some of his puppets, I collected a heap of electrical scraps from my electrician's workshop and also used them for my creatures.

Kunigunde is staring at me right now, with her one oversize Cyclops eye. At 75 centimetres she is the tallest of them all; and the fiercest. A woman of strength, she has four arms. From three of them a stone dangles, the fourth, stretched out high, wrapped in bright red cloth, holds what looks like a gun – it is in fact an electrical voltage tester, with a long spiky tip sticking out. The yellow cable is twined round her body, the other tip pointing downwards to the earth. Her hair, fiery orange wool, falls down her back in a thick tail, topped by what could be a hangman's rope. A pearl earring on one side and a blue heart of glass pinned to her breast, she looks like a cross between a warrior and a pirate. The black-and-red striped neck-scarf marking her fighter figure is fancifully matched by the Mexican cloth belt running from her waist down to the bottom.

'Hello there, I am Kunigunde,' she said when, jumping out of my bed in the middle of the night, I had assembled her, out of an impulse, feeling so irked and burdened by the heavy load of two men in my life. Kunigunde – Teutonic strength is what her name emanates: 'We can handle you.'

'Tod der Mütter' (death of the mothers), a double-headed figure, fragile and wobbly, consists of a body of mashed wire mounted on a dented lid of a can of paint. Clothed scantily with flimsy rags, she was spurred on by my mother-in-law's death. At 94 she died much later than my own mother but with her death I felt another mother had passed on, and so I mourned 'my mothers' in the plural form. Including, as the puppet showed me, my grandmother. The two faces, which I had sculpted in plaster, were very dissimilar. One round like a ball, her eyes staring motionless, her head topped by a cylinder-shaped bulb, a silver-clad wire dangling from one oversize ear; the other one, which I had moulded while looking at a photo of my mother-in-law, emerged, to my great surprise, with the exact features of my long-dead maternal grandmother, whose dress I had worn for my wedding: the long face, the nose, the grey hair and the pearls in her ears. I was so moved when I recognised her, gazing at me with mild melancholy eyes. Images of her in the last years of her life emerged, half-blind, skittering across the street, her walking stick feeling the ground ahead. People turning their heads, greeting her politely. 'Ach, der alte Nazi,' she would mutter under her breath, once we had passed, remembering the time she had been spat at by the Nazi mob.

Here she was, reappearing under my hands.

A necklace of dead fuses dangled from the two heads. Lives bygone. A little bell jingling at my grandmother's scarf, a bright red cravat around the other mother's neck, uncut; the female bloodline flowing into the ground towards me. I could feel the pain my mothers had gone through in my own body. And yet they had given me a life to live.

The puppets also possess magical qualities. Once Franz was over in Berlin at Easter time. I made a little Easter bunny for him, in white satin, the long upright ears a faint pink; tiny round pin heads, also white and pink, as eyes, a bowtie and pink ribbon around its neck; and at the back, as tail, a bell. The bunny was feathery light and when you picked it up, it tinkled. A cute little darling for my darling son.

'Take it with you,' I said, 'as your talisman. As long as you carry it close to yourself you will be safe.' By then he had started to work as a journalist in the Congo.

'No,' he replied, 'with all my travels, it might get lost. It is better you keep it here for me.'

'All right,' I said, 'I will. As long as I see both its ears standing up, I will know you are safe. The moment one ear droops, I will know you are in danger.'

Both ears are still standing up firmly.

Several years later another doll appeared which seemed destined for Franz. The figure is standing stately in a mass of sumptuous African cloth, dark green with golden ornaments. The head is round, the face brown, the eyes, tunnelled beads, are staring into nowhere; the open mouth, thick-lipped and red. A dummy, daft, asinine. Yet, from his jewelled neck, a long golden chain runs over his breast down to where his feet would be, and, dangling from it, hardly visible against the leopard patterned shawl, a tiny gun (found object from my sons' toy box).

'Oh, monsieur, who are you?' I said when I saw him standing in front of me.

He refused to introduce himself, just his bland stare.

Okay, no answer, I said to myself, and, alerted by the mingling of gown, gold and gun in the man's style, I called him 'Power to the People'. Though with the animal skin on his head, folded into a garrison cap, he could not deny his resemblance to one of his kind, the renowned Mobutu Sese Seko, on whose former territory my son was now reporting about warriors of these days fighting for power to the people – or so it seemed.

Once they knew I might use them for making puppets, people started sending me bits and pieces of all sorts. Another puppet with powerful magic was 'Madame Minou', a cat that came crawling out of the patches of brocade an elderly cousin of mine had sent me. The brocade, stiff, ornamental and of a noble golden colour, became the body, and on top a head of white silk covering a bunch of crunched paper. The head had pointed ears and a little protruding nose, which clearly told me: 'I am a cat.'

The face acquired oval sequins for eyes, beaded embroidery along the ears and upward pointing whiskers (tiny pink beads on wire). With a broad pink collar around her neck, a rose attached to her breast and an upwards-curling brocade tail at her back, she looked at me with a pleasantly proud mien.

'Madame Minou will be your name,' I told her, having recently learned that the French call their cats 'Minou'.

Off she went, neatly boxed, to my cousin, who, with great surprise, unpacked her brocade curtains transformed into an adorable companion. Up to this day Madame Minou sits, very upright and dignified, in my cousin's drawing room, feeling quite at home on the rococo sofa and among cushions of similar make as her own bodice, holding polite conversation with elderly ladies over tea and scones.

Madame Minou's magic powers, however, only made themselves known a couple of years later. This was when I had decided to get a real-life cat as a companion. I found one through a classified from a couple whose two cats had not been much amused by the addition of a baby to the family. I took the very handsome, shiny-haired female, and the name she came with was Minou. Since then the real Minou is the cosiest part of my life at seventy.

Many people who saw my puppets proclaimed that they must have been inspired by my connection with Africa. I do not feel they are, apart from the general penchant in cultures all over the world – including Africa – to ban threatening emotions by giving them a figural shape: dolls, masks and the like. Apart from that some of my dolls happen to be clad in African print – when Max saw Kunigunde for the first time, he exclaimed: 'Hey, she is wearing my shorts!' I had used some faded leftovers from the Zimbabaloo pants he had worn as a boy in Zimbabwe.

One of my puppets, however, a prominent and stately one, demanded to be called 'Mother Africa'.

Seventy centimetres high, her spine is formed by a thick metal pipe on a heavy base, her head of milky wrapping paper crunched into a ball, topped by a snippet of Kente cloth. It is her eyes that give her a fierce and yet ludicrous look: one a big green African glass bead; the other a sardonic joke from my children's trick box: a glowing cigarette butt fixed onto a round, black, orange-ringed patch. It was a gag the boys loved to use on innocent guests who were smokers. They'd surreptitiously sneak it onto the table in front of the guest who, oblivious, was smoking and chatting to the others. Seeing the patch, the guest would instantly get a fright, thinking they had burned a hole into the tablecloth with their cigarette – the boys would thoroughly enjoy the reaction.

In Mother Africa's face, this former joke article gave her a somewhat haunted and haunting gaze – mysterious and preposterous at the same time, as was her figure as a whole. All sorts of found objects were attached to her spine. She had a belt of firecrackers around her waist, a bell dangling from her neck and, further down, bulging from a hole in the pipe, a red rubber bulb, a sort of hand-pump, which looked like the womb hanging outside the woman's body (some people seemed to recognise male genitals). A stiff mantle of coarse netted flax surrounded the whole figure and all its accessories. Finally, I attached several Zimbabwean dollar notes on its outside, millions and billions, which I had kept from the time of that crazy devaluation of currency in the 2000s.

What a sinister spectacle of an African bride!

Like all the others, Mother Africa had not been premeditated but emerged from my probing, playful fingers. Yet, once out in the world, she gave cause to some learned 'readings'. An Italian scholar chose a detail of a photo of the puppet for the cover of her book *Afro-Europe*. This is what she put into her acknowledgments:

This image, I believe, beautifully conveys the proximity and interdependence of the two continents of Europe and Africa. The smaller doll [one of the found objects] rests on the shoulder of the bigger one, her balance completely depending on the stability of the sustaining body, and yet she looks elsewhere, like a defiant and ungrateful daughter. By reversing the North-South positioning and by restoring Africa's heterogeneity and richness through the asymmetric and vivid visage of the bigger doll, this image proposes a new cartography which challenges Eurocentric iconographies and provides an unusually truthful representation of the geo-political order.

Hear, hear!

For many years, Mother Africa had an honorary place in my university office. Statuesque and bold, she stood on her pedestal in a corner, winking with her cigarette butt at whoever came in to discuss the role of women in African literature.

Unlike my brother, who had been suicidal, I always fought against the Kraken.

I fought for life.

'How are you feeling?' the chief psychiatrist asked when I came for a consultation after I had been released from hospital.

'I want to *live*,' I replied.

'But are you not living?'

'No, I feel dead.'

'I hate death,' my friend had exclaimed hearing about the death of my father. And yet he had always been on the brink of it, had looked into the abyss of annihilation, had tried to ward it off through his writing. He had explored the 'black sunlight', the explosive energy of life that can tear you apart.

Was this what had attracted me to Dambudzo? Had he conjured forces that lay dormant in me? Had I while being with him fought against being swallowed by them? Had my shield now given up on me and cracked? Could I now finally let go and mourn the deaths of those close to me, the losses my life had endured within a short time? My father, my mother, Dambudzo, and my own unborn child?

The Valley of Death or: Busting the Kraken

THE KRAKEN HAD MANY FACES.

It was the ugly virus that was creeping through my veins.

It was the dark cloud of depression that kept eclipsing the sun.

It finally twisted its cancerous tentacles into my guts and my lymphoid system. I fell prone to a lymphoma.

Towards the end of the 1990s my life in Berlin was solidifying. The once life-threatening virus had been 'caged in'. New antiretroviral drugs had been developed. They did not eradicate the virus from the blood, but drastically diminished its population. Every day I now swallowed what is euphemistically called 'a cocktail' of pills. Many colours, many forms, many sizes – I did not really mind, I knew the threat was banned.

Yet, the new drugs had heavy side effects.

I developed what was called a 'buffalo hump', a thick layer of fat that had accumulated at the root of my neck. I discovered it one day when I felt stiff in the neck and asked Max to massage my back.

'Mama, you have a hump,' he cried out. I had not noticed it before.

Lipodystrophy, a disorder of fat distribution under your skin, was one of the side-effects medical science had not foreseen. It was a gradual process. I had not at first noticed how my bodily features changed. While the hump on my back was growing, my cheeks were becoming hollow – they lost their under-skin bolster. My calves also lost their fat, you could see the veins protrude under the skin.

I had to undergo surgery, three times altogether, to diminish the hump – yet my neck never got as slender as it used to be. My cheeks did not fill up again.

Defeating the virus came with a price.

I will have to conclude my story with a last mythical tale: My descent into the Valley of Death.

In November 2001 my brother took his own life. He was 52. It was not a cry for help as on earlier occasions. He did it after careful consideration and preparation by injecting himself with an overdose of insulin.

Extended phases of severe depression had made it impossible for him to continue his professional life as a doctor. After splitting up from his wife, he had started his own practice but eventually went into early retirement, claiming 'occupational invalidity'.

It was a momentary relief. He was no longer under pressure to be in his rooms every morning, talking to patients, trying to cure their illness, when he himself felt utterly miserable. But the uplift did not last. A phase of extreme manic elation was followed by the steep downfall into weeks and months of depression. Feelings of guilt, of hopelessness, and the prospect of spending the rest of his life in the company of other incapacitated people made him read up on the philosophical question of Freitod (voluntary death).

When I received the news, I was shaken. I could understand his decision, which he had explained in letters to his partner and his two sons, but still, I was struck by the tragic irony: my brother, who had been the Grim Reaper's messenger fifteen years earlier, delivering the 'verdict' to me and my husband – 'Positive, you are both positive' – departed and we lived.

At the time that he was preparing his death, he knew that his initial pessimism had been proved wrong: The prospects for HIV patients in our part of the world had vastly improved.

What he did not know was that I almost followed him. On the night that I received the news of his death I myself was already very ill.

A non-Hodgkin lymphoma was forming in my colon. This is a very aggressive and fast-growing cancer of the lymph system. If not stopped, it would kill me in a short space of time. There had been symptoms in the last couple of weeks, loss of weight and acute states of exhaustion, but I had attributed them to the exertion around my brother's death. I only noticed the blockage in my guts when no food could pass through anymore.

One night in January 2002, after a meal at a friend's house, my stomach was cramping as I had never experienced it before. When I called an emergency doctor, he sent me straight into hospital.

'I cannot give an exact diagnosis,' he said after feeling my abdomen, 'but you need immediate clinical examinations.'

What did I think at that moment? Was I worried?

Victor still lived close by in another part of our flat. When we had come to Berlin, we had designed the rooftop of a building together so that we each had our own flat connected by a bridge. By then, our lives had moved apart and we had agreed to separate. This did not mean that we did not care for each other and give support whenever it was needed. But Victor was out that night. He only heard my anxious messages, my cries for help, on his answerphone the next morning.

Numerous medical examinations followed.

'Can you see that lump there?' the physician said, pointing with the flash on the monitor to something fuzzy. I was lying on my side, undergoing my first colonoscopy – many more were to come in the next couples of months and, at decreasing intervals, throughout the five years after my chemotherapy. It is a very painful procedure and yet I found it amazing to follow on the screen what the camera lens was projecting from within the depths of my body. I felt less helpless being able to see what the examining doctor saw, as he guided the thick tube with a flash showing the way through my intestines, like a single headlight of a train in a tunnel. I saw how this train was furrowing its way around three corners – the colon is rectangular, and getting the tube around the bends are the most painful bits of the procedure – illuminating my inner corridors, which looked thick and pale and caved in like subterranean catacombs.

It filled me with awe.

I was reminded of my first epiphany of such sort decades earlier, though not painful and under quite different auspices, when I used a speculum to watch the slime over my cervix. Franz's conception had been 'inspeculated' in that way.

Was it ironic that I was thinking of my previous physical introspection at that moment when I was not begetting life but rather tracking down what eventually could become an agent of death?

Another sharp pain. I winced, emitting a squeal, as the gastroenterologist manoeuvred the endoscope around another bend.

'Gosh, look at this,' he said, turning to his assistant. The camera light was now illuminating the upper section of my colon.

'Do you see this?' he said, addressing me this time. 'It looks like a cauliflower? No wonder you cannot process food anymore. Your colon is completely blocked.'

I tried to focus my attention on the monitor, away from the pain. The image flickered but, yes, I could recognise something, a huge amorphous shape, pale like the surroundings, with a fuzzy outline. It looked gruesome.

'What is it?' I asked.

'Well, we are taking samples and sending them to Histology. They will tell us what it is. But it is certainly big. The scale on the monitor shows us that it measures twenty centimetres.'

'An eccentric growth on the skin of my country.'

As ever, and as so often happens, a Marechera line emerges from my mind when I think back to that moment. An eccentric growth had flowered inside my intestine, a cancerous growth, as it turned out, another Kraken to fight against.

I felt numb. But I was glad they had found something, however terrifying it looked.

Studying my innermost catacombs also took me back to the moment when I had gone to see my brother for the last time. The mortuary attendant had unlocked the door for me, leading to what I remember as a long cellar-like corridor with small nooks branching off.

'Are you sure you want to see him?' he asked.

'Yes, that is what I want.'

There was nobody else around. It must have been late in the day. I entered into what really felt like the Underworld: it was sombre and cold, dead bodies behind closed doors. One door was open. One glance and I yelled out loud, wailed, howled. 'No!'

The attendant waiting for me at the entrance will have heard, maybe even expected, my cry – was he used to it? It definitely was not a good place to let relatives have a last look at the body of a beloved person. It had been so different with my father and with my mother. My mother had looked very beautiful and at peace. But the sight of my brother was terrifying.

I stood at his feet. He looked so much taller and thinner than he had been, his face hollow, the nose sharp, the lips showing a similarity with my maternal uncles that had not been there before. Like Frankenstein, I thought, clutching my bag, biting my lips.

What would he have thought if he had known that I might shortly be following him?

Again, as almost fifteen years before when we were waiting for the results of the HIV test, the period of waiting was the most trying.

The histological findings of the colonoscopy had been unclear, so it had to be repeated. This time I chose to have anaesthetics.

More waiting.

Finally, my doctor phoned me. The diagnosis had been confirmed.

'It is a non-Hodgkin lymphoma,' he said. 'There is a prevalence of this type of cancer among HIV-positive patients even though their immune system, thanks to effective antiretroviral medication, seems intact. There is no explanation for it. A very trying time lies ahead of you. You will have to undergo chemotherapy. However, the good news is that this particular type of lymphoid cancer is, if the chemo works, curable. Once it is out of your body, it will not recur. It does not lie dormant. It does not form metastases, as other forms of cancer do.'

My doctor's words reassured me. I trusted him and his belief in me to overcome the illness.

Bastard Death and his horrid adjunct, the Kraken, had again reached out for me. When we buried my brother, I was about to follow him.

Yet I was able to escape. I was able to emerge from the Valley of Death.

I busted the Kraken.

Out of the Closet

THIS, DAMBUDZO, HAS BEEN MY life since you departed. Some of my life.

The boys grew up, bright and strong. They finished their schooling in Berlin, bilingual in English and German. After passing their German Abitur they both went to university in the UK, Max also later in New York. They have German passports but Germany is not their home. Their hearts remain in Africa.

Victor and I eventually went our separate ways and divorced. After our return from Zimbabwe our lives drifted apart. So did the narratives of our lives. I cannot speak for him. I can only speak for myself.

As I am writing, I am approaching my 70th birthday, bringing my lifetime to doubling yours. I mean yours in body and flesh, skin and bones. Your spiritual life has not ended. I have been able to let it fly out of my rucksack into books, into minds, into people.

The university was a great platform to make you known. Whenever I included your work in my teaching, my students jumped at it, at least some did. So different, so raw, so honest they found it. It helped them feel more secure, as Germans, as white Europeans, dealing with Africa. It helped them to feel freer around that terrible conundrum of RACE.

'I would question anyone calling me an African writer. ... If you are a writer for a specific nation or a specific race, then fuck you ...'

A liberation for many.

Your words, your works have spread. Now and then I receive an email from 'Dambudzo Marechera'. How eerie this feels. It is sent from 'your' Facebook page. You have not lived to know this age of digital communication. Would you have liked it? Would you have 'posted'? Now others post for you and about you and 'like' you and 'share' you and create a page for you so that all your thousands of fans in the whole world can read you and about you.

Hardly a month goes by that I am not contacted by scholars, editors and publishers. Some want to know some detail, like: 'Was Marechera gay?' 'No,' I answer. 'What makes you think so?' 'The floral jacket he is wearing on some of the photos.' I smile. That jacket – you nicked it from my wardrobe, like a few other pieces. Now seeing you in it, the gender-aware critic reads it as 'cross-dressing'.

Articles have been published, books, dissertations written, reading and discussing your work in this or other direction. I could not keep track of them all and did not have to. I am glad people read you, as much as they might twist their tongues around the most fashionable theoretical jargon.

In all those years, Dambudzo, of speaking and acting for you and about you, commissioned by the Trust – or can I say, by the trust you had put in me? – I have had to wear two faces.

There was the public face of your biographer and editor, of the teacher, the critic, the Dambudzo Marechera 'authority' as people started to call me, the face of the committed scholar who would safeguard your legacy, commended by many, envied and reviled by others.

Behind that public face, only known by some, imagined by others, was the private one, the face of the woman who had loved you and had lain in your arms, had seen you die and had her own physical grievances to bear. For many years, even decades, the two faces led separate lives. One spoke out loud and clear, the other whispering timidly or gleefully. Often when I would be asked, at conferences where I spoke about you, or in the classroom when I was teaching your work, 'What did he die of?' I hesitated. In the very first years I would say, 'He died of pneumonia', which was the official version, and then fall silent. Later, I answered, after a pause and in a subdued tone, 'Of AIDS.' Often, I would add, apologetically, as if it had been your fault, 'It was only 1987, and at that time one was just starting to know that the disease was also spreading in Africa.'

Over the years, around the turn of the millennium, when I knew I was safe because the new drugs kept the virus at bay, I felt less inhibited. I would still keep our love affair in the closet when I was teaching your love poems. But I found it easy to separate the critic from the lover. It came naturally to me to act in my professional role when analysing your poems, just as it had been my professional role back then when I conducted the interview with you about those poems. 'Amelia is not black,' you said, and, while you were implicitly referring to our love affair, Amelia was just a literary figure, much larger than life, whom you compared in the same interview to Shakespeare's 'black lady'. So, she was me and not me.

And yet, it took more than thirty years until my two Marechera faces blended into one. The trigger arose out of a symposium in your honour, 'Dambudzo Marechera – A Celebration', convened in May 2009 at Oxford University. It was just before my sixty-second birthday. I had come with eighteen of my students, who absolutely wanted to be part of it. It was a splendid event, full of the intimacy of people who felt inspired by you and your work. There were young scholars and old teachers – Norman Vance among them, your tutor from New College. There was James Currey, your father publisher; Alastair Niven, who had banned you from the Africa Centre; as well as Robert Fraser, your drinking and conversing partner. There were filmmakers and artists showing and displaying their work, theatre performances, readings, tributes, memories, and a few academic papers – all full of you.

One of the scholars, I think from South Africa, touched in his paper on 'Marechera and his white women', a topic that had always intrigued male readers and critics. In the discussion that followed someone in the audience confronted me with the outright question: 'So what was *your* real relationship with him?'

I do not think I was particularly surprised. Somehow, I must have expected it.

I smiled enigmatically and said: 'Well, I suppose it is time that I write my own story.'

And so I did.

And here it is.

My story, our story.

Acknowledgements

The following sources have been used for quotations in this book:

By Dambudzo Marechera:

The House of Hunger, London: Heinemann 1978.
Mindblast or The Definitive Buddy, Harare: College Press 1994.
The Black Insider, Harare: Baobab Books, 1990.
Cemetery of Mind, Harare: Baobab Books, 1992.
Scrapiron Blues, Harare: Baobab Books, 1994.

Other:

Flora Veit-Wild, *Dambudzo Marechera: A Source Book on his Life and Work*, London: Hans Zell, 1992.
Flora Veit-Wild, 'Me and Dambudzo', *Wasafiri*, 27,1, 2012, pp. 1–7.
David Caute, *Marechera and the Colonel: A Zimbabwean Writer and the Claims of the State*, London: Totterdown Books, 2009.
Tinashe Mushakavanhu, 'Through the Eyes of a Child: A Conversation with Max Wild', in: *Dambudzo Marechera: The Doppelgänger. The Scofield*. 1, 3, 2016, pp. 173–175. http://s55615.gridserver.com/

Acknowledgements

The_Scofield_Issue_1.3_Dambudzo_Marechera.pdf
Chenjerai Hove, *Up in Arms*, Harare: Zimbabwe Publishing House, 1982.
Musaemura Zimunya, *Thought Tracks*, Harlow, Essex: London, 2982.

The most comprehensive source on Marechera and his legacy is provided by the digital Dambudzo Marechera Archive of Humboldt University, Berlin at https://hu.berlin/dmar. The site offers free online access to a multitude of documents, photos, audio and video materials, including unpublished writings, testimonies and interviews. Each source can be downloaded. To view all photographs relevant to this memoir go to: Featured Collections | Life and Afterlife | Photos of Memoir.

For Flora Veit-Wild's life and work, see also www.floraveitwild.de and the short film *Gestalten* at https://vimeo.com/422783003.

I thank Fiona Lloyd and Alison Lowry for their imaginative and resourceful editorial assistance.

www.ingramcontent.com/pod-product-compliance
Lightning Source LLC
Chambersburg PA
CBHW051603230426
43668CB00013B/1962